Endorse

Christi and I have known Pastor Glo... ... ...
1997. She is a Proverbs 31 woman! She has very courageously walked in
the anointing and ministry God called her to despite great persecution
simply for being a woman of God.

With a great sense of humor, she has documented a lifetime of the consistent goodness and love of God displayed in practical ways through her
life and ministry. As you read it, it will bless you, entertain you, and build
your faith. Enjoy!

—MYLON LE FEVRE
MYLON LE FEVRE MINISTRIES, TEACHER,
AUTHOR, GRAMMY AWARD WINNER

Gloria Gillaspie is a precious lady who has been a dear friend for many
years. Her support and love for our family and Daystar has been evident
throughout the years.

In *Arise! Shine!*, Gloria takes you on a journey of her experiences with
the miraculous and a stand for Godly justice. With profound insight and
poignant grace, she has led a life that exemplifies a true woman of faith
and is now sharing her story to encourage and lead those who read it to
believe all things are possible!

—JONI LAMB
CO-FOUNDER OF DAYSTAR TELEVISION NETWORK

You cannot read *Arise! Shine!* without your faith being strengthened to do
greater things for God. Throughout the Old and New Testaments, God
has used women of faith to do the impossible. The story of the life and
ministry of Gloria Gillaspie chronicles many of the miracles that she has
witnessed in over fifty years of service to our Lord. Our ministry lives have
often paralleled in many ways. We just recently passed our fiftieth year
as founder and pastor of Calvary Cathedral International in Fort Worth,
Texas. Gloria is a woman of prayer who is hungry for spiritual revival.
Her church was birthed by reaching out to troubled youth. She has a
heart for missions and a passion to minister faith and grace to the body
of Christ. She is a woman of grace who loves Jesus and loves people. We
were thrilled when our lives paralleled again last year when my grandson,

Robby, married Gloria's granddaughter, Lauren. Joy and I deeply appreciate our friendship and relationship with Gloria. I encourage you to read and be blessed!

—Pastor Bob Nichols
Calvary Cathedral International

Gloria Gillaspie's life has been a fulfillment of Acts 1:8: "But you will receive power when the Holy Spirit has come upon you, and you will be my witnesses in Jerusalem and in all Judea and Samaria, and to the end of the earth." Scores of people in Burleson, Johnson County, and around the world have come to know the Lord because she has been obedient to the leading of the Holy Spirit. Gloria's witness to a lifetime of God's miracles will encourage you and challenge you to draw ever closer to Him, our Lord and Savior.

—The Honorable Arlene Wohlgemuth
Executive Director of the Texas Public Policy Foundation
She served 10 years as a Texas state representative
for District 58

WOW! As I read Gloria Gillaspie's book, I was moved more than I can say. I believe you will be also. Her love for God and her family is quite apparent. She followed God faithfully from a small beginning, a place for young ones to be led to God, to taking the reins as pastor of a full-gospel church. She stood strong, and God smiled down on her; though many obstacles and fiery darts tested her, God allowed this for successful growth of a ministry, and she stood through them all. As this book unfolds, it reminds me of Esther from the Bible and Joan of Arc from history. To me Gloria stands as they did. God has blessed her and stood by her; again—WOW! What an understatement.

—Chuck DeHaan
Award Winning Western Artist and evangelist
recipient of the Golden Spur Award for cover art by the
Western Writers of America. Collector's Mart Magazine once
listed him as the top Western artist in the country, and he was
selected as the State Artist of Texas for 1986-87 by the Texas
Commission on the Arts

Pastor Gloria Gillaspie has been a strong supporter and a good friend to me for more than thirty years. She is a wonderful person and a true believer. Pastor Gillaspie has had a positive influence on the lives of those she has interacted with, and she has been an inspiration to literally thousands of people—myself included.

Lighthouse Church, the ministry she founded, had a strong faith-based foundation, but she also understood that to truly affect her community, she needed to get involved in the political arena.

Included in the pages of *Arise! Shine!* is the story of how Gloria welcomed me, a fresh faced political novice who was running for Congress, into the Lighthouse Church. She took the time to get to know me and what I stood for and gave me the opportunity to share my values with her congregation. It helped me win in 1984, and her friendship has been valuable ever since.

Pastor Gillaspie's spiritual journey and ministry has had a profound impact on Burleson and the surrounding area. I am glad she is sharing her story with everyone, and I know you will enjoy it as much as I did.

—The Honorable Joe Barton
U.S. Congress, Sixth Congressional District

The connection I have with Pastor Gloria is a supernatural one. Her miraculous and overcoming life has spilled over into mine. So here I find myself again amazed that I have a part in her incredible story. A born story-teller, she finally and authentically put pen to paper trying with all her might to express how she has seen the goodness of God in the land of the living. I read this book in one night because I couldn't stop reading once I started, and I tell you that though most of her life is inexpressible, she has managed to write from her heart in a way that will bless all of us for years to come.

I thank God for this written testimony and for her passionate heart for all things Jesus and His kingdom.

Arise and shine, sweet lady. Your children rise and call you blessed.

—Troy Brewer
Senior Pastor, OpenDoor Church

This book is a "great read" for all believers as Gloria shares her personal story of faith and her pursuit of God's call to the ministry. She shares her journey with testimonies of God's faithfulness and the miraculous manifestations of His power, which will encourage and strengthen you for your own individual walk with God.

I highly recommend Gloria's book and encourage you to read it often so that her revelation of God's faithfulness and limitless love will become your revelation as well.

—Dr. Jerry Savelle
Jerry Savelle Ministries International

ARISE!
SHINE!

GLORIA GILLASPIE
with MAX GLOSSUP

**CREATION
HOUSE**

ARISE! SHINE! by Gloria Gillaspie with Max Glossup
Published by Creation House
A Charisma Media Company
600 Rinehart Road
Lake Mary, Florida 32746
www.charismamedia.com

Design Director: Justin Evans
Cover design by Justin Evans

Contact the author: PO Box 1403, Burleson, TX 76097

Library of Congress CataloginginPublication Data: 2015957360
International Standard Book Number: 978-1-62998-504-6
E-book International Standard Book Number: 978-1-62998-505-3

While the author has made every effort to provide accurate telephone numbers and Internet addresses at the time of publication, neither the publisher nor the author assumes any responsibility for errors or for changes that occur after publication.

First edition

16 17 18 19 20— 987654321
Printed in the United States of America

"Arise, shine; for thy light is come, and the glory of the LORD is risen upon thee. For, behold, the darkness shall cover the earth, and gross darkness the people: but the LORD shall arise upon thee, and his glory shall be seen upon thee. And the Gentiles shall come to thy light, and kings to the brightness of thy rising".

—ISAIAH 60: 1–3

"Let your light so shine before men, that they may see your good works, and glorify your Father which is in heaven".

—MATTHEW 5:16

Contents

Acknowledgements

MANY PEOPLE, MORE than I can count or try to list, have had a significant impact on my life. It is amazing how many people have a part in who we become.

I especially thank my parents, Clyde and Frances Lewis, for raising my siblings and me to know God. They always believed in us and encouraged us to fulfill our dreams.

My husband, John, and our children, Shanda, Richelle, Stuart, and Otis, faithfully walked with me through the trials and the victories, the good times and bad, and were my greatest fans.

The people God brought for me to pastor locked step with me, and together we accomplished great things for God.

This book would never have happened without Max Glosup and his wife, Janet. She first had the vision for him to help me write my story. They spent countless hours transcribing from my taped recordings. Max took my story, organized it into its final narrative form, and added some historical context.

The late Steve Powers taped many of the early sessions. I am thankful for him and his wife, Michelle. Without them the project may never have gotten started.

I offer my utmost gratitude to those who reviewed the book and wrote such glowing endorsements: my friend and state representative, the Honorable Arlene Wohlgemuth; another friend from the political arena, U. S. Congressman Joe Barton; Daystar Television co-founder and host, Joni Lamb; award-winning western artist and writer, Chuck DeHaan; teacher and Grammy Award winner, Mylon Le Fevre; Pastor Bob Nichols of Calvary Cathedral; Dr. Jerry Savelle of Savelle Ministries International; and Troy Brewer, my pastor and Senior Pastor of OpenDoor church.

Finally, I wish to express my appreciation to all the other people who are mentioned in the book, those who encouraged me, blessed me, and supported me at some point during my ministry. There are so many.

About Me and My Book

THE CHRONICLE OF the Lighthouse Church in Burleson, Texas, and my life's story are two slightly different perspectives of the same narrative. Together they are one story of Christ's work in Burleson during the last two decades of the twentieth century and the beginning of a new millennium.

This book is my personal journal of miracles that God has performed and that I have been blessed to witness over the last fifty years. It is based on my memories and observations. Most of it can be corroborated by personal witness and testimony of others, but I have made no attempt to catalogue my life's experiences with extensive footnotes or explanations. God's miracles cannot be proved to someone who chooses not to believe any more than they can be disproved to someone who sees God's handiwork in each morning's sunrise.

My ministry began as the Steppingstone Youth center in 1976, but my service to the Lord can be traced to my childhood. In my teenage years, my sisters and I sang in a gospel trio, and later I was youth pastor at a full-gospel church in Fort Worth. Those early experiences were my training for a life-long ministry as pastor of a church.

In the year 2012, as I began writing this book, the city of Burleson was celebrating its sesquicentennial, and I was reminded that no one's life story is exclusively their own. Each life is a culmination of the stories of all the people who preceded us, those who guided and influenced us—our parents and their progenitors. My family's history has been closely linked to Burleson and the Bethesda-Briaroaks neighborhood nearby. I'm even related to Burleson's founder.

Henry C. Renfro is often credited with establishing the township of Burleson. His father, Absalom Renfro of Tennessee, served in the Virginia 75th under Captain Currin during the war with France in 1812. Absalom's nine children were born before the family migrated to Texas in 1847. Henry, the sixth child, was born in 1831, and Malinda Elizabeth, the seventh, was born on January 28, 1834.

Malinda married William W. Bockman on December 26, 1852. The Bockman family's traverse to Texas had been similar to that of the Renfro's, except they started out from Georgia. William had been born in rural Georgia on October 20, 1836. Bill and Malinda named their third daughter, the seventh child of nine, Margaret. She was born on January 4, 1867, in what would later become the Briaroaks region of Johnson County. At the age of seventeen, she was wed to John William Floyd.

The Floyds, like the Bockmans, had migrated from the southeast, setting out from Catoosa County, Georgia, in 1854. First, the family settled in east Texas. As soon as he was old enough, John entered what, I suppose, you could call the family business. Like his father, he became a schoolteacher and practiced for two years in east Texas before the family migrated to the Johnson County area in 1880, after the death of the family patriarch.

After he married Margaret in 1884, they settled on a farm and later expanded the acreage. John became the first schoolmaster of the Bethesda School, which was originally called the Crill Miller School. He taught first through eighth grade classes. Years after leaving the school, his students remembered Mr. Floyd whacking the wall of the school with a large stick to call them in from recess because the school didn't own a bell. John, as most teachers did at the time, taught reading from the Blue Back speller, a textbook used to teach reading and spelling using characters and stories from the Bible.

At twenty, Maggie gave birth to my grandfather, Ercel Royce Floyd, on November 18, 1887. In 1912, Ercel married Bettie Alice Lancaster, who, like him, had lived her entire life in Texas. Their third daughter, my mother, was born on August 9, 1917, in Johnson County.

My father's family tree was similar only in the sense that his forebears migrated from the East, a story shared by many of America's Caucasian pioneer families. With family ties to Meriwether Lewis of the Lewis and Clark Expedition that opened the Northwest Territory, they were a different bunch of people. Winfield Scott Lewis, my great-grandfather, settled a farm in Oak Grove, east of the current Spinks airport. With his sons, he raised horses and operated a horse track on the property. He trained thoroughbreds that ran at Arlington Downs. Today, all vestiges of the Lewis track have disappeared into weeds or subdivisions, and the only remnant of the fabled Arlington Downs, once teeming with more than six thousand spectators every race day and sometimes touted as one of the two premier racetracks in the state of Texas, is a historical marker at what was once a watering trough.

As a teenager, my grandfather, James Dudley Lewis, youngest of the seven children, rode as a jockey in many of the races at Arlington Downs. When the land in Oak Grove was parsed between Winfield's heirs, some sold their property and moved to other nearby communities. During the division, it has been said, the family donated the land for the present day Oak Grove Baptist Church.

My father worked in sales for the Lind Paper Company, but at the same time, he was a farmer, and he operated a Ferguson tractor business with Weldon Noe near the intersection of Renfro and US 81. In the evenings, he called on clients who had come by to look at the tractors and who had left their contact information during the day.

Christianity was the predominant religious influence in both my mother's and my father's families. Historically, this has been true of a majority of American families. As we arrive at the new millennium, the influence of Christianity and the associated Christian values and ethics have begun to ebb, and a tide has washed in a culture of narcissistic humanism, a religion that elevates self to god. To some extent, this book is a journal of the effects of that new morality on the church over the last half-century. I haven't dwelled on this observation, and I've attempted to avoid proselytizing, but it would be hard to miss my opinion that a nation that turns its back on God can hardly expect to continue enjoying the blessings that were heaped on our forebears.

More than anything else, this book is a simple journal of my ministry and the miracles God has performed in creating and sustaining it. He selected me for the ministry at what became the Steppingstone Church and was later renamed the Lighthouse Church of Burleson. I never had a desire to pastor a church, but as I look back over the years since I acknowledged that the full-time ministry was God's call on my life, I can tell you that He slowly guided me to my ultimate calling through a series of events that were miraculously strung together. I value them more than I would a necklace of diamonds or pearls. As Christians we answer God's call each day, and with each decision we make that ratifies our commitment to Him as Lord and Master of our lives, we add another gem.

This is my attempt to display my most prized possession, Christ in my life, to you. There is no radiance in our lives without Jesus Christ, and this little book is my way of sharing Him with you, now that I have set aside my ministry as pastor after thirty-two years.

You are radiant, too, if you have Jesus Christ at the center of your life. So arise, shine. Let everyone see the glory of the Lord through you.

Chapter 1

Peanuts

IN 1950, US 81 bisected the country. In Texas, it sliced southward through rustic metropolises: Fort Worth, Hillsboro, Waco, Austin, San Antonio, and Laredo. The highway almost paralleled the Missouri-Kansas-Texas (KATY) railroad's North-to-South line, which had only been completed fifty years earlier in the first year of the twentieth century. Twelve miles south of downtown Fort Worth, the two-lane "highway" intersected Texas 174. A southbound traveler who took 174 and continued through Cleburne could drive for hours across a landscape as rugged and untamed as Texas's reputation. The small farming community of Burleson, the crossroad between somewheres and nowheres, perched smack dab in the vertex of the intersection of 174 and US 81.

Just South of Burleson, off 81 and at the end of one of the innumerable, unnamed dirt roads that led to a farm house, Clyde Lewis worked his chicken farm, raised a crop of peanuts and children, and just for fun held down a sales career for a paper company in Fort Worth. In the evenings, he made calls on farmers who had left contact information during the day seeking to know more about the Ferguson tractors that Clyde and Weldon Noe sold as a side job.

Clyde's father tended to the farm, planting peanuts year after year while also sowing the seeds of Christian discipleship deep into the hearts of his grandchildren. Clyde and his wife were charter members of the Gospel Tabernacle, a fundamentalist Baptist church founded by Lavada Reed, our pastor.

Clyde worked at the church every Saturday, contributing to the upkeep of the building or grounds in some way. He was superintendent of the Sunday school for many years while we children grew up. Mrs. Lewis, Frances, my mother, went to prayer meetings and was one of the church's prayer warriors, a vast right-wing conspiracy that met in small rooms, church sanctuaries and homes to plan and plot and pray for the fate of the nation and the

1

world. They believed that prayer could change the future and more impor-
tantly change people's hearts.

Clyde and Frances' children remember that our parents took us to church
all the time. When we weren't in school or working, we were worshipping.
Tuesday and Thursday evenings, after a hard day of work, the five children
were carted off to church. And, of course, on Sunday we were decked out in
our finest to worship in the morning and again in the evening. It was normal
to spend the entire day in worship. That's what Sundays were for. The Lewis
family was devout. Many families were, and because of that, stores were
closed, even in the cities, on Sundays. It was rare to find a gas station open
on Sundays in any Texas community in the early 1950s either.

The Gospel Tabernacle's Sunday services ran long. There was no rule in
the Bethesda community just South of Burleson that Sunday morning's
worship service had to end at high noon so that men could rush home for
the weekly duel of shoulder-padded Titans on television. There was no race
for the door at the end of the service to beat the family in the next pew to
a favorite restaurant. Even if there had been restaurants in Burleson, they
wouldn't have been open on Sundays. Like other businesses, they would
have closed. Their proprietors would have been sitting in church along with
everyone else. Blue laws made sure that stores closed down for Sunday,
too. Families went home for lunch. The television had not yet replaced the
family Bible or the dinner table as the hub of communication in the suburban home.

Bettie Sue, my sister and the eldest daughter, had an exceptional
musical talent. As early as age five, she played piano in church services.
Sister Lavada lived in Fort Worth where she bragged about her protégé-
prodigy. Sometimes visitors would drop by the Gospel Tabernacle just to
hear Bettie play.

In 1946, when Bettie Sue was nine and I, the middle daughter, was seven,
we went to Vacation Bible School and revival meetings hosted by a nearby
Baptist church. It wasn't the church we normally attended. During one of
the services early in the week, I stood beside Bettie Sue during the altar call.

I felt the conviction of the Holy Spirit. I felt the weight of the world. I
wasn't thinking of my sin exactly, but the weight of conviction was unbear-
able. Even a seven-year-old can realize that we are born with a sinful nature.
I wanted to step out into the aisle, go to the front, and profess my belief in

Jesus Christ, but I hadn't been able to move. I was very timid, and I stood there on the brink, unable to take that first step into the aisle until Bettie Sue nudged me aside as she passed to go to the front of the church herself.

When I stepped out of the way to let her by, I just kept going. Instantly, I was crying. I cried the entire, ecstatic trip. I felt the Holy Spirit, and I cried while they took my confession of faith. I cried while they took my name and filled out the card. I couldn't stop crying, and the VBS workers began to think there was something wrong with me, but I was saved that day. It was a deep experience, and I still remember it vividly.

Beginning that night I suddenly had an insatiable thirst for the Bible. I read all the time. I read through the New Testament and then the Old Testament, soaking in the words, even though I didn't always understand what they meant. It felt good to read the Bible. It warmed me like hot cocoa on a cold night. I read all summer.

When school started, I wanted to share how I felt with all my classmates and friends. At that time, there were no laws or rules that prevented a grade-school student from sharing feelings about salvation with classmates, and godless bureaucracy had not yet assumed absolute control of the school system. My bus arrived at the schoolhouse about thirty minutes before classes started, and I went in with all the kids and sat down on the front desk and called the others over and told them about the Lord and what had happened to me. I told them Bible stories and encouraged them to go to church. They really listened. A lot of them started going to church.

When Bettie Sue was ten and I had barely turned eight, we started singing duets in church. It wasn't long before we were invited to perform in other churches. The Gospel Tabernacle sponsored a program at KCLE, the AM radio station in Cleburne, and we became regulars on the show, at least our voices did. With our youngest sister, Mary Lavada (named for the pastor), we recorded the program's theme song, "A Song in My Soul." The station played it before the Tabernacle's thirty-minute program every Sunday at 7:00 a.m. and on Tuesdays and Thursdays at 3:00 p.m. It wasn't long before our trio was singing to the piano accompaniment of Bettie Sue at school, too.

We didn't rate star status, though, especially at home where we were still expected to help out on the farm. We didn't have much. The country was still recovering from the depression and World War II. The broiler houses were populated with over 3,500 birds at a time, and the chickens had to be fed. We fed them from a wheelbarrow, dipping out the feed and pouring it into the feeders. It took about an hour in the morning and an hour in the afternoon. We raised them from chicks and sold them at eight or ten weeks old as broilers or fryers. Once they were shipped off to market, a new shipment of baby chicks arrived and the cycle started over. The chicken farm alone was constant work, but the farm produced a crop of peanuts every year, too. Grandpa harvested the peanuts by plowing them up. There was no end to the work to be done on the farm.

Despite the hard work, the farm was just a source of extra income. My father was a sales representative for a paper company in Fort Worth. He worked incessantly. He called on grocery stores and big companies and sold all kinds of paper products. That was really our main source of income. When he and Weldon sold a tractor, it was a reason for celebration.

Not long after my sisters and I began singing in services, things at church began to change. Lavada Reed started attending prayer services at Bethel Temple, a Pentecostal, spirit-filled church in Fort Worth. She hadn't been going there long before she was baptized in the Holy Spirit.

When Jesus left the earth and ascended into heaven, he instructed the disciples to remain in Jerusalem where the Holy Spirit would be imparted to them. The disciples met fifty days after Christ's ascension into heaven for the Feast of Weeks, also known as Pentecost. During the conduct of business, the disciples selected Matthias to replace Judas as one of the twelve apostles. Then, while they were celebrating and praising God, tongues of fire appeared above the head of each person, and the disciples were overcome with the joy of the Holy Spirit. They began speaking in tongues (as the Spirit gave them utterance). Anyone they spoke to heard them in his native language. Anointed with the Holy Spirit, they ran about the streets telling everyone about the wonderful things that had happened to them. They seemed drunk to some of the people they accosted. The Bible describes them as acting as though they had been filled with new wine.

Pentecostals believe that it's possible to be filled with the Holy Spirit in this way today. Dancing, singing, praising, speaking in tongues, healing the sick, and prophesying are outward signs that a person is overflowing with the Holy Spirit. Pentecostal Christians will often manifest one or more of these fruits of the spirit.

Once Pastor Lavada had been baptized in the Holy Spirit, things at the Gospel Tabernacle were never quite the same. She began teaching her Baptist congregation about the power of the Holy Spirit, and one by one, the members of the Tabernacle were all baptized in the spirit, too. They began prophesying in tongues. I remember when I first heard people speaking in tongues. When messages were given in tongues, just hearing people speak made me cry. It was as though the Lord himself were standing in our midst.

Everyone praised and rejoiced when anyone received spiritual baptism. When the Holy Spirit moved, people shouted and danced. This sometimes went on for hours, sometimes long after the regular church service was over. It was nothing to start at 7:00 or 7:30 in the evening and for the worship to continue until 10:00 or 11:00 p.m. An old-time revival hit that church, and it continued for years. I grew up in that. Every church night was revival night, a celebration of the freedom from sin we receive when we surrender ourselves to Jesus Christ.

Sister Lavada taught that Christians are redeemed from our old sin nature, and that we have been made righteous through Jesus Christ (2 Corinthians 5:17, 21). The Gospel Tabernacle celebrated that redemption and Jesus Christ as the redeemer, but there were times during the next few years when some members of the church challenged pastor Lavada's teachings. I remember one church elder who insisted that the church should teach nothing but conviction for our sins.

"We are all dirty rotten sinners," he said.

But that is not Christ's message. Even though the Bible tells us that "all have sinned and come short of the Glory of God," it points out that we are freed from the condemnation for our sins when we acknowledge that Jesus Christ sacrificed his earthly life to pay the price for our sins. To concentrate on the fact that we are sinners misses the point of Jesus' life, death, and resurrection. "God sent not his son to condemn the world, but that the world through Him might be saved" (John 3:17).

Chapter 2

"I Can't be a Member of a Church with a Woman Pastor."

Pastor Lavada was an exceptional woman and leader. As respected as she was, however, it was not unusual for elders to challenge her authority or try to dictate how she should conduct services. That happens in any ministry to some extent, but sometimes it seemed that some of the elders wanted to dictate every detail of the services.

Today women are more accepted as pastors than they were in the forties and fifties. But for a woman to take the shepherd's role in a church, especially a woman teaching that we should celebrate our redemption rather than wallow in our sinfulness, was more than many people could bear. Men who seldom uttered more than an "amen" during a sermon by another alpha male didn't hesitate to challenge Lavada, sometimes even right in the middle of her message.

But she was getting her revelation from scriptures. The things she taught are common in preaching today, but few ministers were preaching them then. My mother and father recognized Lavada's message was ordained of God. She took her teachings from the Word rather than trying to twist the Word to support preconceived notions.

Her teachings made me feel like I was valuable to God, and when we value who we are in God, we have a strong weapon to fight off temptation. We realize we have this treasure in earthen vessels, that we are the temple of the Holy Spirit, and that we're special. We are set apart for God.

My parents never disagreed with the pastor or put her down. If they had, it would have made the children question what she was preaching, and we probably wouldn't have received the message. Through my adult years before I became a pastor (at forty-three), I observed other people in the church who did not respect the pastor of their church. They would put down the pastor, disagree with him, and even become angry if the pastor's message deviated from their personal convictions. They would complain about the pastor or critique the sermon in front of their children. The lack of respect was perpetuated in their progeny.

After I became a youth minister, I tried to influence those teenagers who made negative comments about the pastor or who repeated their parents' criticisms. It was hard to deal with the negative things parents sometimes said. The children were inheriting their skepticism and cynicism, which undermined their respect for ministers and the church in general.

Chapter 3

Bread and Jam

CHURCH REMAINED THE center of my life through high school. A forward on the basketball team, cheerleader during football season, and member of the 4-H club, I was a typical, busy teen. Although the basketball games conflicted with the Tuesday night church services, my parents consented for me to participate because there were two weeknight church services. I was allowed to play basketball on Tuesdays as long as I made it to church on Thursdays. A little different from most teens, however, I didn't see the weekday church obligation as a sacrifice or a burden. It was a blessing. Even though I was very involved in school activities, they never interfered with church time, and I never felt like putting Christ first was a sacrifice.

All my friends knew where I stood, too. I couldn't help noticing that they reminded each other not to tell certain jokes around me or not to curse in front of me. I never told them not to; they simply respected my beliefs. They knew that I went to church. There were others in our group who went to church, too. My sisters and I were different, though. Everyone recognized it, but we were anything but outsiders. Each of us was deeply involved in community activities. I joined in on everything, everything at least that I didn't feel was forbidden by my faith. When I was invited to attend a party or participate in an event my parents might not approve of, I gratefully, and as graciously as I could, declined: "I've got a call on my life," I explained more than once.

I didn't fully understand what that meant, but that didn't make it any less true. When I went out with someone I hadn't dated before, the conversation inevitably required me to say something about my hobbies and interests. By the time I was a teenager, I had read through the Bible twice. All I did was talk about church. That didn't seem to keep the boys from asking me out though.

By 1955, our sister trio had become well known locally. We were invited to sing at the Battle of Songs at the Will Rogers Auditorium in Fort Worth. Battle of the Songs, organized and promoted by Fort Worth native W. B. Nowlin, was a head-to-head competition between the most famous gospel quartets of the day. The battle could be waged in any venue, but Fort Worth was as common to the competition as the stockyards were to cattle. Mary, Bettie, and I shared the stage with the likes of the Blackwood Brothers, The Statesmen, and Oak Ridge Boys. We often won first place in area competitions and talent shows. Later, we spent a summer singing for WBAP TV, channel 5, the NBC affiliate in Fort Worth.

We were invited to perform at the Big D Jamboree, a cross between the Grand Ole Opry and the Louisiana Hayride. The weekly Jamboree kept the lights burning on Saturday nights in the Million Dollar Sportatorium near downtown Dallas, a rebuilt version of the original, constructed in 1936 and consumed by fire in 1953. Legends about how the fire started and who may have started it still haunt the South side of downtown Dallas today. On Saturdays, the locker rooms of the Sportatorium, home of world famous wrestling every Tuesday night, became the anterooms where musicians waited their turn in the arena.

The Jamboree was never broadcast on TV even though it was considered the regional launching pad to national stardom in country music. KRLD radio transmitted the shindig to the Dallas-Fort Worth area, and we performed at the jamboree several times in 1955.

On Saturday afternoons at five o'clock, before the Jamboree got rolling, we stopped by the KRLD television studio and sang on a live television show that was a preview of the night's program. Then we headed for the Sportatorium where we waited until called to perform. The Jamboree started at eight. We usually had time to sit and watch the big name stars and their crews make ready for the evening's festivities.

LEWIS SISTERS AT THE BIG D JAMBOREE (GLORIA AT LEFT, MARY, BETTIE SUE)

Chapter 4

Chicken Feed

In April 1955, the Johnson County Broiler Association chose me to represent the local wing of the chicken industry in the statewide beauty contest at the Texas Poultry Festival in Gonzales. They wanted me to compete for the title of Texas Broiler Queen.

Mother had been bedridden for much of that spring. She had been in the hospital briefly, and during her convalescence, the children had shouldered her daily chores around the farm. There was no way she could help me prepare for the competition. I was sixteen and was expected to take care of myself.

I didn't have a formal gown and had to borrow one that Bettie Sue had worn to the prom a few months earlier. Bettie Sue was only one size bigger than I was, but that was enough to make a difference in the way the gown draped over my younger, smaller frame. There was more dress than girl, and I suspected that I might be mistaken for an empty dress hanging on a chicken wire frame.

The night of the competition, I was the houseguest of a prominent family in Gonzales. They lived in a large old house, three stories high; the kind of house you might see on a city tour of historic homes. The family I stayed with had a daughter who was in college. She stood nearby as I stepped into my dress and got ready for the reception.

On seeing me in the dress for the first time, the daughter exclaimed, "Oh, your dress is too big." She laid her arm across my shoulder, and like a hen taking a chick under wing, led me to her mother who had me remove the dress; then, with a needle and thread, this prominent member of the community stitched and adjusted the dress to fit. I felt thrown together but was very appreciative of the help, and I was reminded of Christ when he washed the feet of his disciples. He that is greatest among us is the greatest servant. That was a Christian act, and it was a blessing to me that I'll never forget.

Even with the adjustments to the dress, I knew there was little chance of winning. There were so many beautiful girls who were decked out in expensive gowns and jewelry. But supporters from Burleson and my hostess kept encouraging me, saying, "Smile, smile, smile all the time." And so I did. I smiled constantly.

The competition required each girl to give a speech, and I had no reason to suspect that I should speak about anything other than the chicken industry. I was, after all, representing the farmers constituting the Johnson County Poultry Association, and I had appropriately titled my speech "Chicken Feed."

It was a prepared lecture, as far from extemporaneous as chickens are from dinosaurs. I had researched the feed that the Lewis farm fed its chickens. I had compared the weight of chickens when taken to market after being raised on brand X instead of brand Y. Selected as one of the first speakers, I told the audience about the chicken industry and my first-hand experiences, and I bragged about the brand of feed that the Lewis chickens were raised on. I talked about feeding the chickens. I described my project and filled my speech with cold statistics that could be appreciated in a boardroom or by a group of chicken farmers.

After I had finished and sat down, I listened to the presentations of the other contestants. Pretty quickly, I realized that if my chance of winning had been a chicken, my speech had probably wrung its neck. It seemed that beauty queens weren't supposed to talk about the industry. The girls who followed recited their curricula vitae to the judges. They were impressive, too. They sounded like the career summaries you might see on the playbill of a Dallas theater production. These girls had been around; many of them already had an impressive list of accomplishments.

"I was homecoming queen," said one.

"Most likely to succeed," boasted another cheerleader, who had condescended to appear to the gathering of chicken farmers.

"Friendliest...Class President," one after another recited her qualifications.

"Drum Major"

"Most studious."

I had been a cheerleader, too, although it had never occurred to me that a group of chicken farmers would be impressed by my juvenile credentials. These were hard-working men who I had assumed would be much like my father. Obviously, I had been wrong. Although my list of personal accomplishments probably wouldn't have seemed puny if I had stacked them against the other girls', I hadn't given myself a chance. I kept smiling although it was becoming more painfully obvious with each new presentation that I should have focused on my personal accomplishments. Long before all the girls had finished, I felt a little embarrassed. I didn't belong in the competition. I hadn't understood what was expected at all.

I couldn't wait for the tortuous presentations to end so I could go home. Then a wonderful thing happened. Almost before I realized it, I was holding a bouquet. My hosts insisted that I call home and let my parents know I had won. I wanted to call, but long distance calls were expensive, and I was hesitant. I didn't want to wake mother either.

At the dance in honor of the queen of the festival, I listened while a young rock-a-billy sensation sang "I'm Left, You're Right, She's Gone" and "Mystery Train," two songs he recorded in 1955 for Sun records. It was still a year before his recordings would roll to the top of the charts and rock the music world. Even though my sisters and I had sung at Big D Jamboree, at home we listened to Doris Day and crooners like Sinatra. We didn't listen to country music and didn't know the new artists of rock-a-billy music. It was the first time I had ever heard of the young performer. After he had finished his set, the polite young man and I danced together.

I couldn't have kept the contest a secret if I had tried. I hadn't told any of my girlfriends that I had entered the contest, but I had missed school on Friday to travel to Gonzales. Before the weekend was over, WBAP radio's Farm Report sponsored by the Red Chain Feed Company had broadcast my speech and had announced to the entire farming community that Gloria Lewis had won the title of Miss Texas Poultry Queen. By the time I got back to school on Monday, everyone knew about it. I was a little surprised that my friends squealed when I finally remembered the name of the young performer who had sung at the party and with whom I had danced. Later that summer I saw Elvis Presley again. At that time, my sisters and I were performing at the Big D Jamboree, and he gyrated on the stage on one of the nights that we were there.

MISS TEXAS POULTRY QUEEN

I was awarded one hundred dollars along with the title Miss Texas Poultry Queen. The first thing I did was give my tithe. I gave ten dollars to the church. In 1955, the remaining ninety dollars was a lot of money by the standards of most people in suburban and rural America. I bought a pair of shoes for two dollars and ninety-eight cents, a skirt for two dollars and ninety-eight cents, and a blouse for one dollar and ninety-eight cents. You could buy a lot of clothes for ten dollars. Finances were just different then. You could buy a new car for twelve-hundred dollars. I bought all my school clothes for the next year, and I dressed better than I ever had. I was so blessed. I felt that the Lord had provided because of the financial situation at my house. I didn't ask daddy for a dime for the whole year following the contest.

After I had tithed ten dollars, the local feed company sent me another ten dollars. I got my tithe back immediately, and I gave another dollar, tithing on that ten dollars.

Harry Rand, a vice president of the Red Chain Feed Company in Fort Worth, lived in Burleson, which was beginning its evolution into a suburb of the Dallas-Fort Worth metroplex as families, particularly families of defense workers, began flooding to places with a small town atmosphere to raise their children. The paradox was that each family that moved to the small town made it bigger, and inevitably, I suppose, they brought their culture with them rather than leaving it behind in the city.

One of the small town's streets would later be named in honor of Rand, but that year he was just another fan of the Lewis sisters. He asked us to sing at the company's annual convention in Fort Worth. Then he asked us to create a jingle that the company could use in its radio spots. Bettie Sue and I composed the lyrics and music, and the company used the song in its radio advertisements for the rest of the year, with our trio singing it, of course.

Chapter 5

Satisfied Mind

HARRY RAND WASN'T our only fan. Hank Locklin, a country singer who popularized the song "Please Help Me I'm Falling" and wrote "Send Me the Pillow That You Dream On," two favorite tunes through the sixties and still popular today among fans of classical country music, was among the promoters of the Big D Jamboree who offered us a contract. Several songwriters and promoters tried to get us to record their songs. The glamour, fame, and wealth of a music career lay at our feet. All we had to do was pick it up.

We had to get the studio by five p.m. on Saturday for our televised performance. Then we rushed to the Sportatorium to get some practice with the band in time for the Jamboree, which lasted from eight to midnight. On most Saturdays, Sonny James, a rising country star known as the "Southern Gentleman," accompanied us to the large anteroom where he parked us saying, "Now y'all can wait here until time for you to practice with the band." We had no way of knowing he was protecting us or even that we needed protecting. James made sure we had soft drinks and snacks, and he kept us away from the ruckus that rivaled the Sportatorium's Tuesday night wrestling fare for ribaldry and raucousness.

No one knows better than my sisters and I how much James deserved the moniker his contemporaries had saddled on him. He was nice. We didn't realize that he was protecting us. We didn't suspect until one night when he told us, "You know, y'all can go as far as you want to in this business, and I'll help you in any way I can, but y'all are really too nice of girls to get into this business."

Not long after that, on a Saturday night when Sonny was making an appearance at the Grand Ole Opry and was off duty as our guardian angel, there was no buffer between us and the other performers. No one waited on us so that we didn't have to go out and scrounge for refreshments. No Sir Galahad insulated us from the behavior of other groups and bands. We just wandered around and sat and waited for our turn to practice. We were out with everyone else. Other singers practicing with their bands and going over their songs cursed without inhibition. We had never been exposed to the litany of cussing and nasty jokes. My dad never used bad language. I was never around it. We didn't understand some of the words or a lot of the innuendo that thickened the air along with the cigarette smoke and the boozy odors. The filthy flirtations of leering Lotharios were wasted on the innocent trio. We may not have understood everything, but we knew it was foul.

We had planned to sing a recent hit called "Satisfied Mind." A Porter Waggoner rendition of the song was still climbing the charts. "Satisfied Mind" was not quite a gospel song, which could be said of a lot of country music, but was about how few rich men are really happy with their possessions as they come to the end of their lives. The song was about seeking the things of the world but eventually coming to the conclusion that only God can give you a satisfied mind.

The promoters wouldn't let us sing it. So, we selected a couple of other current hits, and they rejected each of them, too. *That's not right*, I thought, but the rules governing access to music weren't written by us or for us. We finally settled on a song that didn't threaten to bruise the promoters' most sensitive appendages, their money belts.

Throughout the evening, we never discussed what had happened. We noted each other's revulsion to lewd comments or jokes left hanging in the air, but we didn't speak about it. Each of us silently took notes. It was as though we had seen into the heart of the country music industry for the first time and found that it was soulless, empty, and fouler than a chicken yard.

I began to think that all these stars who were wealthy and famous had bartered their souls for success. Our eyes were opened. Three girls—fourteen, sixteen, and eighteen—were more mature spiritually than the adults around us.

On our way home that night I was the first to say what we were all thinking. "I'm never going back." My sisters told me that they had already made the same decision themselves; they just hadn't said it yet.

The Lewis Sisters never performed at the Big D Jamboree or in any other professional venue again. When we quit going, scouts called trying to get us to come back, but we were finished with it. We decided that we wouldn't do gospel music outside of church either. We had seen the slimy underbelly of the music industry, and in the wisdom of innocence, we had each made the same decision about our lives. We continued to sing in church and at local events.

Later on, we found out that far too many people in the music industry, even among the gospel quartets of the Battle of Songs, made lifestyle compromises. Even as teenagers, we recognized that the individual talents God had given us were to be used for His glory. All of the fame and money in the world wasn't worth our souls. We left the music business with satisfied minds, confident that all the glitter and gold of the professional entertainer could not match the satisfaction of singing a gospel song for the sake of praise alone. Although we weren't permitted to sing the song that night, the song "Satisfied Mind" would have been perfect for our last professional performance. The song was written from the point of view of a person who, perhaps nearing the end of life, had lost the treasures he had accumulated in his youth, only to discover the true treasure of a life well lived, the value of loved ones and friendships, and the comfort of company and family as he grew older. My sisters and I already knew that the only real satisfaction comes from a life lived for Jesus. Fortune and fame are no comparison in the final count.

I didn't want to get involved in all the things of that world. No one was telling me what to do and what not to do. Mother and Daddy had our two younger brothers to attend to, in addition to the farm and the multiple jobs. They weren't going with us when we performed in Dallas. They weren't standing nearby telling us how to behave. We had been taught who we were, and each of us knew she was being given a choice. People worked and scraped and compromised to compete in that world, but here we were, three teenaged girls, and each of us decided for herself that she was too good for that. Thank God for pastors and parents who teach their children the boundaries of propriety and provide them with examples of a moral lifestyle. It's what we learned from our parents and our pastor that led each of us to her personal decision. We had given our lives to the Lord.

The Battle of the Songs waged on for a few years, but eventually lost its tune. The Big D Jamboree jammed on for about twenty years, but was jammed out long before the landmark Sportatorium, for years the favorite wrestling venue in the Southwest, was demolished in 2003. A disproportionate number of wealthy music stars who rollicked in the rockabilly style ebbed into anonymity, poverty, misery, or tragedy.

Today, Mary, Ercel, one of our younger brothers, and I pastor churches. Grady and Bettie are very active in the ministry of their local churches. We have satisfied minds.

Chapter 6

Feed the Children

AFTER MY MARRIAGE to John Gillaspie, whose family lived south of Burleson in Alvarado, I continued going to the Gospel Tabernacle. John sometimes went with me, but I attended church just as I had all my life, still under the tutelage of Lavada Reed, the only pastor the Gospel Tabernacle had ever had. It was the church where my sisters and I had sung as children. It was as much like home as the farm, and Lavada was as much a friend as she was a mentor and spiritual guide.

I taught Sunday school at the little church. Almost from the first time I stood in the center of a room of children, I understood the gravity of what I was doing. I didn't have to remind myself of Jesus' admonition about leading children astray. I knew I was assuming responsibility for leading them into a closer relationship with Jesus Christ. When you realize the significance of your Christian influence on the lives of others, it can be overwhelming. Every action you take, every word you say can lead another person closer to Christ or drive him or her away. What an awesome responsibility it is to be a Christian.

Not long after my marriage, Lavada was forced to surrender her ministry. Her husband, an employee of a major oil company, was transferred to Ohio. There were tears enough to fill a milk can when my family said goodbye to Sister Lavada. She had played an elemental role in the Christian development of the entire Lewis clan, but God had separate plans for her and for each of the Lewis children.

After Lavada's departure, Tony Wise came to the Tabernacle as pastor. Tony's ministerial luggage was stuffed with prophecy and healing. He taught the power of faith. He only occupied the podium at the Tabernacle for one year before he was called to pastor a large church in Fort Worth. For the year he was at the Tabernacle, he influenced my life profoundly.

Chapter 7

Richelle's Miracles

I F YOU EVER hear any old wives' tales about how the first childbirth is the most difficult, don't believe them. Shanda, our first daughter, was born on October 9, 1957. She arrived without complications, and the baby was a blessing to our lives. Soon I was pregnant with a second daughter, but things didn't go as smoothly with that pregnancy. Richelle was early. She only weighed five pounds at birth and wasn't very healthy. She had a lot of problems typical with premature babies.

Even after we had taken her home, John and I spent a lot of time at the doctor's office. She was sick much of the time. After a few months, she couldn't keep anything on her stomach and she still wasn't gaining any weight; a month before her first birthday she weighed less than thirteen pounds.

I had believed in faith healing since Lavada had introduced it at the Gospel Tabernacle. Our family believed in miracles and in the power of the Holy Spirit. Both Lavada and Tony Wise taught that healing is possible today basing that belief on the words of First Peter 2:24: "Who his own self bare our sins in his own body on the tree, that we, being dead to sins, should live unto righteousness, by whose stripes ye were healed" (KJV).

As spirit-filled Christians, we believe that miracles, like those performed by Jesus and his followers, are still possible today. Many wonders and signs were done by the apostles (Acts 3:43). They healed the sick in the name of Jesus, assuming authority over illness and even life itself in His name. We have the same authority in Jesus' name.

In Acts 3, Peter and John healed a man who had been lame since birth.

> Peter, fastening his eyes upon him with John, said, Look on us. And he gave heed unto them, expecting to receive something of them. Then Peter said, Silver and gold have I none, but such as I have I give thee. In the name of Jesus Christ of Nazareth rise up and walk.

And he took him by the right hand and lifted him up; and immediately his feet and ankle bones received strength.

—ACTS 3:4–6 KJV

The Gospel Tabernacle sometimes devoted entire services to nothing but healing. Healing is one of the many ways that God's awesome power is demonstrated even in our skeptical, modern world. No less than speaking in tongues, no less than prophesying, the authority to heal and cast out demons is real. It is as real today as it was when Jesus' followers rushed into the streets on the day of Pentecost.

An act of healing is the seed of faith for further miracles. Witnessing a miraculous healing is a great blessing. By the time Richelle was born, I had seen people healed by faith many times. Having seen it with my own eyes, I knew that it was possible and that God could heal my baby.

We had tried everything, including regular doses of prayer and laying on of hands, but even my parents, who never failed to believe we have a right to healing through faith, had said they were concerned that Richelle might not live. Then one Wednesday, I decided that the time had come to seize God's promise. God was going to heal Richelle. I knew it.

Prayer cloths are not an invention of modern Holy Roller Pentecostals. They are Biblical. Paul used them to perform miracles by remote control. Acts 19:12 describes their use. "So that from his body were brought unto the sick handkerchiefs or aprons, and the diseases departed from them, and the evil spirits went out of them" (KJV).

I went to church and got a white prayer cloth. Pastor Wise anointed the cloth, and church members prayed over it. I folded it gently, wrapped it, and put it into my purse. As soon as I got home, I pinned it to the baby's clothes.

Richelle's health improved immediately. That night, for the first time in a week, she held down her dinner. She stopped throwing up altogether. Soon she was gaining weight. Within two weeks, it was obvious that she was going to survive. My family and the entire church praised God. Because I had stepped out and exercised my faith, I received the added blessing of an increase in faith. This is the cycle of faith, the root and the fruit. First, I had believed for a miracle because I had accepted Jesus Christ and decided to believe the words of the Bible. My faith took root in the word of God. Next, I had taken action on that belief, and finally as a result of the miracle, my faith for future miracles was increased. That is the way faith works.

As my faith grew, I found I needed it more, too.

As Richelle became more active and began attempting to stand, it was obvious that she had other problems. She couldn't walk. She could stand, and grasping the bars and rails of her baby bed for balance, she managed to limp around, but she was practically walking on her ankles. Her feet collapsed outward, and she moved around like she was trying to walk up the inside of an egg. It was obviously painful, and she crumpled to the floor crying out in agony and frustration. Days and weeks went by. Richelle's first birthday passed. The family grew concerned because her feet weren't getting any better.

On a Monday in November of 1960, I took Richelle to the local doctor, James Heberle, M.D. After examining her, Dr. Heberle consulted with a specialist and described the baby's symptoms to him. As he hung up the phone, Dr. Heberle looked at me and sighed. Richelle would need to wear braces. The braces would extend from her knees down to a pair of special shoes that would keep her feet from turning out.

"She'll probably always have to wear them," he said, because her ankle bones were deformed. Dr. Heberle's staff made an appointment for me to take Richelle to the specialist on the following Friday.

I couldn't accept the diagnosis that Richelle would be crippled for life. Jesus is the same yesterday, today, and forever. What He did in the Bible, He will do today. He healed lame people. Later, the disciples healed lame people simply by saying "In the name of Jesus Christ of Nazareth, rise up and walk."

You either believe it or you don't. If you believe in healing, you must act on that belief. On Wednesday after the visit to the Burleson doctor, I bundled up the baby and drove to the Gospel Tabernacle. It was a very cold November. I shivered alternately from the cold and excitement as I carried Richelle into the sanctuary. There were only about twenty people at the Wednesday night prayer service.

When Pastor Wise saw me enter with Richelle in my arms, he knew why I was there. At the end of the service, he called, "Everybody gather round. We're going to agree for a miracle." The members of the congregation, including my parents, surrounded me. I held Richelle with her legs draped over my arm. Pastor Wise took her deformed feet in his hands. He held them up, and everyone saw that they were turned out to the sides grotesquely.

We prayed. I closed my eyes and prayed for my daughter's limbs to be straight and strong. I heard others around me praying, too. Then a few stopped praying, and Lorene Green, my aunt, gasped, "Oh!"

I looked down at my daughter and watched as her feet rotated. No longer jutting out at the ankles, they were straightening. She was being healed right before our eyes as if Jesus himself had commanded her bones to align. We praised the Lord.

Many people who were there that night remained close to me throughout my ministry. Pat Shetter and her mother Margaret Green were there. My aunt Lorene and my parents were there, too. They were all witnesses to and participants in the miracle.

I kept the appointment with the specialist on Friday, even though in the two days since Richelle's healing she had started walking. At sixteen months old, Richelle had taken her first steps outside the baby bed. The specialist looked the baby over and then asked her to walk to him. As Richelle stepped toward him, he looked at the notes he had written down when Doctor Heberle had called. He inspected her ankles again. Finally, with a confused shrug, he pronounced, "There's nothing wrong with her ankles." He asked what had happened.

"We prayed for her," I stated.

The doctor didn't say anything more. He hadn't seen the miracle, and he hadn't seen Richelle before. How could he possibly believe a miracle had occurred unless he already believed in miracles? He couldn't take my word for it. It was easier for him to believe that Dr. Heberle had been mistaken or that Richelle had never really been crippled. All he could do was pronounce that there was nothing wrong with the little girl. But at the very least he had to realize that something unusual had happened. Both Dr. Heberle and I had described Richelle's condition in the same way.

Through miracles, some people who otherwise would reject the message of Jesus Christ outright can be convinced that the story of salvation is real. Miracles plant seeds of belief that if properly cared for and nourished will grow into faith. Miracles like those that I have personally witnessed may seem to you to be more the exception than the rule, but I believe that miracles will increase in the days before Christ's return, and the outward signs of God's power will convert many unbelievers.

In 1999, Richelle became the worship leader at Lighthouse Church in Burleson. In 2010, she and her husband, Cory Smithee, left the Lighthouse to become praise leader and pastor of a church in a neighboring city. It blesses me when, filled with the Holy Spirit, she dances in a service. I remember how God healed her ankles. If God hadn't healed her, she couldn't have danced and praised Him like that.

Chapter 8

A Financial Miracle

JOHN, ALONG WITH almost 15,000 other employees of Convair, a Fort Worth division of General Dynamics, found himself without a job in 1959. The fallout from cancelled defense contracts was suffocating Burleson and other dependent suburbs. The manufacturing plant was Tarrant County's largest employer, and at its height had employed as many as 32,000 people. Bell Helicopter furloughed a large number of employees, too. LTV in Grand Prairie, another local defense contractor, terminated employees at about the same time.

The layoffs hit Fort Worth and its suburbs with about the same effect as a Saharan oasis evaporating overnight. Local subcontractors for each of the three defense manufacturing giants went into hibernation to save their businesses. John, a machinist, had to find work knowing that 30,000 men and women were pounding the same pavement, knocking on the same doors, scouring the same newspapers, and making the same telephone calls. Fort Worth was in the grips of a microcosmic depression.

Employers in businesses unrelated to defense were hesitant to hire the high-salaried workers who came looking for work. Layoffs were routine in the defense industry, and local businessmen, who had witnessed the cycle before, knew that aircraft manufacturing industries laid people off when contracts dried up, and they hired those same people back when a new agreement with the government was signed. Business owners knew it was almost impossible for a worker to turn down an offer from the defense contractor when times were good. They knew their business would suffer when the defense companies got new contracts. They would have to scramble to find replacements for the employees they would lose en masse. Companies like Texas Steel, one of the manufacturers where John had applied, turned away defense workers at the door. After two visits to Texas Steel, John was told, "There's no use coming back. We're not hiring aircraft workers. We know if we hire them, they will go back to Convair when they get a new contract."

The buck stopped with the unemployed workers. They were regarded as fickle and uncommitted by the non-defense employers.

John's unemployment check of thirty-seven dollars per week covered the house payment of eighty-seven dollars, but with two baby daughters, it was evident that our unblemished credit record would soon have more holes than a flour sifter. We had phoned creditors and were surprised that in some cases, all we needed to do was write a letter each month to explain why we couldn't make our payments. We weren't the only ones in the situation, and creditors understood the cyclical nature of the defense industry. The workers were reliable customers who would be back at work soon, and the lenders were willing to suffer temporarily along with them. There was a reasonable expectation that the defense industry employees would catch up when they went back to work.

Through it all, we believed that John would find work. If God could heal a baby's twisted ankles, He could certainly lead a man like John to a job.

I had been raised to give generously to the church. My parents had tithed, always taking ten percent off the top, before taxes, before health care, before expenses, and they often gave even more just to keep the small country church going. I was taught to regard giving as one more aspect of worship, as essential as prayer and praise. God, after all, doesn't just inhabit our words and thoughts; He inhabits our work and every dollar that we make.

There is nothing wrong with expecting God to bless our giving. God revels in our worship whatever form it takes, whether it is praising Him in church, praying, merely studying the Bible, or giving. He honors our worship, and He will reward our tithing unless the sole basis for giving is receiving in return. We should not expect God to honor our greed, and He knows our hearts and motivations.

I wanted to tithe, but John didn't understand tithing as a form of worship or as a covenant. I knew that when our finances were in crisis, that was the time when we most needed to exercise our faith through giving. The story of the widow's mite was never far from my mind during the period when John was unemployed.

I went to church one Wednesday night, and at some point during the service God spoke to me. We had seventeen dollars in the bank. It had been set aside for milk, bread, and other necessary items. I heard God telling me that if I would tithe the entire amount and if John would go to Texas Steel the next day, a job would be waiting for him there. Without hesitation, I wrote the check. All seventeen dollars. I had no doubt that God would keep His word. I carried the check down to the altar where people dropped their offerings. I left the service thrilled with anticipation. I was overflowing with joy because I knew I had heard from God.

When I got home, John had already gone to bed. I went straight to the bedroom to tell him the good news.

"You didn't," was all he could say. "You didn't."

"Yes, I wrote a check for seventeen dollars and put it on the altar." After all, I thought, that's all we had. I couldn't very well write it for more.

John sat up in bed and cradled his head between his hands in disbelief. "What am I going to do? What are we going to do?"

I realized that the burden of disbelief is the heaviest load a person can carry. The reality that we had no money suddenly hit me, but I couldn't commiserate with him. I still expected the miracle that God had promised. "You're going to Texas Steel tomorrow to get a job," I insisted.

"They told me not to come back the last time. They are not hiring aircraft workers."

"God said if you would go, you would have a job."

"I'm not going." It was final.

I awoke the next morning as full of faith as when I laid my head against the pillow. John still lay in bed beside me.

"John, get up," I said.

"I'm not going," he moaned.

"You've got to."

"They told me not to come back."

I knew I couldn't force him to go. No matter how much I believed, I could not take a step in faith for my husband. He had to take it himself. "Lord, you told me," I pleaded. I crawled out of bed praying that John would make the effort, but as the sun rose higher and the day grew brighter, the promise that had risen with the new day was fading. An hour passed. Two.

He finally came into the kitchen at ten thirty. "I guess I'll go up there," he conceded. He didn't want to disappoint me, and I loved him for that. Besides, he had nothing to lose. He had no other prospects.

That wasn't the point for me. I had never worried about what we had to lose, only what we had to gain. Even so, it was getting late. I felt John should have gone first thing in the morning. If the company had any openings, they would almost certainly have hired someone else by this hour. There were thousands of people looking for work, but I didn't express a doubt to John. I had a word from God, and that should be enough for both of us.

If I had faltered in my belief, he may not have gone. He left the house dressed casually in blue jeans and a short-sleeved shirt.

He drove into the parking lot at Texas Steel, pulled to a stop, and sat there for a moment convinced that the staff of the employment office would laugh when they saw him coming. When John started across the parking lot, a department manager spotted him. They knew each other well.

"Hey, John, do you want a job?" he called out. "We've got an opening in our department, and you can go to work right now if you want it." John went to work that afternoon.

Our family has been tithing ever since. I had always felt that if I wasn't tithing, I was not in obedience to God. John began to believe it, too.

By giving all I had, I established a covenant with God. He didn't tell me to give five dollars, seven or even ten. It took every bit that I had at that moment to establish the covenant. Jesus paid it *all* for us. All we have can never measure up to the all He paid.

I saw my family's situation as very similar to the Gentile woman that God sent Elisha to during a famine. She had only enough meal and oil to make one cake of bread. She and her son were going to eat it. They expected to starve together soon after sharing that last cake.

Elisha told her to bring him the cake. She obeyed. She gave him all she had. Then Elisha told her that God had said her flour bin and oil would never be empty (I Kings 17). And God honored that one instance of sacrificial giving. God multiplied and gave back to her, providing her with all she needed.

I have asked the Lord, "Why all?" I believe it was because the woman was outside the covenant. She was a Gentile, but that faith to believe Elisha and give everything brought her into covenant, and that was what God did with us. I gave all we had. As Christians, we had a salvation covenant, but this brought us into a financial covenant. God has blessed us financially ever since that day. We are not wealthy, but He has always provided.

Eventually, John returned to Convair. He retired from General Dynamics at the end of 1990.

Chapter 9

My Tonsillitis Miracle

FROM THE TIME I was a child, I had suffered from recurring tonsillitis. I sometimes had several attacks in one year, many of them so painful that drinking water felt like swallowing razor blades. The attacks continued even after my daughters were born. During a severe attack of tonsillitis in the spring of 1960, while I was working at International Service Insurance Company in Fort Worth, I stopped at the doctor's office on my way to work for a shot of antibiotics; I stopped by the office for another in the afternoon on my way home.

One Wednesday evening after my shot, I felt very ill. I'm going to church tonight, I told myself. "We're going to pray. I will be healed." Anytime I had a need for healing, I knew that going to church and having a prayer of agreement with laying on of hands was the surest route to health. We have assurance of this in James 5:14–15:

> Is any sick among you? let him call for the elders of the church; and let them pray over him, anointing him with oil in the name of the Lord: And the prayer of faith shall save the sick, and the Lord shall raise him up; and if he have committed sins, they shall be forgiven him.

Miracles are more likely to take place in a corporate anointing—"For where two or three are gathered together in my name, there I am in the midst of them" (Matthew 18:20). I got the kids ready. No matter how bad I felt, I was going to be prayed for, and I was going to ask God for the miracle that I would never have tonsillitis again.

The church prayed for me that night, and God honored my faith in the same way that he honored the faith of the woman who reached out and touched Jesus' robe. Her faith made her whole. In many cases where Jesus healed someone, He acknowledged their faith and healed them because they had believed enough to take some kind of action. When He said, "Your faith has made you well," it was because the woman had faith enough to reach out and take her healing.

During the service, several members of the church gathered round and prayed for me. I left that night knowing that I had been healed.

Six months later, with no further attacks of tonsillitis, I stood in front of the bathroom mirror and wondered what my tonsils looked like. I hadn't suffered any pain, not even a sore throat. I opened my mouth and then praised God. I didn't have any tonsils. A few months later when I was getting a physical, the doctor asked when I had my tonsils out.

"I've never had my tonsils out," I said. "God healed me and removed them."

The doctor didn't ask any more questions. More than forty years later, I have never suffered again from tonsillitis. How could I? I don't have any tonsils.

The covenant of faith is more than just praying, "Lord, please heal me." It is knowing that we will be healed, not doubting, but standing by faith on God's promises. We take command by proclaiming that we are healed.

Chapter 10

Stuart's Miracle Birth

Tony Wise led the Tabernacle for a little less than a year before leaving for other evangelistic work at a larger church in Fort Worth. I was sad to see him go. After all, he had stood and watched with me as God straightened Richelle's twisted feet. People who share a miracle, just like soldiers who have fought beside each other in battle or people who have survived the same catastrophe, share a bond. Even if they never see each other again, they are related from that moment on. When Pastor Wise left the church, I was full of hope that God would send a pastor to the Gospel Tabernacle who would continue to preach faith in the same way that Lavada Reed and Tony Wise had. Our new pastor loved the Lord, and he taught from the word, but I personally needed to hear a different message, at least at that point in my life.

A year after Pastor Wise left, I was pregnant with my third baby. Early on, the baby was in grave danger. Doctors were not optimistic. In some pregnancies, a condition of the blood causes the mother's immune system to form antibodies to the baby's blood as though it is a disease, and her body's defenses attack what appears to it as foreign matter. The baby becomes anemic because the mother's body destroys the infant's blood cells. The red blood cells die off faster than the infant's body can replace them. Babies that survived the curse called hemolytic disease often were born prematurely. The baby was at constant risk throughout the pregnancy. Today, doctors can usually treat this condition before it becomes life threatening.

Tony Wise had become the pastor of the Meadowbrook Evangelistic Temple, a much larger church than the Gospel Tabernacle. It was located in a community on the east side of Fort Worth, about twenty miles North of Burleson. I visited services there and re-discovered the same atmosphere that I had loved at the Gospel Tabernacle when Pastor Wise was its leader. God's presence was palpable in each service, and the church couldn't get enough of praise and worship.

During the fifth month of my pregnancy, I was told the baby in my womb may be dead. There was no movement. If there was a heartbeat, it was so faint that he couldn't hear it. He said there was no sign of life. "Expect anything. Something could be very wrong." He told me that he wanted to start seeing me every week.

Even though I had seen miracles first hand, I needed to breathe the rarefied air of an atmosphere saturated with faith and worship. I knew I was sick. I was struggling with the pregnancy and needed to hear a message of faith and hope and be in a church where the gifts of the spirit were low hanging fruit. I started making the long drive every Sunday for morning worship and in June, 1962, joined the Evangelistic Temple.

Tony Wise's faith message coincided with the emergence of the faith movement led by Kenneth Hagin and other evangelists in the sixties. Brother Tony's message wasn't exactly like theirs. It was simpler. Pastor Wise preached faith. He was always preaching about somebody being healed in the Word and how Jesus worked miracles.

Miracles were standard fare at the Evangelistic Temple. People, sometimes at the point of death, were healed when we prayed for them.

Jesus healed the sick and raised the dead. His disciples healed the sick and raised the dead, too, under his tutelage but particularly after the meeting at Pentecost when they were baptized in the Holy Spirit. The apostles, Paul, Timothy, Silas, Barnabas, and others, healed the sick through the power of the Holy Spirit even though they were not present at the Pentecost meeting. So the Holy Spirit was never limited to Jesus, the twelve apostles, or to the people present at Pentecost.

Pastor Tony taught that the gifts of the Holy Spirit are available to Christians today. He taught about the operational gifts: prophecy and words of knowledge. A word of knowledge often accompanies a message given in tongues as an interpretation. Paul's first letter to the Corinthians describes the gifts of the Spirit:

> Now to each one the manifestation of the Spirit is given for the common good To one there is given through the Spirit a message of wisdom, to another a message of knowledge by means of the same Spirit, to another faith by the same Spirit, to another gifts of healing by that one Spirit, to another miraculous powers, to another prophecy, to another distinguishing between spirits, to

another speaking in different kinds of tongues, and to still another the interpretation of tongues. All these are the work of one and the same Spirit, and he distributes them to each one, just as he determines.

—I Corinthians 12:7–11, niv

I had been seeing the doctor every week for two months. I was continually ill. Still at 117 pounds in the seventh month of my pregnancy, I hadn't gained much weight. Lots of people remarked that I didn't look pregnant. The baby was riding so low that it looked as though I just had a stomach that pooched. I had no energy, although I was trying to care for my daughters, and I was working. The doctor still couldn't hear a heartbeat, and I hadn't felt any movement of the baby in months. After listening again, he announced that the baby was dead. There definitely was no heartbeat, he said. He told me that my life may be in danger, too, and he wanted me to go to the hospital. He planned to induce labor that day. "We need to take this baby," he said.

The idea horrified me. Without knowing with certainty that my baby was dead, to have induced labor would be tantamount to aborting my child. I told him that I couldn't do that. If there was any chance that my baby might live, I could not let them take it prematurely. "I'm putting myself and the baby in God's hands," I told him. I had been telling him that for two months because I knew that he was worried, and I felt like I needed to reassure him.

"If you haven't gone to the hospital by Saturday morning," he answered, "I want you to come to the office. I'm going to take an x-ray." Doctors didn't like to take fetal x-rays, but he was so concerned for my life that he had to do something to see what was happening.

I returned on Saturday. After the x-ray, I could tell the nurse was worried. In the consultation, the doctor insisted, "I want you to go right over to the hospital and check yourself in." He was convinced I was in eminent danger. The baby's head was in the birth canal.

"No," I said. "I'm in God's hands. He's taking care of me, and I will be all right."

"God, give me a word," I prayed driving home after the doctor's earthbound prophecy that my baby would die. I prayed that evening and almost constantly for the next day. I had seen God heal, and I knew that God could resurrect the baby in my womb. I had seen too many miracles to believe anything else. God could resurrect my baby as dramatically as he could straighten Richelle's twisted ankles, as personally as he had cured my tonsillitis, or with as inconspicuous a miracle as finding a job for John.

"Keep me going. Give me direction," I cried out, but only to God. "I've got to have a word." Even if the Lord wanted me to listen to the doctor and have labor induced, I needed guidance. I didn't believe that's what He wanted, but I needed some assurance that I was doing the right thing. I hadn't told anyone else about the doctor's prognosis. It was a secret between the doctor, John, God, and me. At least as far as I knew it was a secret.

My aunt Lorene knew, too. I hadn't told her, but Lorene was friends with one of the nurses who worked in the doctor's office. In fact, Lorene may have known more than I did. The nurse had confided to her that the doctor was concerned about me. He had no fear about the baby's survival. He felt it was a certainty that the baby was dead. He was concerned that I would die, too.

The next evening, in church, I stood with my eyes closed and my hands raised in praise and supplication along with the rest of the congregation while Pastor Tony spoke a word of knowledge. "My daughter, you have desired a word from me this morning," he started out, and I sensed immediately this was for me. I prayed in the spirit seeking God's guidance, willing to claim whatever the pastor would say next as a prophetic word just for me. "Your baby will live and will be perfect." Tony's voice grew louder. "And the doctors will marvel."

I felt Tony's finger touching my forehead and opened my eyes. There was more to the word, but I don't remember anything else. I had not felt any movement from the baby for more than three months, but immediately I felt a kick. It wasn't a small movement. It was a strong, healthy, vibrant shift. I couldn't help thinking of the New Testament's description of the baby "leaping" in Elizabeth's womb when Mary, who was pregnant with Jesus, visited. I knew that my baby was alive.

The doctors did marvel. Stuart, my first son, was born on September 5, 1962, and he was perfect. A month premature, in fact one month to the day before the date the doctor had calculated, Stuart's organs were fully developed and healthy, although at five pounds he was expectedly small. The pediatrician visited my room in the hospital. "Is this an eight-month baby?"

he asked. After I confirmed, he said that he could tell by the baby's size and the bones. the doctor added that those things were consistent with the baby's age, but his lungs and all his vital organs were perfect like those of a full-term baby. "I haven't seen that before," he said. That fulfilled the pastor's prophecy that the baby would be perfect, and the doctors would marvel. One doctor after another expressed surprise and disbelief.

My baby came alive when Pastor Tony spoke the words of life. The pastor spoke a word of knowledge, a prophetic word, and a creative word. I believe when God gave that word through the pastor, it sparked life in my child. It was a resurrection miracle.

Not everyone exhibits all the gifts of the spirit all the time, but Tony Wise often displayed the gifts of prophecy and laying hands on the sick. I believed in miracles before Pastor Wise came to our church, but during his tenure, the series of healing miracles that I personally experienced would have made a believer of a stone.

Chapter 11

God Healed My Blood

After Pastor Tony's word, I didn't have any other problems with the pregnancy. I felt fine. I knew my baby would survive, too. Just as in the early church, people with other gifts came into our lives. At the church in Meadowbrook, we experienced many of the gifts described in Corinthians. It was almost like going to ministry school all the time.

Despite the miracle of Stuart's survival, my gynecologist warned me that I should not have another baby. He said bluntly that if I did, it was doubtful that the baby would survive, and my life would be in extreme jeopardy, too, because of my blood condition. That's when he finally told me that it had been a miracle that I had survived Stuart's birth.

I intended to do as he said. I didn't want to risk another pregnancy. I did not want to risk losing a child. But our plans aren't always God's plan for us, and God obviously had plans for my family to continue growing. I was soon pregnant with my fourth baby.

Dr. Turner wasn't happy. Deeply concerned and a little frustrated with me, he told me to stay off my feet throughout the pregnancy and reminded me that he had warned me about the dangers of having another child. I assured him I was all right and that God would take care of me. I understood his concern, but I felt a little sorry for him. I knew everything would be ok. God had already blessed my life with one miracle after another. I had no reason to think that he would not deliver one more, if it was needed. "The Lord will take care of me," I insisted.

Despite my conviction that I had nothing to worry about, I stayed home and tried to follow the doctor's advice. God doesn't expect us to ignore earthly authorities or common sense. So I stayed off my feet as much as I could even though I had three children who needed care.

I still went to church as often as I was able. I wasn't far into my pregnancy when a visiting evangelist pointed me out in the congregation and prophesied saying, "God is showing me that he is healing your blood. Are you aware you have a blood disorder?"

"Yes," I replied.

He instructed me to go to the doctor and have my blood tested to confirm that I had been healed.

During my next pre-natal visit, they did the routine blood work, and when the doctor got the results, he seemed confused as he said, "Your blood is perfect." Then he added, "You're not even anemic anymore." He paused before he tacked on the most unbelievable part, at least for him, "You know, once you have developed this condition, there is no cure for it. There is no drug you can take, and it doesn't just go away. But that is what has happened here. At least as far as I can tell that is what has happened here."

What else could I say, except, "I told you the Lord would take care of me." He did. He does. And He will.

Chapter 12

Reveille: My First Call to Ministry

EARLY IN THE pregnancy, I realized that God was calling me to a ministry at Meadowbrook Evangelistic Temple. I was certain God was calling me into the youth ministry, but a talented and committed couple was in charge of the Temple's young people already.

I felt God's call was very specific. I was supposed to lead the Meadowbrook Temple's youth group. I would never have interfered with the young Christian couple, and I would willingly do anything I could to help them. This was the first time God had called me to a specific ministry, and I was excited about that, but it confused me that the position was already filled.

"Make use of the time to prepare," God said. I began studying the Bible with the intent of preparing lessons. If God had a plan for my life in youth ministry, I wanted to do everything I could to be ready. I used my time to outline lessons. I knew without a doubt I would need them later. I still let thoughts about the youth pastors nag me. I had to tell someone about my confusion. So I spoke to my aunt Lorene. I had turned to Lorene a lot since Lavada Reed's departure, and after I had received the word about the youth ministry, I asked Lorene to study the Bible with me regularly.

"I don't think you should tell anybody else," Lorene advised. "The church has a youth pastor, and they might get the impression that you were trying to take their place."

I assured Lorene that I hadn't intended to tell anyone else. I explained that I had told her only because we were so close. By the time my second son, Otis, was born on December 15, 1963, I had developed a curriculum and formulated a plan to expand Meadowbrook's youth ministry.

Chapter 13

Pneumonia Miracle

OTIS WAS BORN healthy and whole, without complications and on schedule. It was snowing three nights later, on my birthday, when we took him home. We had moved into a new house on Murphy Street in Burleson a month before the baby was born.

It was a cold winter. John was putting in long hours, seven days a week, on the evening shift. Defense industry work is either boom or bust, and in 1963, it was booming again. Unfortunately, that meant John couldn't be home with me in the weeks following the birth.

Typical of middle class households in the sixties, we didn't have a clothes dryer. I washed clothes and hung them on a clothesline strung across the back yard. Clothes dried quickly in the heat of summer and in the winds of fall, but winter was different. With four young children, I spent a lot of time with the laundry. Life had become a constant relay between the washer, the clothesline, and the kitchen. One afternoon, sheets, towels, diapers, clothes, everything had been hung on the clothesline, and it started raining. The soaked clothes froze on the line.

Whether from exhaustion, the incessant running in and out between the warm house and the freezing back yard, or a contagion that I had picked up in the hospital, I got pneumonia. I hadn't been diagnosed, but I was too sick to drive Otis to the doctor for a scheduled visit. When I called to cancel the appointment, the doctor diagnosed my condition over the phone. I could hardly talk, and I was coughing.

"You have pneumonia," the doctor said. "Go check yourself into the hospital."

"I can't. I have these kids to take care of." I suffered with the illness for the next couple of days until the baby got sick, too. Coughing and burning up with fever, he was having as much trouble breathing as I was. When my cousin, Doris Couch, came by to see the baby, I could barely stand to answer the door. Coughing, I pulled it open.

Doris immediately realized how sick I was. She knew the pharmacist and called him for advice about the best medications. Although it was a Saturday night and the store had already closed, the pharmacist returned and pulled the medicines. I started taking them right away. We prayed. We called the pastor to have the church pray for us, too.

If my cousin hadn't helped us, Otis could have died. I was in no condition to take care of him. I was as sick as he was. In a daze with fever, I was not thinking well and may not have been able to keep track of the medications or the proper doses.

Both the baby and I began to get better with Doris's nursing, the medication, and prayer. Although God used Doris, the healing from pneumonia wasn't any less a miracle than the realignment of Richelle's feet or God breathing life into Stuart while he was still in the womb. In this case, God had used a caring human mediator to deliver His healing. It was just a different kind of miracle. Maybe God wanted me to realize that He performs miracles in a lot of different ways. The miracles where God uses others often are overlooked. That really doesn't diminish them. They are just as profound as any of the miracles where God's hand is obviously at work. Sometimes, a miracle is in the eye of the beholder.

I continued to prepare for my ministry. Once I was able to return to church, I learned that the couple that had been leading the youth at Meadowbrook had resigned. They were moving out of town. When they turned in their resignations, they told Lorene, and she passed the word to me. That was convincing confirmation that God had called me into youth ministry at the Meadowbrook church. It was a miracle, too. God had called me to the ministry knowing that new opportunities were opening up for the young couple. Then He had set everything in motion for me to prepare for the ministry He had given me. Sometimes God's timing is a miracle.

I had said nothing to Pastor Wise. I was convinced that if God had selected me for a ministry, the circumstances would align perfectly in God's will, and Tony would somehow confirm God's hand in it. I didn't ask for the job. Lorene asked for me. She let the pastor know that I had been interested in leading the church's youth ministry, and she told him how I had been preparing for it.

Throughout my life, whenever I received a word or a miracle from God, I waited for a confirmation before acting or speaking about it. The second confirmation, as I knew it must, came from the pastor. In mid-January, 1964, Pastor Tony phoned and asked, "Would you like to lead our youth?"

I accepted the position because I saw the invitation for exactly what it was: God's confirmation that He had whispered the same secret to Pastor Tony that He had whispered to me, even if God's still, small voice had sounded a lot like Aunt Lorene's to Pastor Tony.

There weren't many teenagers in the church. Most of the church members were young married couples with small children. Nevertheless, I dove into the unpaid job with all the enthusiasm that could be expected of a former Texas high school cheerleader. I surrounded the three teenagers who regularly attended church and began organizing. We started visiting other teenagers who had previously attended, and we invited them back. Sunday school attendance doubled within three weeks. We visited the newcomers' friends who didn't already attend church somewhere. Then they started recruiting others.

"Kevin is a good prospect," one of the kids would volunteer, and the next week a team of young missionaries appeared on Kevin's doorstep inviting him to church. Once a week, we visited young people and witnessed to them right in their homes. Visitation paid other benefits, too. It gave us a chance to fellowship and share our faith with each other. Often we wound up at a fast food place where we had refreshments and talked about the problems that young people faced. It became a social event, sometimes a Bible study, sometimes a praise, worship or prayer session. Many young people we visited started coming to church.

I was learning as we went. While I had no formal training, I was prepared for the ministry. I had been preparing throughout my pregnancy. I guess, in some ways, I had been preparing all my life.

Jesus walked alongside his twelve disciples for three years. They had various educations and backgrounds. He trained them personally. Paul, and others who may never even have seen Christ, were educated, but they had no formal training in Christian ministry, they only had the call. There is no reason to believe that God ranks his missionaries by educational level or training, and that's partly because of the very simplicity of the message: believe that Jesus Christ is the son of God, that He died on the cross as the sacrifice for our sins, and that we inherit eternal life by simply acknowledging that truth. Your witness to Jesus Christ's effect on your life is really all you need to be a modern day apostle, but it doesn't hurt to study the Bible so that you can lead others to Him using God's own words.

We really got into the Word in our Sunday school class. The kids liked it. They enjoyed the study of the Word and learning scriptures. We talked a lot about witnessing and leading people to the Lord, and many of the kids were as excited about our mission as Christians as I was. By the end of 1964, between thirty and forty teenagers regularly attended Sunday school and church.

I got my brothers, seven and ten years younger than me, into the act, and before long many of the young people participating in the Meadowbrook Evangelistic Temple's youth program were from Burleson. The Lord did everything a step at a time. He worked through Brother Wise, the teenagers, and through me to build the youth ministry, and the participation continued to grow over the next ten years.

The title of youth director was an honorary one. I wasn't compensated for my labor, at least not in the currency that puts steak on the dinner table, but I was happy to serve in any way I could. I taught Sunday school. I played the piano in church services and organized all the youth activities.

Chapter 14

Vision of a Ministry

O N A SATURDAY night in 1966, I sat up late at the kitchen table. The children were in bed, and I was putting the final touches on Sunday's lesson. The evening's shadows had relinquished their grip on the day and dissolved into the darkness. I had the lights on but could feel the darkness, not just the darkness of night, but spiritual darkness. The sense of doom was palpable.

I worked alone, quietly and intently, when all of a sudden I was caught in a vision. It was like dreaming, but I wasn't asleep. I found myself in a waking nightmare. I was surrounded by a pressing throng of somnambulists who were oblivious to me, or their own peril, as they herded past.

I looked forward and saw a crowd of people walking toward me. They walked past like they didn't see me. I heard screaming, and I looked over to my left. I saw those who had just passed me walk right off a cliff. They didn't seem to care until it was too late. They were oblivious to all the others in front of them who were crying out as they stepped over the threshold of eternity. Once they started falling, nothing could be done. Over the cliff they went, one after another, mindless of the others who were falling right in front of them and beside them. They fell off the cliff into darkness. Pitch black. Outer darkness.

I didn't see hell, only darkness, but when they fell off the cliff, they shrieked in such agony that it was as though they had been set afire. I didn't see them bursting into flames, but I could tell by the horror in their screams that they had awakened from their dreams to find themselves damned. It seemed impossible that those who had not yet reached the cliff were oblivious to the horror. One after another, they marched blindly behind the people in front of them right over the edge of the cliff. I warned them that they were heading for the cliff, but they ignored me, or they didn't see me. I waved my hands and tried to get their attention. They kept flowing toward the cliff like zombies.

Then I looked to my right. No one was going to my right. On a hill were three crosses, just as you might imagine the scene at Calvary. I saw Jesus on the cross, and I turned back to the people and tried to stop them again.

"Stop. Go back. Go to the cross," I yelled, holding up my hands. I stood in front of one young man and tried to block his way. "Turn back, turn away." But he kept walking. I was powerless to stop him. I tried to grab a teenage girl. She didn't struggle to resist; she kept walking and slipped right out of my grasp as though I wasn't there. I began to cry because I could see the chasm they were blindly walking into and they couldn't. So many had already walked past me and fallen over the cliff.

I cried and pleaded with them to open their eyes. Finally, one boy noticed me. He looked at me curiously at first, then he began to listen, and as soon as he started listening, his eyes grew wide as he realized he was walking toward the precipice. I told him to look at the cross. When he did, he started walking in that direction. Others paused and listened to me, and when they did, they turned and started climbing toward the cross, too.

To most of the people in the stream of lost souls, it was like I wasn't even there. They never saw me, never heard me. But out of the hundreds or, I don't know, maybe even thousands, some awoke. Occasionally, one would listen and change course.

As the vision faded, I found myself still sitting at the kitchen table in front of my Sunday school lesson. I wept. I cried for all those people who are willfully deaf to the word. I scribbled the words to a song. It described what I had seen. It was really poignant. The chorus was "turn away, turn away from the world of sin and look to the Lord today." The song described my vision. The Lord gave me a melody for it, too. I sang it as a duet with my sister at the Meadowbrook church, especially at Easter, for many years.

JESUS THE SAVIOR

What darkness on
That fateful day
That Jesus died for all.
The earth did quake
And thunder roll
When Jesus hung all alone
What great love of God
To give His son

To pay such an awful cost
Twas for the sins
Of you and me
That sent our Lord to the cross.

Turn away. Turn away.
From the world of sin
And look to the Lord today.
He's calling you from sin and strife
To give you peace and life.

His crown was of thorns
His throne a cross
His scepter was a reed.
But to this end
Was Jesus born
To meet our every need.
He finished the work
And on the third day
He arose our Lord and King
He's seated on high
To give you and me
The gift of eternal life

My eyes had been opened. I sat at the table weeping for all those people who had failed to listen. I finally understood what it is to dedicate your life to God and what I had meant when I told my classmates as a teenager in high school that I had been set aside for special work. I understood what being a Christian is really about. It isn't about my salvation alone. It is about the salvation of all those who are doomed if someone doesn't speak out and try to wake them and turn them in the direction of the cross. There are too few standing in the stream, warning others that they can save themselves by simply opening their eyes and looking to Jesus for their salvation.

That vision was my call. God calls each of us in a unique way, and I knew this was mine. I knew what I was supposed to do. I was to stand in the stream and cry out.

I have never thought of myself as an evangelist. I have never been one of those itinerant ministers who travel from church to church preaching revival. I'm not an evangelist in that sense, but I am an evangelist in the sense that I am commissioned to win the lost for Jesus. After seeing that vision, I couldn't have done anything else with my life.

How can anyone who sees the precipice ahead remain silent? If any one of us saw someone who was sleepwalking, drugged, or dazed and who was walking mindlessly toward a cliff or onto a busy highway, we would scream out, block their way, try to grab them and stop them. Even if there was nothing that we could do, we would at least gasp in horror. How is it then that any of us who believes in the cross will stand idly without a sense of loss or compunction and allow our families, friends, neighbors or even perfect strangers to walk mindlessly into eternal darkness? We must cry out.

God's call to me on that Saturday evening was the same as His call to every Christian, anyone who professes to believe that Jesus died on the cross and in doing so paid the full price for his sin, her sin, my sin, everyone's sin.

I sat at the table and cried, still hearing the screams, and I knew that I had to wake as many as I could.

In class the next morning, I told the teenagers about my vision. I told them to bring their friends to church, and in my lessons for the next several weeks, I taught them about witnessing. I had a mandate to win the lost. Although I was shy, I had never been reticent about sharing the gospel with others, but now I understood the urgency of getting through to each person I could as I had never felt it before. I realized that the Christian walk is not a complacent one. It is a desperate struggle to reach out and grab the hand of each passerby who is heading toward the cliff.

I began meeting with some of the kids during the week. I took the young people out, and we witnessed to people on the streets and at shopping centers. That became the thrust of my youth ministry. I wanted to teach young people who had been saved how to grow in the Lord and how to lead other people to Him.

We had a lot of good experiences. Many people wanted to hear what we had to say. They were hungry. They asked questions and wanted to know more. Then there were those who wouldn't even let you talk to them. It was just like my vision. They slid past as though they were already ghosts.

Arise. Shine. Share the good news of our salvation.

Chapter 15

Otis Saved from the Jaws of Death

MY YOUNGEST, OTIS, was small for his age, but trouble could spot him coming from a mile away and invariably rushed to meet him. It embraced him like a long lost brother. Otis wasn't bad, he was a cherub, but bad luck stuck to him like slick on a snail. When he was three-years-old, we had a sofa with a wooden frame. We laid pillows at each end to cover the wood. One afternoon, Otis and Stuart got into a scuffle on the sofa, and Otis fell to the floor knocking out his front teeth.

The dentist pressed the teeth back up into his gums, and they stayed even though they looked very long. Later, Otis was out playing and jumped off the patio table and didn't land quite right. His face hit the floor, and his teeth popped out again. This time the dentist wasn't able to put them back. So from the time Otis was three until he was nearly seven, he didn't have three front teeth, but everybody remarked about how cute he was.

At first, part of his cuteness was his size. When he was four, he was still being mistaken for a two-year-old.

"How old is he, about two?" newcomers to the church guessed.

While I was secretly concerned, I told myself and others that Otis was just small for his age. He was bound to grow out of it.

In April, after Otis's fourth birthday, the kids were spending a few days with their grandmother at the farm. The girls, now in the second and third grades at Mound Elementary School, were out for spring break.

My brother Ercel was still in high school. He wasn't around that afternoon, but he had a new dog, a German shepherd. He had found it about eight months earlier and was very attached to it. He and the dog were almost constant companions. The dog was very playful. It rollicked and played with Ercel and other kids all the time. But that dog did not like Otis.

It was a time in rural America when children could still wander along a country road without an adult to watch over them every second, and the four galloping Gillaspies decided to go to the pasture to play. They were exploring along a dirt road and had turned down a path that was barely more than a pair of tractor ruts.

As they started down the hill, the dog appeared out of nowhere and charged toward them. It attacked Otis, biting his legs and knocking him to the ground. The dog's teeth cut deep into the tiny limbs. The animal seemed intent on killing him and lunged repeatedly at his throat. Shanda, only ten-years-old herself and no behemoth, forced her way between them, but her efforts only drew the dog's ire. The shepherd attacked her. It bit her legs and hips and tore her clothes. The diversion probably saved Otis' life. The dog was much bigger than he was, and it wouldn't have taken long for the animal to tear my baby boy to shreds. Instantly, the four children were locked in a life and death battle with the dog. If the dog hadn't been so fixated on Otis, there's no telling how much damage it could have done to all of them.

Frances, my mother, heard the screams all the way up at the farmhouse. She raced down the hill picking up a stick somewhere along the way. As she got close and saw what was happening, she beat the dog away from the children who were scattered like a patch of busted watermelons. She stripped Otis from Shanda and tried to carry him. Although it was hard to tell which of the children was most severely injured, the dog was unrelenting in its vicious attack on Otis. It continued trying to tear Otis from mother's arms as she carried him all the way up the hill to the house. She fought the dog with the stick, battling for each step and simultaneously trying to protect the whole terror-stricken brood.

Only when she got them in the house could she assess the damages. Shanda bore the marks of her sacrifice for months. Her hips and legs were covered with bruises, punctures, lacerations and knots where the dog had bitten her. But the bloody punctures covering Otis were horrifying. He was lucky to be alive.

Grief stricken, heart sick, and horrified, Ercel got rid of the dog.

When Ercel's dog attacked Otis, Shanda sacrificed herself for her baby brother. She stepped in and fought against the powerful animal until mother arrived and took up the fight. God used Shanda because she had the courage to stand in the breach and face an overwhelming power that she knew she could not overcome on her own. Just as Frances came running to the children's rescue, God will rescue us, but we have a responsibility to stand in the breach and defend our brothers and sisters by telling them that Jesus Christ is the way, the truth, and the life even while they flow past us, oblivious to the message. God is looking for us to act.

Chapter 16

Appending Otis

BOUT TWO MONTHS later, in June, I was at work when I got a call from my younger sister, who had been babysitting the children. Mary was concerned about Otis.

"He hasn't felt well all day," she said. "A while ago he started screaming." He had stopped screaming and was quiet before she called. "But I don't know what's wrong with him."

It was obvious, as Mary caught her breath to continue, that his condition was severe and getting worse. My sister would not have bothered to call so near time for me to get off work unless she was one breath short of panic. "I can't leave right away." I explained that I would get off work in fifteen minutes. It was about four thirty, and I left work at four forty-five with the three girls in my car pool. I scrambled out of the car at five fifteen and rushed into the house barely turning to say goodbye to the girls.

Otis was quiet, but I could tell at a glance that he was terribly sick. Wan and pale, he seemed nothing like himself. It was a Friday afternoon, and I called the doctor's office immediately, knowing as I dialed that the office was already closed. The only options were to rush him to the emergency room or wait until Saturday morning and take him to the clinic. He had a little fever, but not extremely high. So I called my parents, and they thought he might have a virus. They decided to come by. They went by the store and got some lemons and fruit juice on the way over. My father showed up with peppermint candy. Peppermint candy could heal any childhood ailment according to my father. It worked on everything from the flu to a stubbed toe and cured halitosis in the process.

We gave Otis some Tylenol for his fever and prayed for him. He seemed to be doing okay for the time being. We had decided he must have a virus because one had been going around, and several kids on our block had been sick that week.

Despite our diagnosis, I sat up caring for him most of the night. I had never seen any of my kids so lethargic even when they were very ill. I was worried and wouldn't feel comfortable until the doctor could tell me that Otis was just suffering from some common childhood malady or had gotten a bug that was making the rounds.

Otis awoke several times. I soon lost count of the number of times I got up to care for him. The next morning I took him to the doctor first thing. The only doctor's office in town opened at nine in the morning and closed again at noon on Saturdays, a small window of opportunity. Added to that, almost everyone else sitting in the waiting room had an appointment. We didn't. So we had to wait until there was an opening in the clinic's busy schedule. They didn't call us until noon, when they were ready to close.

When the doctor took a look at Otis, it almost seemed cursory and anti-climactic. He pressed the baby's stomach. It was as hard as a rock. That was all he needed to make a definitive diagnosis. He announced almost casually, "His appendix has ruptured. He's a very sick boy." The doctor immediately called Cook Children's Hospital in Fort Worth and arranged for Otis to be admitted as soon as I got there with him. A surgeon would be ready to operate.

We drove to the hospital where nurses drew blood and orderlies whisked him away so that doctors could perform a series of tests to determine just how bad his condition was. Almost as soon as the tests were completed, a doctor returned to the family. Most of us had gathered outside the emergency room. Otis's white cell count was 26,000.

"A normal range," the doctor explained, "would be between 8,000 and 11,000, and such a high reading indicates a severe infection. Peritonitis sets in at about 18,000. Otis is in critical condition." He hesitated and took a breath before going on. "I'm sorry," he commiserated, "I think surgery would be useless."

All I could do was cry. We called the church, and the pastor came up. We gathered together and prayed in the intensive care room. For more than two hours, the family haunted the ICU where Otis was spending his last few hours. Although the doctors had given us no hope, we prayed anyway. Friends from the church dropped by, and others who had gone to the church to pray were updated regularly: there was no change.

Then, a little more than two hours after Otis had been moved into the ICU, the doctor returned for a second consultation with John and me. "I have decided to go ahead and do the surgery," he told us. The hospital staff had been monitoring Otis closely, and something made him decide to do the operation. He didn't explain why he had changed his mind, but that was the first answer to our prayers, a small miracle.

Even so, the doctor didn't proffer much hope that Otis would survive the night, even less that he would recover if he made it off the operating table. In fact, it almost seemed that he was going out of his way to refrain from encouraging us. He didn't want to get our hopes up.

We prayed and waited while Otis was in surgery. Gangrene had set in, and the infection had spread throughout his body. After the surgery, the doctor told us that his appendix had been diseased for a long time. That may have been the reason for his stunted growth. He had been poisoned by his own appendix for much of his short life.

When the nurses returned Otis to ICU and I was permitted to sit with him, his body was so swollen that he looked like a fat baby. Well-meaning visitors dropped by, and almost without exception, they observed that Otis looked fat and healthy. Their comments were meant to console and encourage me and the rest of the family, but they only heightened my concern. He wasn't fat. His whole body was swollen.

As Saturday bled into Sunday, the doctors still weren't optimistic. They had made a heroic effort, but Otis was still very sick. We sat with him all day, and by Sunday night with no sign of improvement, John and I were exhausted. I had lain down on a bench outside intensive care. John, down the hall in the room reserved for Otis, had fallen asleep. I was dozing when a nurse nudged me and said, "Mrs. Gillaspie, I think you need to come back to the room."

Otis was dying.

I wiped the tears from my eyes before I entered the room. Smiling at my small son, I struggled not to cry in front of him. All I could do was say, "Jesus." That single word was my prayer. Other than that, my mind wouldn't work to pray.

By two o'clock Monday morning, Otis started convulsing. The nurses frantically tried to get hold of the doctor, but when they finally got through to him, he didn't have any new suggestions. There was nothing more they could do except try to make him comfortable.

There was nothing that doctors and medicine could do, but people had been dropping by the church to leave prayers for Otis ever since Saturday afternoon when news began to spread about his illness. There was almost always someone at the church praying.

After I had been in the room with Otis for a while, all of a sudden there was a noise. He had passed wind. I asked the nurse about it. She hadn't noticed the sound, and she dismissed the possibility that his gastrointestinal system might be functioning at all. "His intestines don't work," she explained. She described how the surgeons had lifted the intestines out and washed them during the surgery because they were covered with poison. It would be days before his intestines would function again. It went unstated that he wasn't expected to live that long.

Immediately after that, he began to have a bowel movement. Not being a nurse, I didn't realize the significance of that, but the nurse did. Soon other medical staff appeared in the room. They were excited, and it was as if they were rejoicing more as the mess grew. I didn't know what the celebration was all about, but it was unbelievable how much green excrement came out of that child.

"It's a miracle," each different nurse agreed as she passed through the room. "He may be all right after all."

By breakfast time on Monday morning, Otis was much better. The doctor visited and seemed surprised that Otis had survived the night. In the afternoon, they moved him out of ICU. He still had a tube plugged into his stomach, and intravenous lines sagged above his head as they rolled him away, but he was improving. Later that evening, while people from church were visiting, the doctor entered to update us.

"You're very blessed," he said smiling, almost jubilant. "You have a miracle."

Otis remained in the hospital another six days. The nurses found excuses to drop by repeatedly and often would hang around a little longer than they probably should have to visit. They kept talking about a miracle. The head nurse who had been on duty Saturday when Otis was admitted had taken Sunday off. When she came back on Monday, she confided to me that she hadn't expected Otis to be there. All her experience had led her to conclude that there was only one possible outcome.

"As far as I was concerned, the child was about to die," she said bluntly.

All the medical professionals repeated the stanza, "Do you realize what a miracle you had?"

And I answered, "Yes."

During the week of Otis's recovery, while I prepared the next Sunday's lesson with the Bible open in my lap, the surgeon who had operated on Otis entered. Seeing the Bible, he said, "It works, doesn't it?"

Shortly after Otis had been admitted, police officers had questioned us. They wanted to know how his body had become so scarred. The attack by Ercel's German shepherd had only taken place a few weeks before, and Otis was still badly bruised. The punctures from the incisors had started healing and looked a lot like recent cigarette burns. Doctors and nursing staff at the hospital had taken note. Many of the wounds were in places that would normally be covered by clothing, and as obligated by law, they had contacted the local office of Child Protective Services to have the family investigated. We tried to explain that the scars were punctures from dog bites, but if not for Brother Tony Wise, who had prayed for Otis shortly after the dog attack, we may have had a hard time getting Otis released back into our care.

God has miraculously spared each of my children at some point in their lives, and I believe it's because He has a special mission for each of them. He has already done good works through their lives, but there is a lot more to come.

In March, 2008, Otis, already a successful businessman, became part of the full-time ministry team of the Lighthouse Church, joining Richelle, Richelle's husband Cory Smithee, and me. He had already served as the children's pastor for ten years and as youth pastor. Richelle and Cory left our church to plant a full gospel church in Mansfield, Texas. Shanda led the Lighthouse church's door-to-door outreach ministry and was youth pastor for several years. Stuart battles for Christ on a different front. As a member of the Burleson City Council, his is one of the strongest voices for God's principles in local politics. They're all standing in the breach.

Chapter 17

Oh, Calcutta! A Sign of the Times

IN THE MID-SIXTIES, a sign boasting that Burleson was the nineteenth fastest growing town in Texas was posted on the highway just north of the intersection of US highway 81 and state highway 174. The railroad-stop community founded in 1882 and named for Dr. Rufus Burleson, who was president of Baylor University from 1851 until 1861 and again from 1886 to 1897, was being gobbled up by the ravenous Dallas-Fort Worth metroplex. Along with innumerable small towns that had once been independent villages with unique identities, Burleson was slowly being digested and regurgitated as a suburb of Fort Worth. Many of the families moving to the growing community were overflow from the city. Burleson's schools were bursting at the belt buckle because the population was growing so fast. It wasn't just young couples that were buying homes in the additions springing up all around the small town. Many of the families already had two, three, or four children, often teenagers. Burleson inherited all the blessings and the plagues of a metropolis, including access to entertainment as varied as shows in New York or Los Angelas.

I didn't limit my reading exclusively to the Bible, although I could have been content with that. I kept up with local events in the same way that most people did in an era pregnant with the electronic revolution. The communications gadgets that would take over American life during the next thirty years were still merely gleams in the eyes of science fiction writers and scientists. Flat screen televisions that could hang on the wall like pictures and two-way visual communications were as fanciful as nuclear submarines were when Jules Verne wrote of Captain Nemo. My contemporaries and I read the newspaper to get most of our news about the world.

When *Oh, Calcutta!*—a celebration of sex that opened off Broadway in 1969—exposed itself in Fort Worth, it was as controversial as it had been when it was performed anywhere else in the country.

In his column for the *Fort Worth Press*, one of two Fort Worth newspapers, the local columnist Jack Gordon left the question hanging: "Is this artful satire on a nation obsessed with sex or more work of the devil?" I responded with a letter to the editor attempting to answer the question from a Christian perspective. I gave the devil his due, conceding the artful satire critique, but I suggested that any satire about society's sexual obsession is itself an extension of that obsession.

"The answer is both, but could this also be a sign of the time?" I observed, continuing:

> Jesus, telling of signs relating to his return to earth, said in Matthew 24:37, "But as the days of Noah were, so shall also the coming of the Son of man be." Genesis 6:5 describes the conditions of Noah's days, "And God saw that the wickedness of man was great in the earth and that every imagination of his heart was only evil continually." The success of this show and others like it proves the evil thoughts and imaginations of the people of our day. The Bible seems to be describing our generation in II Peter 3:3, "There shall come in the last days scoffers walking after their own lusts." And in II Timothy 3:13, "But evil men and seducers shall wax worse and worse, deceiving and being deceived."

I had merely attempted to apply Bible prophecy to a nation preoccupied with sex and explain how the trends in modern entertainment were relevant to that observation. Even though debate about *Oh, Calcutta!* as art or sin was raging throughout the entire United States, and even though I had only written a letter that attempted to explain my view on a question that the columnist had raised, some "moral liberals" were outraged at my explanation and instead of making the debate about *Oh, Calcutta!*, they pointed the fickle finger of liberal vigilantism at me and lynched me in their letters to the editor.

"Moral Liberal to Moral Conservative" one letter was headlined. "I am not sure whether she is serious in that silly letter or whether she is just putting us all on," one response from a reader said. "I have a feeling, though that she takes herself quite seriously. She piously suspects that the production of *Oh, Calcutta!* is a "sign" telling us that we are living in the last days before judgment, in a generation of extreme evil, with very little restraint upon the base appetites of sinful man."

Then it got personal. "I'm not sure where or when the species Morals

Protectorus developed, but I think it has outlived its usefulness. The world has had enough undeserved guilt shoved on it from moral watchdogs like this one who shout righteously from their splintered pulpits telling us how evil we are, trying to keep mankind in line." The letter then suggested that I should "resign from [my] post as monk and protector of public morals" and view some of the contemporaneous films and plays.

In 1972, the man's criticism stirred the morally conservative community (those with moral compass enough to distinguish prurient eroticism from art) to my defense. A number of letters were written to the editor of the *Fort Worth Press* defending my right to an opinion. There were many people who still took a critique based on a Christian perspective very seriously.

How things change.

In the intervening years since *Oh, Calcutta!* premiered, every developing form of communication and entertainment has opened new avenues for abuse. With each new technological triumph, we find new ways to debase ourselves. Images of sex that were confined to closed theaters and darkened strip clubs in the seventies are now commonplace even on broadcast television. DVDs, cable TV, satellite TV, and the internet are littered with sexual garbage. The constant barrage of indecent proposals should be enough to appease even the most prurient appetites, except that there seems to be no limit to depravity, and in the years since *Oh, Calcutta!* premiered, our appetite for "art" has exploded like the American waistline. Even pet food and cleaning product commercials use sexual images, intimations, and double entendres to hawk products. We have become a nation truly obsessed with sex. The "seducers wax worse and worse, deceiving and being deceived," and the moral liberals still fail to recognize the incongruities within their arguments. Each year we fall further from Christ's example for how we should live our lives. Today, it's OK to base a literary critique on Marxist, Feminist, modernist, or humanist points of view, but don't you dare base a critique on Christian thought or morality because the seducers have control.

Chapter 18

And Now for the Rest of the Story

THE CRITIC WHO found my opinions so objectionable was another Burleson resident. In fact, he lived just a few blocks away from me. I didn't know him, but you may have heard of him. Rex McGee had graduated from Burleson High School in 1970. He was only a few years older than the teens that I taught in Sunday school and was already enrolled at the University of Southern California as a film major in 1972. He returned home for Christmas that winter and got together with a group of old friends.

At some point in their discussions, my name surfaced, and one of Rex's friends, who was also a good friend of mine, suggested that we should meet. This was just a few months after our shootout in the Fort Worth newspaper. Despite our obviously differing points of view, I was happy to get an opportunity to meet the man who had been so critical of my letter to the editor.

I'm not sure exactly what Rex was expecting, but based on discussions we've had over the years since then, I suspect it was a pale, doddering, schoolmarm-ish little lady brandishing a ruler in one hand and a Bible in the other, with gray hair pulled so taut across her head that it squeezed the blood out of her brain and a severe bun at the back that looked like a knob to tighten it further still. I suspect he expected me to be dressed in gingham and lace with a neckline that choked my chin and a hemline that dragged across the floor hiding an old pair of black boots. He has admitted he was surprised when a thirty-four-year-old showed up, dressed to the nines with styled hair, a pant suit, and make up.

Rex remained in California after graduating and became an assistant producer on many films directed and produced by Hollywood legend Billy Wilder. After several years, Rex returned to Texas and moved into a one hundred-year-old house in Cleburne bequeathed to him by a beloved aunt. After his homecoming, Hollywood came calling again, and Rex wrote the screenplay *Pure Country*, a star vehicle for George Straight. Later he scripted the Hallmark Hall of Fame teleplay, *Where There's a Will.*

After his homecoming, Rex and I had many opportunities to discuss our differing perspectives and opinions about our culture. We discussed religion, theology, and sociology. Over the years, he has taken a more critical look at the culture of Hollywood, and in many ways, Rex returned home all over again to the values instilled in him during his childhood. I'm not going to say that we agree on every topic, but our talks have always been stimulating. We have challenged each other's ideas, always respecting our differences. I consider him a dear friend.

As of this writing, Rex has re-written and is producing *Pure Country* for the stage. In May of 2013, Rex invited Shanda and me to a rehearsal. We were honored because there were very few people in attendance who were not in the industry, and Rex seemed genuinely interested in our opinions about his play.

Chapter 19

Suffer the Children to Come unto Me

OUR NEIGHBORHOOD WAS growing fast. By 1973, there were kids everywhere, and they all knew each other because they went to the same school. They were the products of hard-working, dedicated parents.

In many cases, both parents worked in Fort Worth. Left to their own devices and consciences, the unsupervised teens formed small, after-school gangs, not gangs with names, but loose groups of bored, undisciplined children. When a family went on vacation, these ad-hoc gangs broke into the vacated home, spray painted the furniture and walls, and ran up phone bills making long-distance, prank calls.

My hobby was working in my yard, and I had honeysuckle growing along the back fence. I cultured beautiful rose bushes, too. I was very proud of my flowerbeds, but the unregulated teens either negligently or deliberately destroyed my flowers routinely. They knew my schedule better than I did and took strategic advantage of my absences. I would come home from church, and my garden would be trampled, completely torn up. I would be furious. God often had to calm me down.

Many parents in the neighborhood suspected a particular group of boys was creating most of the havoc, but they seldom thought their own children could be part of that group. Accusations bred contumelies; insults fired feuds. Everybody blamed everybody else's children. The events were reported to police, but little could be done when police rounded up the usual lists of suspects and didn't get much cooperation either from the children or their parents.

One Sunday evening I had packed up the kids and left for church, and after driving about a mile, I remembered that I had left some of my lesson materials on the kitchen table. I turned around and headed home. As I pulled into the driveway, I spotted three boys in my back yard. I had seen them all before. They were often rounded up or interviewed as the usual suspects when some of the more egregious vandalisms were reported to police.

They were in my back yard smoking marijuana. I marched back and bawled them out. I don't remember exactly what I said, but they had ears to hear and I rigorously exercised that God-given gift. I didn't use bad language or anything like that, but I told them how bad the things they had done were. I had caught them in the act.

My back yard was fenced, and I suspected that the boys had passed through my garage to get there. "You are trespassing, breaking and entering, destroying private property," I scolded them. "Don't you ever come back in my yard," I concluded my tirade.

I was still in a huff when they sauntered away. Even then, when I had caught them red handed, I didn't call the police. I didn't want to get them into trouble. Instead, I got into my car and drove to church. The Lord began to convict me as I made the twenty-minute drive. I remembered a verse of the New Testament, "The wrath of man does not produce the righteousness of God" (James 1:20, NKJV). I heard that over and over again as I drove. I was convicted because I knew I had reacted out of wrath and anger.

By the time I got to church, I was overwhelmed with conviction for the way I had responded to the situation. As soon as I got there, I kneeled and prayed for forgiveness and guidance. I knew God was convicting me, and I had not handled the situation with faith and patience.

When I got back home, I barely had time to get the kids into the house before the doorbell rang. I opened the door and was surprised to see the parents of one of the boys standing on our front porch. I smiled at them. I was certain they had come to apologize for their son's behavior, and that was a relief.

But sadly, they weren't there to apologize for their son or to have their son apologize to me. They were there for me to apologize to him for bawling him out, even though he had trespassed in my yard, smoked pot on my property, and possibly even participated in the vandalism of my garden on one or more occasions. At another time, maybe just a few hours earlier, I would have defended myself, but I was already convicted for lecturing and berating those kids instead of trying to help them.

I made no defense. I knew I had handled it poorly. As the parents continued, it became obvious that the boy had told his parents only that I had bawled him out and that I had been mean to him and his accomplices. Somehow, he had conveniently forgotten to mention the marijuana or that he and his friends had either scaled a fence or broken into my home to get into the backyard. He had neglected to tell them that he and his cohorts had been trespassing on my property and trashing my garden routinely.

Randy, the boy, was visibly uncomfortable. I could tell that he was waiting for the blow that was bound to ricochet off his parents and bowl him down when I set the story straight. I was tempted, but I didn't do what he expected. His parents may not have expected what came next either. I sincerely apologized for my actions. They may have been surprised by my contrition, but they were not satisfied.

Randy was, though. He obviously wanted to end the interview before the whole truth wormed its way into the conversation, and maybe he was even beginning to feel a little remorse. He veiled a personal apology in a half-hearted attempt to defend me from his parent's continuing, excessive verbal barrage.

"I know Mrs. Gillaspie loves us," Randy said. "She always treats us right."

That much was true. I did love them. Always before, I had treated the kids in the neighborhood courteously, and I would often speak to them when I saw them.

"I do love them, and I apologize," I told his parents. "Maybe I was too harsh. I want the best for the kids in our neighborhood. I want to help them in any way that I can."

The Bible says a soft answer turns away wrath. It's one of the easiest Biblical principles to put into practice and see immediate results. God had convicted me of my mistake, and then He had prepared my heart with the best response.

Finally, Randy's parents seemed satisfied with the apology, and as I closed the door, I started praying. "Lord, how can I help these kids?"

God spoke to me, and I became convinced that the best thing, maybe the only thing, I could do was offer them something that they probably weren't getting at home or school and that they certainly weren't getting roaming the neighborhood.

I started offering Bible study for the kids in the neighborhood. I invited them to my home every Tuesday night. I made cheese dip, brownies, and cookies, and I sent my kids up and down the street inviting others.

While they ate, I taught from the Bible. Kids started getting saved in the Bible study, and afterward they wanted to go to church with us. We had a Ford LTD, and there were times we crammed as many as thirteen children and young people, including myself, into that car. I hauled kids to church in Fort Worth for the next two years.

During that time, the study group continued to grow. Kids saved at the meeting were bringing their friends, and it wasn't unusual for me to count forty to forty-five of them on Tuesday nights. A lot of times it was hard to get them to leave because they wanted to talk about the Bible. They were still talking about it the next morning at school, and in classrooms they discussed the things they were learning in Bible study.

Not long ago, I was at a political meeting, and a gentleman who was campaign manager for one of the candidates came up to me.

"Do you remember me," he said.

I didn't.

"I got saved at your Bible study."

I still see lots of the people who came through that Bible study, but even if there had been no more than that one boy, it would have been worth it. One boy who listened, one person who woke from the trance before walking over the cliff was worth it.

Just as God had delivered Otis from the ravages of disease and had given him a new life, He delivered children throughout Burleson from the ravages of a life without Jesus Christ.

Which is the greater miracle? Of all the miracles that God has given us the authority to perform, we must never forget that the miracle of opening our mouths and telling someone about Jesus Christ and then leading them in the sinner's prayer is the most powerful and most important of all.

Chapter 20

Shame for His Name

DESPITE ALL THAT was happening at the church in Meadowbrook and in the Bible study in my home, I was a mother first. My children were in Burleson schools, and as most parents, I was drawn into community involvement through their activities. I had no desire to be an "activist" or to promote any cause other than the cause of Christ in the lives of my children and other children in the community. But my involvement in my children's lives hurled me unwittingly and unwillingly into local politics.

One morning in the spring of 1974, I was studying my Bible. I was reading the Acts of the Apostles. It described Peter and John who were jailed, humiliated, and beaten. They hadn't committed any crimes, and because the high priests were afraid to make martyrs of them, they were eventually released. The two apostles counted their suffering a blessing because they had been found worthy to suffer shame for His name.

I silently prayed, "Lord I want to be that worthy. I want to be worthy to suffer shame for your name." The answer to my prayer was almost audible. I felt the Holy Spirit's response so strongly that I was almost fearful.

"Are you willing to suffer shame for my name?" God was asking me in a voice as clear as a train whistle, even though it wasn't audible. At first a little confused, I couldn't answer. Why wouldn't I be willing to suffer shame for Him? I loved Him that much. Yet something kept me from answering. I think I knew that there was no turning back. My life would never be the same. I hesitated.

Not once but twice he asked, and I couldn't answer. When He asked the third time, it was with finality. If I hadn't answered then, I don't know how my life may have been different. What if God had never given me the opportunity again, or what if I could never summon the courage again to ask for the privilege of suffering shame for His name. When He asked the third time, I was ready to answer despite the uncertainty of where it may lead. Three times I was given the opportunity to say no.

"Yes, Lord," I answered aloud and from my heart, my innermost being. Even as I answered, I knew that something was coming. I wept. I cried like I was grieving the death of a child or a dear friend. Over the next two years, as I experienced the privilege of suffering shame for His name, I never cried. I had done my crying at the moment I made the commitment and understood its costs, even though in that moment I had no way of knowing specifically what those costs would be.

Within weeks, I began to understand the full meaning of such a commitment. The *Burleson Star*, the local bi-weekly purveyor of the community's collective intelligence and sometimes its conscience, reported that the Health and Science Department had asked the school board to approve a curriculum at Burleson's Middle School. The program included instruction on Human Health and Reproduction. Scheduled for implementation in the fall, it would introduce sex education courses for sixth through eighth grades. The newspaper stated that before the instruction could be introduced, the school board wanted input from the parents of students.

My two youngest children, Stuart and Otis, were starting seventh and sixth grades. I didn't automatically object to or condemn the introduction of sex education into the grade school curriculum, but as a parent I felt obligated to find out as much as I could about the new courses.

The news article announced that the school board would hear from parents at the next regular meeting before making a decision. I had little doubt that I would approve of the changes. I respected and trusted the people who held positions of authority in the community and its schools. I assumed that the curriculum would be similar to the health classes taught to me when I had been a student at Burleson High School. However, I took my parental responsibility as gatekeeper very seriously. I took the day off from my job at Geico Insurance to visit the school and check out the curricula. Details were supposed to be available at Hughes Middle School, the only middle school in the Burleson School District at that time.

When I arrived, I told the receptionist why I was there. She handed over an outline of the curriculum, but she seemed almost reluctant to give it to me.

As I glanced through the document, I noted that it listed some of the films that would be included in the lessons. I saw that representatives from Planned Parenthood, already known to many Christians as a socially liberal organization that encouraged abortion and distribution of sexual information that could be described as a promotion of promiscuity, would be delivering two of the six weeks of instructor-led training.

It was surprising enough that any outside organization with a known political and social agenda would be permitted to conduct classes at public schools. An organization that so openly embraced promiscuity was cause for concern. I realized that any curriculum that advanced the beliefs of Planned Parenthood in public schools should be questioned and investigated by parents. I feared that the organization's sexually liberal biases would be proselytized to innocent and impressionable children as absolute truth. I slowly became wary of both the content and objectives of the courses. The titles of the films piqued my curiosity even more.

I left the school more educated and more cynical than I had entered. As soon as I got home, I made a few telephone calls, mostly trying to get information and find out what other mothers knew about the program. Within a few hours, we were evolving into an unofficial committee. A lot of women were concerned about the curriculum. We gelled into a group that would resist any attempt of Planned Parenthood to infuse our children with the organization's doctrines and political biases in the guise of educating them. We traveled to the regional education service center in Fort Worth and asked to see the films that were to be sent to Burleson.

After we had watched several films, the supervisor of the service center apologized to us. He had never seen the films before that day either, and he shared our shock at their content.

"You didn't know these were in here?" I asked.

"No," he answered, "these films are sent in by the federal education department, and they are not subject to our review."

Because the films had been approved by the department of Health, Education, and Welfare, they did not have to be reviewed or approved by state or local school boards. After viewing some of the films, our ad hoc committee was more concerned than ever. We decided that we needed to play a more active role in reviewing films that would be presented to our children. Most of the ladies pledged to return to the service center throughout the year to review films for other curricula, too.

The more immediate concern was the sex education program. I visited the local office of Planned Parenthood to find out as much as I could about the organization's contribution to the new curriculum. "I work with the youth in Burleson," I told them, "and I would like to see some of the materials that you're going to use in the co-educational Human Sex and Reproduction classes to be introduced in Burleson middle schools." I didn't mislead them. While I wasn't a paid professional, I did work with the youth. Ministering to them at church and out of my home was already the central focus of my life.

The organization's staff provided me with curriculum materials and seemed happy to do so. I lugged the packets of information into the house, spread them across the kitchen table, and began reading. Before long, I was in tears.

It was horrible. It was teaching immorality. It promoted homosexuality as an acceptable "alternative" lifestyle. It encouraged abortion as a good way out of an unwanted pregnancy. It instructed young women, if indeed pubescent sixth, seventh, and eighth grade girls can be referred to as women, to seek the advice of their school counselors if they were thinking about an abortion. The counselors could get them to Planned Parenthood, the materials intimated, and a girl's parents would never need to know.

Later, I learned that Burleson schools were one of seven "pilot" school districts in Texas for the sex education program. The Texas Education Agency (TEA) launched most of its pilot programs in a few carefully selected schools. After they got programs past a few complacent communities with as little feedback as possible, it was easier to foist the programs on other school districts. A pilot school was expected to praise the programs so that they could be instituted in other school districts with as little resistance and parental review as possible across the entire state. Programs like the sex education course were cultivated in Burleson and other pilot communities in exchange for additional state funding. There may be better words than "insidious" to describe these strategies, but I doubt it.

As I became more involved, I was alarmed at the number and nature of other pilot projects. Burleson's schools were piloting many of them. One was a program intended to make it a requirement for anyone who sought a state teaching certificate to complete a three-hour course in humanism. I'm not talking about an emphasis on the humanities, which includes English or philosophy or psychology, but humanism, which is essentially a religion that elevates man to the status of god and denies the existence or relevance of the supernatural. The principles of separation of church and state that social liberals had subverted and perverted to expel God from the classroom didn't seem to apply to the religion of humanism. Another of the pilot programs permitted smoking on the high school campus. The school board had designated and approved a smoking area, a big area, and people said that you could walk through it and get high.

The concepts tested at Burleson and similar pilot schools defied common sense. The basic argument seemed to be that since children were going to smoke and have sex anyway, why not give them a safe place to do it and teach them how to do it with as few physical repercussions as possible? Why not teach them how to be responsibly irresponsible. Schools that institute such practices have surrendered to the tyranny of progressive pornography. They have given up on their mission. When the objective of sex education becomes training in the most effective application of prophylactics to control the consequences of sexual activity rather than educating children about the moral issues of sexual promiscuity, an educational system has already failed. I wasn't opposed altogether to sex education and some of the other programs, but the emphasis on controlling the consequences rather than discouraging the behavior was topsy-turvy.

Burleson Independent School District's administrators may have been a little too quick to grab the gold ring. The schools were involved in numerous pilot programs that garnered additional funding but may not have been in the best interests of Burleson's children.

The final decision to adopt the new sex education curriculum would be voted on by the school board at a regularly scheduled meeting. I gathered all my materials, including notes on the films and the courses. I met with the leader of my women's prayer group and requested that they say a special prayer for me in the event that I needed to speak at the meeting.

I expected to walk into a packed boardroom. Surely, a majority of parents were as apprehensive about the school district's meddling in the morality of their children as I. Surely, others had completed similar investigations and found the proposals abhorrent. There would probably be several there who could elucidate their objections more eloquently than I, but I wanted to be prepared just in case those who were opposed to the curriculum needed evidence to back up their objections. I asked the prayer group to pray that God would give me wisdom.

When I walked into the boardroom I was surprised to see so few people. I recognized many who were there. Ed Carroll the tax assessor-collector for the school district sat in the audience with a smattering of other community leaders. Wayne Hutson publisher of the *Burleson Star*, the local weekly newspaper, was there, too, but most of those in attendance were employees, teachers, and representatives of the school district as well as the board members themselves. Though I knew Wayne and Ed as good Christian men, I also knew that in their respective roles, there wasn't much either of them would contribute to the discussion. Wayne was there primarily as an observer and reporter. I knew that many of his opinions would be reserved for the editorial page. Dean Franklin, the pastor of the Methodist church, and Jimmie Koontz, a community leader whom I knew well, were there, too. Both were members of the board.

I was the only one there to speak in defense of the children. To this day, it's difficult to believe. Nobody else had a critique of the program. No one volunteered to speak. So when they got ready to vote on it, the board's president announced, "OK, well there's nobody here to object."

"That's why I'm here," I spoke up.

The members of the board were nice to me. One of them brought a chair, and I joined them at the table where the august group deliberated the fate of Burleson's children. I told them all I had found out. They seemed to grow concerned as I expressed my opinion that the films were pornographic, and I related everything that I had learned about the course materials, too. "I'm not going to describe the content to you," I told them. I left it up to each of them to examine the content and satisfy himself that my analysis was correct. I explained that even the Media Director for the Burleson school district had said he was shocked by the films.

The school board members listened attentively and courteously, and everyone seemed receptive, even grateful, for my research. They all believed me. All, that is, except for the superintendent of schools, who glared at me throughout my presentation and the ensuing discussion.

I had attended the meeting to gain more insight into the curriculum. I hadn't gone to attack anyone, start any battles, or offend the chief administrator of the school district where my four children were enrolled. I had certainly never expected to go to war.

Over the next few weeks, I heard of comments like, "What business does she have opposing coursework that was developed by teams of professional educators in Washington and Austin?" and "Who does she think she is?" I learned that anyone who has the audacity to question, much less oppose, programs that the TEA is attempting to institute can find themselves besieged by criticism. Some of the ladies who had joined me in taking a look at the films or who had expressed similar concerns or objections to the sex education curriculum were in the same boat.

In a community like Burleson with a population of about 12,000, there was no media feeding frenzy. The publisher of the local newspaper, the *Burleson Star*, even agreed with me. Burleson was a hybrid, no longer either a rural farming community or a metropolitan mix of societies and cultures. To question or demur to the accepted norm was to risk being kicked off the community wagon, but the norm was a blurring landscape. As few as ten years earlier, morality was well defined and Bible based. Now you could find yourself walking alone just by standing up for right. The go-along-to-get-along mentality was a strong force, but there was no longer a moral or ethical basis for it. As far as the school district's administration was concerned, if you bucked the system, you could find yourself bucked right out the door, and apparently I had bucked the system. It's not as though I was being mulched by a massive media machine, but the attacks on me were far from subtle. In some ways, they were more sinister than an all-out media blitz. Neither the *Fort Worth Star Telegram* nor the broadcast media in Fort Worth and Dallas had much to do with the farm towns rapidly evolving into suburbs, but the predatory slander that rippled around me was no less dangerous than a pool of piranha in a feeding frenzy.

During this time, many of my friends didn't want to be seen talking to me in public. Many of them called to apologize for not returning my greetings when they saw me. They told me they didn't want to be treated the same way that I was being treated, and they were concerned that if they were seen associating with me it would be assumed that they shared my views, and they, too, would be branded as troublemakers. They were right. They would have been. All the people who reviewed the films and then attended school board meetings to oppose them found themselves the objects of slanderous assaults. As the instigator, I was the target of the most vicious attacks.

The Lord's words came back to me, "Are you willing to suffer shame for my name?" Surprisingly, the words comforted me. They assured me that what I was doing and the stand I was taking were in His will. Before Jesus went to the cross, knowing the suffering he would endure, He prayed to the father, "Not my will but Thine be done," and Jesus said if we would be his disciples, we must deny ourselves, take up our crosses, and follow His example. I felt each stinging, slicing incisor, every ripping jolt, but I had already done my crying.

I was introduced to Ellie Hutcheson, a former teacher from Fort Worth who reviewed text books. She had learned of my resistance, which in the minds of many people in the school district had escalated to a crusade, and of the vituperous siege that had been mapped out against me and anyone else who dared to oppose the pilot program. Ellie sent me a copy of a magazine that school boards receive from the TEA. It instructed teachers and school administrators in dealing with parents and others who dared to question a school's initiatives. I was amazed that the magazine instructed public servants in the strategies of conducting campaigns of slander against parents who dared to speak out.

Do not speak to the issues. You will lose on the issues. Try to discredit the parent. These are paraphrases, of course, but they are not inaccurate summaries of an article from one of the magazines. The theme was not inconsistent with teachers' guides for some of the textbooks used in Texas schools. The guides propagandized that instructors were not just teachers. "You are agents of the change from traditional values to progressive ideas." Is it any wonder children don't learn anything at school when the primary goal of the educational system is to teach them that there are no rules except the existential mores they create for themselves? Do schools really exist to change the basic values and framework of a society? Shouldn't schools perpetuate core moral values of a society? Well, according to the documentation, schools and teachers believed that their function was redefining society rather than perpetuating it. They have been doing that job very well.

We celebrated when the school board postponed final action on the sex education curriculum for several months. I appeared before the board again and repeated my objections to the offensive materials before they finally vetoed the objectionable films, the classroom instruction proposed by Planned Parenthood, and other parts of the curriculum.

Along with several concerned women from Burleson, I returned to the educational service center in Fort Worth several times over the next year.

We watched many films, not just the ones that had been proposed for the sex education curriculum. Some were already being shown as part of other curricula for students of varying ages. Each one heightened our horror. They were scarier than anything we could have paid to see in a movie theater.

Even the superintendent of the service center was appalled. As I was leaving after one viewing, he asked me into his office. "If there are not more people like you," he confessed privately, "we are going to lose this generation."

Although many persons who depended on the Texas public school systems for their livelihood privately expressed their concerns and their agreement with the stand I was taking, when the time came to stand on their principles, they usually stood behind their principals.

"Our hands are tied," the director of the educational service center told me, "We can't do anything. It takes grass roots efforts by people like you." When he and others recommended that I present my case to the state board, I knew God had placed me in a unique position. Marlin Brockette, commissioner of the state board of education, was the brother of the man who owned the insurance agency where I worked.

As I delved into the TEA programs further, I found that the agency was sponsoring a program to introduce humanism into the school curriculum at all grade levels. The program, after approval by state and local school boards, would have required teachers to follow the Values Clarification Handbook, a curriculum designed to teach children to question the morals and values of their parents and to promote a conscienceless society, in which the only value is based on the individual's goals.

The group of Burleson women wrote letters to the state board. In response, the state board asked for our input. We received a letter inviting us to address one of their meetings in Austin. I carried the invitation in a box along with all the other paraphernalia I had accumulated. I lugged that case of documents with me to all the local school board meetings, and it was on the floor at my side when I attended the next Burleson ISD board meeting two weeks after getting the letter.

The curriculum superintendent for Burleson schools was a proponent of the changes. He addressed the local board saying that the state board of education had already passed a resolution to make values clarification mandatory in all grade levels. What's more, he instructed the board, the resolution had been passed by the legislature. He insisted that Burleson schools should start teaching it immediately.

When I heard him say that, I rifled through my materials and pulled out the letter from the state board. I raised my hand and waited patiently to be heard. There was no way to know if the superintendent's statement was merely uninformed or if it was part of a carefully orchestrated campaign of misinformation, but as soon as I was recognized I objected. "That's wrong. It hasn't passed," I explained. "I have a letter here. I've been invited to address the state board on whether—"

Red faced and seething, the superintendent turned toward me, and I never got a chance to finish my sentence. He raised his hand, and for a moment, he seemed ready to slap me.

A board member later told me that he had been fearful for me. No one in the room could have interceded quickly enough to keep the man from hitting me if he had really wanted to. I doubt there was anyone in the room who didn't feel his rage.

By that time, many people hated me. Several thought I was crazy. They believed all the things that had been said about me. But I had never felt hatred like I did at that moment. It was a tangible entity that hovered in the room.

The board did not approve the request to institute values clarification in the curriculum.

Over the next year, the ladies who had reviewed the films and I addressed the state board three times about various movies and about the TEA's plans to instill humanism in the curriculum. The ladies from Burleson, who had simply been curious about their children's education and who had taken the time to investigate, eventually convinced members of the state board to watch some of the films. Once members of the state board had watched, they were as horrified as we had been. Several films were rejected as a result of our efforts.

We read excerpts from the TEA's propaganda to the state board, too. They were appalled and ultimately did not approve TEA's request to make humanism and values clarification mandatory. With God's help, we were successful in every appearance before the state board.

Chapter 21

Bulging Budgets

CONTINUED TO ATTEND the local school board meetings. Before too long I had become a fixture. When the school board began discussing the budget for the upcoming year, I had little interest in the public hearings. Of all things that I never would have a natural interest in, budgeting was probably at the top of the list. The mention of the word made me yawn; my eyes glazed over. Yet I began to feel that I was being directed to review the budget. Even though I'm just not that into columns and rows of numbers, God clearly said to me, "Look at the budget."

State law dictated that school administrators had to make the budget available for public review seventy-two hours before the school board meeting, and I went to the administration building filled with about the same excitement and anticipation that I would have felt if I had been assigned to rake the barnyard as a child.

I had taken my lunch hour, leaving the office of Charles Massey, the Burleson representative of State Farm Insurance, who had hired me away from Geico earlier that year. Although the law required the school district to post the information, the administration staff wouldn't let me have a copy. That didn't bother me too much. After all, it would have been expensive to make a copy for every parent in the school district.

When I returned to the office, I told Charles that I hadn't been able to get a copy. "Charles, they wouldn't let me look at the budget."

"Now that's not right," he barely had time to say before Wayne Hutson, the publisher of the *Burleson Star* ambled into the office, a common afternoon occurrence. The paper's offices were right next door.

"I'll get you my copy," Wayne said. A few minutes later, he walked back into the office with it.

The budget hearing was scheduled that evening, and I knew I only had a few hours to review it. So I left work early, and when I took the document into the house I hardly knew where to start. I hesitated before folding back the cover page and was tempted to plead, "Lord let this cup pass," but instead I started reviewing the endless lists of figures. I wasn't totally unfamiliar with accounting practices. After all, I worked for an insurance agency. I would learn more about budgets when I became responsible for the administration of a church, but at that time, I had no desire to try to make sense of the rows and columns that could only be deciphered by someone whose dreams take place against a backdrop of the light green columns and rows of a ledger. There was nothing, I felt, that I could learn from the school district's budget plan. But God had directed me to do it, and I was determined to do His will even if it made absolutely no sense to me. I squinted at the rows and tried to make sense of each line.

The budget was divided into sections. Normally, it would have been impossible to read through the numbers without falling asleep, but as I reviewed them I soon found some things that just didn't add up. I saw the same figure in one section that I had seen in another with a similar but slightly different section heading. I suddenly realized the numbers were duplicated.

"Wait a minute, I just saw that same amount in another category under a different name," I said to myself as I reviewed the expenses headed "Multi-media." I had already seen the same amount listed under "Film." I thought, well that's the same thing as multi-media, isn't it? I found similar duplications throughout the budget, repeated amounts under different headings. I started listing the duplicated amounts and titles in a spiral notebook.

That evening I slid into a seat at the back of the crowded boardroom at the BISD Administration Building. I couldn't help noticing that there were more people at the meeting for the budget review than there had been at the first meeting I had attended not many months before. There were more people interested in the school district's finances than its curriculum.

The school board president recognized one person after another who had general remarks about the expenses. Almost all the comments were about the bottom line, the total expenses for the upcoming school year, and how they compared to the amounts for the previous year. There may have been comments about the funding for specific programs, but no one commented on or questioned the amounts. No one mentioned the duplications. I raised my hand, but the board's president didn't seem to take note and didn't offer me an opportunity to speak. I kept my hand in the air until finally one member called attention to me. "That lady has her hand up," he said and pointed at me. The school board president seemed almost reluctant to recognize me, but he could no longer ignore me and finally asked for my comments.

"I only have a question," I said. "It looks like there could be duplicate charges here." The finance superintendent turned pale as I was allowed to explain why I thought there were duplications in the amounts. I presented my case directing the board's attention to some of the specific items beginning with the multi-media and film sections. I knew I was no accountant, and I didn't try to represent myself as one. I never insisted that the figures were wrong. I simply voiced my questions. Board members leaned forward and began looking at the figures in their copies of the budget as I called their attention to the duplications. The finance superintendent sat quietly: even when he was asked to answer questions by the school board members, he had nothing to say. He kept his head down and never said a word.

Members of the school board listened, and after further consideration decided to call in auditors to inspect the budget more closely. Over the next few weeks, the auditors turned the budget inside out. When news of the investigation made it into the *Fort Worth Star Telegram*, I was more than a little taken aback by community reaction. Hostility toward me was stirring again.

If I hadn't already been branded a troublemaker, I certainly was now. The elite, those who participated in the decision-making processes of the community, made their impression of me public. I was seen as an uneducated intruder.

Within a few weeks, the auditors delivered their opinion. They had found duplications. Together, the repeated entries amounted to about $300,000, and what that added up to was malfeasance and possibly even embezzlement. The next day the newspaper headlines told the story.

"You have been vindicated," Wayne Hutson announced when he and Charles Massey came into the insurance office with the daily news and gossip.

I had suffered month after month of ridicule and scorn because I had simply followed His direction. I persevered in my commitment and didn't compromise my beliefs. And in the end Jesus delivered me, not simply by vindicating me but by elevating me in a few short months to a position of respect in the Burleson community. People seemed to appreciate that I had exposed the problems with the budget.

As I walked through those trying times, the Lord taught me many valuable life lessons: forgiveness, loving and praying for my enemies, and the value of listening when He speaks. He let me know that many who opposed me and even some who may have ridiculed me were good people. Some didn't understand the issues. Others judged me based on hearsay. In the end, He showed me that when our ways please Him, He makes our enemies to be at peace with us (Proverbs 16:7). In time, some leaders in the community, who had objected to my interference either in the school curriculum or in the budget, began to change their attitudes toward me, and many eventually became good friends.

Chapter 22

Steppingstone Youth Ministry

THE DRUG PROBLEM in Burleson had reached critical mass and threatened to melt down the community. Gangs roamed the streets, not organized, urban gangs, but groups of friends who collected in pockets at the local Dairy Queen, the only restaurant in the suburb besides small mom and pop shops that tended to open for a few months only to close when there wasn't enough business to support them. On the barren fast-food landscape of the early seventies in Burleson, the Dairy Queen was the only permanent landmark. It had been there for years. If you drive through Burleson today along US 174, you'll see it's still there.

Its parking lot is a permanent fixture, too. And in the seventies, every night, especially on weekends, kids congregated there like electrons swarming in a reactor. I learned later that much of the drug trafficking in North Texas was coordinated from that parking lot. Neither the Dairy Queen's owner nor its management had anything to do with the drugs, but the site was a hub for a distribution network that covered most of the state, a policeman-friend told me. When some entertainers, even some very famous rock groups, came to Dallas or Fort Worth for their concerts, they often got their drugs from a dealer in Burleson.

But at my home each week, kids were being saved from drugs. Soon there were so many kids showing up every Tuesday that my house couldn't corral them all. The nuclear group was expanding so fast it would soon burst through the walls, but I couldn't bear to turn kids away. I had to reach as many young people as I could, and as long as the crowd was growing, I knew there were more out there to be saved. There had to be a way to reach out to young people and get their attention so that they would look to the cross.

One evening, as I kneeled in prayer, a revelation dawned. The young people needed a place where they could meet, a place built especially for them. So many were searching for relationships in loosely organized, unstructured ways. They needed a place where counseling was available to help them find answers to their questions about a meaning for their lives. They needed to be taught that they had more to offer each other than the ephemeral pleasures of drugs and sex. Like most people, they knew there was something more. They believed in a deity. They just didn't know how to find Him. They didn't instinctively understand how to accept Jesus as their Christ. Someone had to tell them about Jesus. We needed a venue, outside the church, where they could listen and learn without formalities and pressures.

Word about the Bible study was reaching parents and community leaders as well as the teenagers. The foster son of a local justice of the peace was one of the kids who attended the Bible study. When he told his mother where he spent his Tuesday nights, she had an idea, too. Who could tell community leaders what needed to be done about drugs, vandalism, and a counter-culture movement that was turning many of its children into criminals better than the children themselves? She wanted the kids to fill out a questionnaire so that they could help determine what the community should do about the problem. She asked her son to see if I was willing to distribute the questionnaire at the Bible study. Within a few weeks, the kids' responses made one thing perfectly clear: teens in Burleson wanted a place where they could meet. "These kids want a place to go," I explained to the justice.

I had heard about a place in Fort Worth called the Cornerstone. From the teenagers' descriptions, it seemed to be similar to the center that I had in mind. Teens met there for Bible study, fellowship, and entertainment. I told the justice of the peace about it, and she visited the Cornerstone with me the next week. We talked to the director and to some of the kids who went there regularly. It was apparent that this was exactly what Burleson needed, too.

The more I thought about it, the more it took root: kids needed a place where they could receive God's word and study the Bible, but they also needed to get wholesome, Christian-oriented entertainment, an alternative to the Dairy Queen parking lot.

I soon realized what God was calling me to do. Just the word "church" was enough to alienate some kids, the ones we most needed to reach. They would scatter before organized religion like jackrabbits before a prairie fire. So the youth center couldn't be a church, but it certainly should be a place where God's love was expressed. Its programs shouldn't be as structured as a Sunday school class, but it shouldn't be an unsupervised meeting in a parking lot either. It wouldn't be a place where God's Word was twisted into dogma or diatribe, but it would offer the Good News to anyone who wanted to listen. It would be a place designed simply to get the attention of teenagers, a steppingstone to a relationship with Jesus Christ, a way for those who understood the problem to stand in the flow and offer these young people something to hold onto.

Chapter 23

Multitude of Counsel

WITHOUT KNOWING WHERE the finances would come from, I started organizing. God had spoken to me. I knew what He wanted, but I still consulted with Pastor Wise because I needed to get a confirmation and blessing. I feel very strongly about that. A passage in II Corinthians says, "In the mouth of two or three witnesses shall every word be established" (II Cor. 13:1), and when you get a multitude of counsel you can be sure that what you're planning is in God's will. The counsel of others is encouraged in Proverbs 12:15, too: "The way of a fool is right in his own eyes: but he that hearkeneth unto counsel is wise."

The Bible also says that by the multitude of counsel, plans are established (Proverbs 15:22). So God may give us an assignment (call us) with visions or that still small voice, but it is through counsel with other Christians that we confirm that calling and stay on course. Not only does it help us to stay on course; it helps us proceed with our plan in God's timing.

I asked Pastor Wise if he could confirm the things the Lord had laid on my heart. I was the youth minister, and what I was proposing would involve the youth at our church.

Brother Tony said, "I believe it is a call from God. I surely can give my blessing."

Next, I spoke with John. We talked about looking around for a house somewhere in Burleson and converting it into a youth center. We could knock out the walls so the kids could meet together in one room. We wanted to finance it ourselves, but we had house and car payments. Finally, we decided we could take on an additional responsibility, but we were concerned that we would not be able to get a loan.

Thanksgiving was approaching, and the idea had taken such a hold that I could think of little else. My family gathered at my sister's house for the holiday, and I told the group about the youth center. I told them that the younger generation was turned off by religion and church. They're always saying, "We don't believe in organized religion."

It's not that they didn't believe in God; it's that they didn't believe in church. It was easy to get them to go to Bible study. After they got saved, most wanted to go to church. "We've been studying at my house," I told my family over the holiday table. "But I don't have room for all these kids. They need a place."

My parents listened and nodded agreement. They asked questions when I told them about the Cornerstone, and I described the problems and temptations that children in the 1970s had to confront daily. They agreed that the pressures on each generation change as society changes.

They were good friends of a loan agent at a local bank. She handled loans for people to make home improvements, buy houses, automobiles, and small businesses. I asked my father if it would be a good idea to contact her, since she already knew me and the rest of the family.

When Mom and Dad went to church at the Gospel Tabernacle on the Sunday after Thanksgiving, they listened to a guest speaker who seemed to echo my concerns for a lost generation. The evangelist described the problems that youth, not just in Burleson but throughout the nation, were facing every day. He described a completely different world than many of his listeners had grown up in. "Free love" and "turn on, tune in, drop out" were the mantras of a society increasingly influenced by eastern religions, sexual obsession, drugs, and humanism.

Many teenagers were rebelling against their parents' culture and values. The generation that had won the Second World War was obsessed with possession. Accumulation had become the American god. It wasn't too hard to understand why the post-baby-boomers' god was self. The god of greed had been supplanted by Narcissus. Humanism was the religion of the seventies. It was proselytized in schools, in every form of media, and it had received the seal of government approval when prayer was outlawed in schools and abortion became the law of the land. The guest speaker told the congregation that something must be done to help the youth, or the generation would be lost.

Mother and Dad could hardly contain themselves. Each of them, without telling the other, had been thinking about what I had said for three days.

After they had settled into their easy chairs following the Sunday meal, Mom said to Dad, "We're supposed to buy that property."

"Yep, that's what I've been thinking."

At church that night, they made a commitment to purchase the property. They called me with the news when they got home that evening, and we began looking for property the very next week. We knew a real estate agent in Burleson. He started looking for something that might work as a youth center.

The town was growing fast. Property didn't stay on the market long. New homes pop-corned over the landscape. Existing property was gobbled up, and nothing was available that could meet the needs of the youth center.

But God's plan was still on schedule. Bids were being taken on a small house sitting on two lots a few blocks from downtown Burleson. The house lay directly across the street from Nola Dunn Elementary School. The owner had died without an heir. His wife had died a few years earlier. His brother, Ray Green, my uncle by marriage, was selling the property.

Once they heard about the house, my parents thought it would be perfect. With two lots, there would be plenty of room for a building, even a large one, and for the kids to play volleyball or other yard games. My parents placed a bid for the property.

While we waited for the results, the teens in my study group, my parents, and I tried to come up with a name for the youth center. One day my father was driving, between calls for the paper company, when the name hit him: Steppingstone. We had always said it would be a steppingstone to Christianity.

The Steppingstone's bid won. We bought the property and after cleaning out the small, frame house and knocking out walls, we started meeting there in January, 1976. Six young people from Meadowbrook Evangelistic Temple helped me set out refreshments and prepare the building for the first meeting.

Soon it was clear that with my continuing commitment to the church in Meadowbrook, my growing involvement in the community, the weekly Bible study, and with my children becoming more active in athletics, cheerleading, and dozens of other clubs and groups, I couldn't manage additional activities at the Steppingstone on my own. Clinton Elder, who had attended

Baylor University before becoming a staff member at the Cornerstone in Fort Worth, signed on to conduct a weekly worship service.

The Steppingstone was open on Saturdays so that it wouldn't interfere with teens' attendance at church with their families on Sundays. The youth center, after all, wasn't created to compete with church, but to offer a ministry that would complement it and eventually lead young people who had dropped out of church or who distrusted organized religion back to the church.

It was best, I felt, that someone trained in the ministry should conduct the more formal Saturday worship services, and I planned to continue leading the weekly Bible study.

STEPPINGSTONE CHRISTIAN YOUTH CENTER, THE LITTLE HOUSE.

Chapter 24

Dedication

I N MARCH, WE decided the building needed a public dedication. I had become acquainted with many community leaders over the previous two years and had developed strong friendships with some. Many were eloquent speakers. I knew a few world-famous church leaders, too, but there was only one person I considered to deliver the dedicatory. I asked my pastor, Tony Wise, to do the honors.

We planned an afternoon program and had it printed. The formal dedication took place on April 25, 1976. The *Burleson Star* reported the event with the headline, "Total Commitment Emphasized: Vision for Teen Center in Burleson Becomes a Reality."

"The Steppingstone, now within the view of anyone passing by 301 S. Dobson, is the manifestation of a vision for a teen center in Burleson, with a spiritual emphasis," the article began. It named me as program director and teacher. It was official. Now teenagers in Burleson were meeting for Bible study in a place they regarded as their own.

The article acknowledged the leadership of Clinton Elder and Curt Jewett, a Burleson High School graduate who was in charge of a share session on Thursday evenings. Several members of the clergy in and around Burleson were present at the opening service. Steve Sill, pastor of First Christian Church of Burleson and president of the Burleson Ministerial Association represented the alliance at the meeting. Warren Keith, pastor of the Bethesda Gospel Tabernacle where my parents still attended church, and the Reverend Harold Nichols, pastor of Grace Temple in Fort Worth, were also there.

"I have been praying and asking God what He is going to do through this ministry," Brother Wise started. "This ministry is like David going out against Goliath. Gloria, the youth of Burleson will slay the giant." He described how David grew from a shepherd boy to a king. He grew in authority with every new challenge. Pastor Tony predicted that the

Steppingstone ministry would grow and become a force for Christ in Burleson just as David had grown to be a force for Jehovah in the world.

The Steppingstone's Goliath wasn't a Philistine giant, Brother Wise said. It was everything that stood in the way of delivering the message of salvation. Goliath is anything that makes us afraid to do God's will. All the soldiers of Israel were afraid to go out and battle him. Only David, who knew God was with him, had the courage to face such a formidable enemy. God had been with David when he killed a lion that attacked his flocks, and the young man knew God would be with him when he fought the giant.

David had no training in combat, no skills with the sword and shield. He had no experience other than an expert use of the slingshot. He refused the accoutrements of battle that the army tried to saddle on him. He rejected the armor, sword, and spear. David, a teenager, went out to battle Goliath armed only with his faith and the skills that God had given him. He found the stones for his sling on the battlefield. David defeated Goliath through the power of his faith, not through the power in his arm. And those first steps in faith led to a lifetime of authority.

Brother Tony said the Steppingstone would grow into a ministry that had authority. I had no plan or desire that it should be anything more than it was then, a place for young people to gather and talk to others about Jesus. Today, the church that sits on the property once occupied by the little house doesn't have more authority just because it dwarfs the original building. I believe through our intercessory prayer and fasting that we have assumed authority over the spirits that continually try to capture our city. It is a struggle that will only end when Jesus returns. You never finish conquering the devil.

Pastor Wise knew that the youth ministry at Meadowbrook church would be affected by the time I devoted to the Steppingstone. Yet he blessed the Burleson ministry, which quickly became a full time job. Burleson was my mission field.

GLORIA LEADING BIBLE STUDY AT THE STEPPINGSTONE CHRISTIAN YOUTH CENTER.

Chapter 25

Shout it From the House Tops

FOLLOWING THE PUBLICITY in the *Burleson Star*, opposition to the ministry rose like an obfuscating fog above a mountain meadow. High school teachers told students they should avoid the youth center. Youth pastors told their youth groups not to attend for fear we would lead them into speaking in tongues or some false doctrine. For months, the youth group had grown, now suddenly, the ministry was labeled a bad influence. Some church leaders even referred to our organization as the "grinding stone," as though we were deliberately honing the hearts of our teenage proselytes against the churches and their doctrines. Kids stopped coming.

For several weeks, the only young people who came to our Bible study were the ones who had been with us since we started—my kids and their friends. I began to have doubts and was becoming discouraged. I thought maybe I should just give up and close down. Even my father told me that it would be OK to close the Steppingstone.

On the way to the youth center one morning, I stopped in at Hilley's Pharmacy. The store had been a mainstay in the community for years. It had a soda fountain and snack bar where you could order anything from a banana split to a hot lunch while reading a magazine you had just picked from the rack. Walking by a bookstand, I noticed the book *Shout it from the Housetops* by Pat Robertson, founder of the Christian Broadcasting Network (CBN). I watched his television program, the *700 Club*, each morning. The jacket described the book as Pat's auto-biography, and I thought I would enjoy reading about his life. I even wondered, as I browsed through the pages, if Pat had ever experienced struggles in building his ministry.

When I arrived at Steppingstone, I felt very discouraged. I almost didn't want to go inside the building. Maybe that's not the way to say it. I wanted desperately to go inside. I wanted desperately to do God's work and to see fruit from that effort, but I was fighting a losing battle against the people I had expected to be allies. I sat there, leaning over the steering wheel, with no energy to get out of the car.

The Steppingstone Youth Ministry could have ended right there. I looked over at the book lying on the seat. On impulse, I picked it up, opened it, and began reading, not at the beginning but the place the book fell open to. I realized almost immediately that God was guiding me with Pat's life story. The book described a time early in Pat's ministry when he experienced discouragement. Opposition and lack of funds brought him to the point of giving up. In his case, God spoke to him through his board of directors. They told him that he should continue building the network. The fact that many people in the community had rejected his ministry without knowing anything about it didn't diminish the need one iota. Pat knew he was doing God's work, and God would provide the resources.

His story renewed my resolve. I praised God as I got out of the car and walked into our little building. The Steppingstone ministry originated because of a need in the Burleson community. The need hadn't evaporated just because support had. The fact that this was God's work hadn't changed either. If some churches wanted to ostracize our ministry, let them. There was nothing I could do about that but pray for them. If God wanted the Steppingstone to succeed, the only thing standing in the way at that moment was me.

The remainder of the year was a string of constant challenges and attacks, most ending with blessings and victories.

One of the challenges was that my children became the targets of school authorities who hoped to destroy the ministry. At Tuesday night Bible studies, gospel tracts were handed out for our youth to give to friends as witnessing tools. They took the tracts with them to school to witness to other students. I was at work one morning when Stuart called. He was very upset. He was calling from the principal's office because his teacher caught sight of the tract in his shirt pocket. The gospel tract was confiscated, and he was sent to the office for being in possession of religious material on school property. I asked to speak to the principal. He verified everything Stuart had said and warned me not to allow my kids and others attending the youth center to bring religious materials including tracts onto school grounds.

God blessed us with a victory in direct response to that threat. Soon after we had dedicated the building, I was contacted by a ministry asking to bring a former Hell's Angel from California to speak at the Steppingstone on a Saturday night. He also asked that I try to get him into the high school for an assembly. When I contacted the school, I was directed to the teacher who sponsored the student council. He told me that any religious event had to be endorsed by the students. Soon a teacher contacted me and said the students had given their consent.

On Friday morning, the entire high school was brought into the gym. When Ron, who was about six feet, seven inches tall, with bulging biceps and rippled musculature, began to speak, some boys began to hoot and holler at him, trying to drown him out. He strode toward the bleachers and challenged them to come down and face him. Singly or in a group, it didn't matter to Ron. When there were no takers, he threatened to go into the bleachers and get them. That silenced the hecklers. Ron began to preach like a man on fire. No one moved. He spoke to the students about disrespect for others and themselves. He rebuked their attitudes toward drugs, alcohol, and sex. He told them that their casual slough of conscience and values in a vain effort to conform and appear cute to their peers would destroy their lives. They were killing their futures.

The next night at the Steppingstone, hundreds showed up, packing out the building, spilling onto the porch and into the yard. We turned up the public address system so that the music broadcast throughout the neighborhood. Dozens received Jesus as their savior as a result of that outreach. I was so excited. I felt it was the beginning of revival.

Ron didn't share my excitement. He told me he had spoken at a school in Los Angeles when riots were erupting up and down the West coast, yet he had not felt darkness like he felt as he drove into Burleson. He felt it during his presentation at the high school. He prophesied that unless there was a spiritual breakthrough within thirty days, God was going to judge Burleson for its pride and rejection of the truth. If there was no change, then we should take our family and move away.

Instantly, I knew this word was from God. That very night I called the intercessors and asked for everyone on the prayer team to start a thirty day fast with daily prayer to break the devil's hold on our city. I put my foot down and told the devil he could not have our town! I was not going to leave.

He was. We fasted and prayed like Jesus instructed us in Mark's gospel: this kind (of demons) go out by fasting and prayer.

In the meantime, the First Baptist Church had scheduled a revival that coincided with the fourth week of our fast. Shortly before the revival was to start, the scheduled evangelist had a medical emergency and had to cancel. The church contacted a young evangelist, Wayne Copelin, from Fort Worth, and asked if he could fill in. As it happened, that was his only open week. He had been reserving the week for a vacation, but he agreed to preach for the revival.

He spoke at the First Baptist Church's Sunday services, and Monday morning my phone was ringing. Prayer intercessors who attended FBC told me that God had brought a breakthrough.

I attended on Monday night, and it was true. Copelin was a fiery evangelist with a clear message. He told all the students to take their Bibles to school. He challenged the FBC teachers to display their Bibles on their desks! And they did.

After the service, a deacon's wife and I were standing to the side at the altar area. Brother Copelin saw me and immediately walked to us and bluntly asked, "Who are you?"

The Holy Spirit fell on me, and I blurted, "I'm one who has been fasting and praying for this!"

"I knew it," he said. "I knew somebody had been fasting and praying for revival. I have never before felt such power when I preached."

Young people witnessed to their friends and brought them to the revival. Over three hundred young people were saved that week, and there's no telling how many others were revived and privately rededicated their lives.

The next week a member of the school board came into the office. He was laughing. I asked what he was laughing about, and he informed me that the school district had contacted its lawyers and had been planning to bring a case against me and the Steppingstone for the Gospel tract incident. They didn't expect to win, but hoped to shut the Steppingstone down. They knew that the Steppingstone didn't have the financial resources required to defend ourselves in an extended court battle with constitutional implications.

He was laughing because the district had decided to drop their lawsuit. Since the teens and teachers from the First Baptist Church had started taking their Bibles to school, the school district and board members were forced to concede, at least behind closed doors, that they couldn't sue the Steppingstone without suing the First Baptist Church, too. That was something completely different. They couldn't sue FBC!

God sure has a sense of humor.

Those events changed the atmosphere over Burleson, but there would be more battles and victories to come.

Chapter 26

Newsworthy

I WAS VERY AWARE of the extent of the drug problem in Burleson's schools and on its streets. My four kids, two policemen friends, and many young people who were getting saved and escaping from the drug culture were all telling me in detail what a serious problem drugs were.

I found that the youth who had a drug habit before coming to the Lord had a much greater battle. They had to overcome physical and psychological addiction as well as temptation. They needed extra help. I developed a counseling program to strengthen them and help them focus on God and the word. I encouraged them to bring their friends who had problems with drugs to attend the program.

In general, people in Burleson were in denial that there was a drug problem. To the shock and dismay of the "head in the sand" crowd, a nationally broadcast news program, 20/20, on the ABC network, reported that Burleson was a major center of drug activity and distribution. In Texas, it was second only to Houston.

That was an eye-opener for many community leaders. The high school and middle school opened their doors for my program and allowed me to present it in their assemblies. That led to an opportunity to reach many more young people. The Steppingstone's counseling program grew in authority. It offered a way to fill students with God's Word and enable them to stand against the temptations they faced daily.

A change had truly come to our city. God had turned attitudes toward me and the Steppingstone from hostility to favor. What a mighty God we serve!

Despite the overwhelming evidence, there were other town leaders who refused to acknowledge that there was a problem. I even heard someone remark recently that they didn't believe there is or ever was a drug problem in Burleson.

Chapter 27

Arise, Shine

IN 1977, I was in prayer one day, and, as I often did, I prayed for the youth. I said, "Oh Lord, all these young people are lost." I begged Him to overcome the darkness and save them.

The Steppingstone was reaching out to a community that seemed, at times, to think it had become too mature for God. Drugs were everywhere. In the 1970s people were being turned off from church and religion. Many no longer trusted organized religion of any kind. That grieved me because I knew how important the church is in reaching the lost and in teaching those that are saved.

Some churches seemed to have lost the vision of their mission. They taught that we can't expect things to get any better. The emphasis seemed less on saving souls and more on preparing for the end, as though the two activities were mutually exclusive. Some churches were teaching that we should only work on trying to get our families saved because Jesus is coming soon. We're going to be caught up with Him and we don't want our families to be condemned. But Jesus' great commission to win the lost, all the lost, will not be suspended in the last days. It will be more important than ever. We have a lot of work to do.

As I prayed and pleaded my case to the Lord, my Bible fell open to a passage in Isaiah:

> Arise, shine; for thy light is come, and the glory of the LORD is risen upon thee. For, behold, the darkness shall cover the earth, and gross darkness the people: but the LORD shall arise upon thee, and his glory shall be seen upon thee. And the Gentiles shall come to thy light, and kings to the brightness of thy rising.
> —ISAIAH 60:1–3

Then He spoke to me and said, "I will answer your prayer. Your desire for the lost to be saved is from me. I gave the vision to you."

I got a new revelation. No matter how dark things are in the world, the light and the glory of the Lord shine through. We overcome the darkness. We carry the presence of the Lord wherever we go. We are the bearers of the light. Isaiah 60 became my life chapter and the foundation for my ministry, first for the Steppingstone, and later it was the inspiration for changing the name of our ministry to the Lighthouse church.

We are charged to bring the light of Jesus Christ to the rest of the world. Today, with global unrest, wars and rumors of wars constantly threatening the political stability of the world; with the United States and the entire world perpetually on the brink of financial collapse; with monstrous earthquakes, floods, fires, hurricanes, killer tornadoes and other natural disasters occurring across the globe with unprecedented costs in human lives; with televised beheadings, human immolations, terrorist bombings, and Face-booked brutality that only demonstrate the depraved depths that mankind falls to in a society that does not know God, the only light that continues to shine is the light of Jesus Christ projected by those of us who have found the truth.

The second half of God's mandate to hold forth our light for mankind is found in the New Testament. The Apostle Paul's letter to the church at Philippi commissions us to shine forth with our actions in the example of a Christian life:

> That you may show yourselves to be blameless *and* guileless, innocent *and* uncontaminated, children of God without blemish (faultless, unrebukable) in the midst of a crooked *and* wicked generation [spiritually perverted and perverse], among whom you are seen as bright lights (stars or beacons shining out clearly) in the [dark] world, Holding out [to it] *and* offering [to all men] the Word of Life, so that in the day of Christ I may have something of which exultantly to rejoice *and* glory in that I did not run my race in vain or spend my labor to no purpose.
> —PHILIPPIANS 2:15–16, AMPC

As Christians, we hold forth our lives as the proof of God's Word. We must keep speaking the truth and taking the truth to anyone who will listen. We can't be discouraged if they reject it, if they refuse to hear us and just keep walking toward the edge of oblivion. There are always more people who haven't heard the good news.

I understood God's glory in a way I never had before. Jesus communicated to me that there is going to be a great revival, a great outpouring of the Holy Spirit. Praise God. There will be a great revival just before Jesus returns, and I pray each day, "Let it begin in me."

The revival of the church became the central theme of my ministry when I later became a pastor, but that day my revelation was that we were going to need a bigger building. My house hadn't been big enough, and neither was the building known as the Steppingstone Youth Center. The ministry was larger than the little one-room building that barely cast a shadow larger than my car's in the morning sunlight. The kids already needed more room, and it was clear that God wanted Steppingstone to reach out to every young person in the city.

We didn't have any finances, but I started planning a new building anyway. There was no earthly reason to expect that the under-funded Steppingstone Youth Center could, or ever would, be able to support construction of a new facility, and I didn't yet realize that my concept of a place for youth to come to worship was slightly smaller than the blueprint that God had already designed for the Steppingstone. Maybe if God had revealed the complete vision for the ministry all at once, it would have seemed too enormous. That may be why we have built this ministry a bit at a time, jumping from one steppingstone to the next.

Chapter 28

A New Church Home

COLD. ON THE first Sunday in the new year, I got the children out of bed and started getting ready for church. It was just like any other Sunday, except it was snowing. The twenty-five mile drive to Meadowbrook over streets that were little better than slabs of ice would have been enough to keep me in Burleson that morning even if I hadn't planned to take the children with me. I was determined we would worship together as a family, but it would be irresponsible to load up the kids and try to drive to church in Fort Worth. Missing church altogether was not an option.

I planned to go to a church that was just a few blocks from home. The kids were looking forward to it. They knew many of the children who went there. As they were getting into the car, I was rethinking where we should visit.

"I feel like we're supposed to go to the First Assembly of God church," I told the kids. I had met the Assembly's pastor before. He had read about the youth center in the *Burleson Star* and had visited our home where he asked if I would consider coming to the church as their youth pastor.

"Oh, no," I had answered, "I go to Meadowbrook and work with the youth there."

Remembering the invitation, I decided to visit. The kids objected. They were afraid they wouldn't know anyone at the Assembly.

People who lived right outside Burleson couldn't get into town. Cars had skidded off the highway everywhere. Few people were at church that morning, but I enjoyed the service and felt at home there. I told the kids about my feelings as we drove home. That set off fireworks that should have thawed the streets.

Stuart and Otis balked at the suggestion that we might leave Meadowbrook and start going to church in Burleson. "We don't want to leave Meadowbrook." That's where they had gone to church all their lives.

"OK, OK," I yielded, "I just really enjoyed being at the Assembly."

The second Sunday morning in 1977 started out as a replay of the first. We got up and saw we had another snowstorm. "So," I said, "I think we'll go back to the Assembly."

The boys grumbled a little, but they knew it would be lunacy to drive into Fort Worth; besides, I had outvoted them. By the time everyone was dressed and fed, the sun had come out. There was still a lot of snow on the ground; the roads weren't really impassable, but it was safer to stay in Burleson. There was a larger crowd at the Assembly of God church than the previous week. The boys found that a lot of their friends from school attended the church. Even before the children piled into the car to go home, I was thinking seriously about finding a church closer to home. It seemed only fitting, since the Steppingstone was in Burleson, that I would go to a local church. For two Sundays in a row, it had snowed. Someone in Montana or Minnesota may not see that as a message from God, but in north central Texas where two snowfalls a year, much less snow on two consecutive weekends, border on apocalyptic, the message was clear. I knew God was telling me to start taking my family to that church.

The children confirmed it. On the way home that Sunday, one of the boys said, "Well, Mom, if you want, it's all right with us to start going to church here." Richelle agreed. She was still in high school. She would later marry a young man, Cory Smithee, who was a member of that church. Shanda was already married; she and her husband began attending, too.

"We'll see what your daddy says."

John had been working nights. He wasn't getting to bed until about two in the morning, and he hadn't been able to go to church with the family on those first two frozen mornings of the year. When we got home from church, he was just getting out of bed. He didn't seem surprised when we wanted to talk to him about transferring to a church in Burleson.

"Well," he said, "if that's where you want to go, that's OK with me."

So, we started going to First Assembly. The pastor had offered me the job of youth pastor, but that had been several months earlier. In the meantime, he had found another youth pastor who, with his wife, was building the church's youth outreach. I took over the youth Sunday school class and worked closely with them.

Within a few months after I had started attending the First Assembly of God church, the youth pastor asked if the church could hold the Assembly's activities at the Steppingstone. I thought it was a great idea. I had been leading the Tuesday night Bible study, but now I would be able to turn that over to him so that the church could sponsor a Tuesday night youth service, and I could concentrate on the weekend activities. The youth minister had put together a band that made a regular appearance at the Tuesday night meetings, and the Tuesday Bible study, already a big event, got even bigger.

In addition to the main event on Saturday night for the teens and college-age crowd, we added Friday nights for the pre-teens. The younger children were asking to come on Saturdays. Rather than turn them away, we put together an exciting program on Friday nights just for them. It was not unusual to have more than one hundred kids attend. Many children were saved, and many later attended Steppingstone church.

The Steppingstone's outreach overlapped with that of the Assembly of God church, but they were still distinctly separate ministries. I was integrally involved in each. With my direct involvement in promoting the weekend activities, the Steppingstone sponsored several city-wide youth events throughout the year, and the ministry continued to grow.

We went to the parking lot of the bowling alley and held services from time to time. The band set up in the back of a flatbed truck. The bowling alley was just off Texas Highway 174, the main avenue of business through Burleson. The music could be heard by people passing by on the highway as they headed from Cleburne to Forth Worth on weekend evenings.

The band members were Christians, and they witnessed or gave their testimony between sets. I usually went to the podium near the end of the evening to offer an invitation. I asked the audience to pray, letting them know that if they were ready to receive the Lord, helpers were posted all around. If someone raised their hand, I directed him or her to one of the Christian young people, or I would have the Steppingstone team members wave their hands as I told the crowd, "If you want to pray, you can go talk to one of these people."

All through the evening as the band played, I walked through the crowd talking to as many young people as I could. It was surreal. I knew I was fulfilling God's purpose for my life at that moment. My vision was taking place almost literally as I pressed through the crowds talking to the teenagers. Some had come because they were genuinely seeking meaning for their lives.

In some cases they came just because they had heard the music and had nothing better to do on Saturday night; they were caught in the flow.

I waded against the stream of young people trying to get them to look toward the cross. Many paid no attention. But some listened to the lyrics or to me or to one of the young Christians who tried to talk to them, and the greatest miracle of all, the miracle of salvation, happened regularly. Sometimes fifteen or twenty young people would be saved in one evening. God blessed the effort.

Adults attended the Steppingstone's worship services and brought their children with them. Sometimes they asked where I went to church, and on Sunday morning, I would see them at Burleson's Assembly of God. The church was growing because of our youth ministry.

Chapter 29

Christian Concert Playbills

THE STEPPINGSTONE WAS the hub of the ministry, and the bowling center was a common venue, but we organized youth-oriented concerts anywhere we thought we could attract a few young people. Usually, local bands played at our concerts. Sound of Salvation, from Burleson, and Bliss, a group formed by a youth pastor and his wife—Rick and Carol Eubank—and Kathy Lewis, performed at Steppingstone many times, but we began attracting nationally known performers to Burleson, too. The young artists had a lot in common with their audiences. They were products of a generation of spiritual nomads. They had been adrift and had floated toward the precipice because once they rejected the material idols of their parents, they had no anchor, no philosophy or moral code to hold fast to in a world inundated by narcissism and greed.

Many of our visiting musicians had been saved after surviving depression or drugs. Most had miraculous testimonies. All of them could relate to the challenges that young people faced in the seventies and eighties. One of them was Terry Clark, who had completed a tour of Europe in 1975. He performed in Burleson on December 4, 1976. A native of Texas, Terry was involved in the growth of contemporary Christian music for several years. He had sung with Children of Faith who recorded an album in 1974. He later recorded with Maranatha Records. Terry had turned to Christ after he found he was unable to cope with life's pressures on his own, the *Burleson Star* reported before one event. He had tried drugs while stationed in Germany with the army and eventually suffered a complete mental and emotional breakdown. Although doctors said his condition was hopeless, Christian friends prayed, and he recovered miraculously.

The playbills read like a Who's Who of youth-oriented, contemporaneous Christian music. Tom Autry and Tim Sheppard topped the bill of Freedom Song Fest, a Fourth of July praise celebration at Burleson High

School's stadium, emceed by (Deacon) Don Evans a disc jockey at KPBC, one of the Dallas-Fort Worth metroplex's Christian radio stations.

In 1977, Autry was the premier artist of Star Song. His music was an amalgam of praise, worship, jazz, and gospel with a sing-along quality that drew his audiences in, the *Burleson Star* reported. His first album, *Tom Autry*, was number eleven on Southwest Region's gospel charts when he appeared at Songfest. Despite the mid-summer heat and competing Fourth of July celebrations across the Dallas-Fort Worth area, scores of kids showed up.

A group known as Pure Faith performed for the last hour of the celebration between ten and eleven o'clock that night. The group's multimedia production, which combined live music with slides on a jumbo screen and electronic sound effects, overviewed the spiritual history of man from creation until the death and resurrection of Jesus.

By God's grace, Freedom Songfest was the first of many concerts at the high school. I say by God's grace because if not for God's intervention, there may not have been others. We had taken an offering, but the receipts weren't nearly enough to pay the fees of the professional musicians. The next day, I looked over all the bills for the rental of the stadium, performers' fees and expenses, and all the related expenditures. I had assumed the responsibility for payment of all those fees, and the offering fell far short of the total cost, which was staggering. I said, "Lord, I'm not ever going to do anything like this again."

I regretted the comment immediately and fell under conviction for it while God spoke to me. Instead of allowing me to wallow in doubt about my personal finances, He demanded that I extend myself even further. It was almost as though I was being chastised for the faithless thought. I felt him saying, "You need to turn the finances over to me," because He was directing the events and circumstances. The Lord gave me a directive to call David Wilkerson's ministries and ask them to come to Burleson. I didn't have a clue how I was going to pay the expenses of Freedom Songfest, and suddenly God was asking me to commit to something even greater. Another costly campaign might bankrupt my family, but how can you hesitate when you know the Lord is directing you to do something? I picked up the phone, called David Wilkerson's ministries, got through to the manager who scheduled all the crusades, and invited David Wilkerson to Burleson. I told him about the Steppingstone Youth Center. I told him about the drug issues and about a series of recent teenage suicides in our community.

The Reverend Wilkerson, who is probably most famous for the book and movie titled *The Cross and the Switchblade*, had recently written a book about suicide, and the spate of teen suicides in Texas may have been the clincher for his crusade team. One call, that's all it took, and one of the leading evangelical organizations in the United States had committed to come to Burleson. I was amazed and inspired.

When I set the phone back down, I still didn't know what I was going to do, but the pile of bills lying in front of me didn't bother me as much as it had a few minutes earlier. God respects such acts of faith. I had acted on His command, and He immediately rewarded my faith. A car drove up to the door of the Steppingstone. I had never seen the driver before, but he said he had been at the concert the previous night. He didn't have his checkbook with him at the concert, he said, and he wanted to make a donation. He handed me a check that covered the entire balance owed for the Freedom Songfest. I was able to pay every debt. Not one more cent had to come out of my pocket to cover the expenses.

I can't help believing that if I had not picked up the phone and done as God was leading me to do, that car would never have arrived, the check would never have been written, and perhaps an important outreach of the Steppingstone ministry would have ended that very weekend. When God calls you to do something, even if it makes absolutely no sense to you at the time, do it. Don't lose out on a blessing because you fail to act on God's word.

That wasn't the end of the special events sponsored by the Steppingstone Youth Center. Tom Autry returned for an encore performance on August 13. My brother, Ercel Lewis, spoke at an outdoor service on the Friday night before Autry's performance.

Tim Sheppard, another leading Christian vocalist of the time, had shared the top spot on the July flyers for Freedom Songfest. Tim, who had won an international songwriting competition in 1975, returned on Friday, November 12. He wrote the song "Would You Believe in Me," recorded by the Imperials on their Grammy Award winning *No Shortage* album in 1975. Many of his early songs were recorded by the Imperials.

I knew that the Steppingstone didn't have the resources to provide the logistics for such a massive undertaking as the Wilkerson crusade. So I asked the pastor of my church if he could call a meeting of the Burleson ministers to help with the planning and support. "We'll need all the churches to come together for this," I told him. He agreed, but I don't think he believed, at first, that the crusade was coming to Burleson. It was such a small community, and the Wilkerson crusade was playing in major metropolitan centers with sometimes tens of thousands of young people attending. The pastor contacted David Wilkerson Ministries himself to confirm that they were coming, and I'm pretty sure that, as he began contacting some of the other pastors in Burleson, he ran into the same disbelief. David Wilkerson's crusade in Burleson—that was a miracle in itself.

The Crusade made it to Burleson in 1978. After the Burleson school district added a new gymnasium/auditorium at the high school, the Steppingstone rented it, and it was packed for the crusade. Dallas Holm and Praise returned with the Wilkerson Crusade. Dallas was known for his song writing. He authored and recorded, "Rise Again," "Hey, I'm a Believer," and many more top Christian songs, many of which are still popular today.

The Lord did so much through the Steppingstone Youth Ministry. No telling how many young people were saved over the next six years while the Steppingstone's reputation grew and attendance surged, but the count wasn't important. Each individual soul saved was invaluable. Many of the young people who were at the Steppingstone eventually started ministries, and the collateral effect is still being felt today all over the globe.

Looking back now, it seems entirely appropriate that God required an act of faith to launch that ministry.

Chapter 30

Bandidos

REVVING UP

Engines roared
The earth shook,
And Gloria stood
With only a book
Before the threat
In the leader's look.
Unafraid and calm,
While engines growled
She offered snacks.
The gang just scowled
There to claim
Their property,
The souls inside
Seeking safety.
She smiled and said,
"Come in," to the crowd,
But they just sat
In a darkling cloud
Of angry engines
Mean and loud
Until at last
Christ won the day
When they popped their clutches
And all as one
Gave their engines a final gun,
Ran through the gears
In an awesome choir
Of guttural rumbling, silent curses,
And smoking tire,
And drove away.

Motorcycle gangs were the terror of stop six, an area of Fort Worth named for the Cowanville stop, the sixth stop on the inter-urban train line that ran between Fort Worth and Dallas until the 1950s. By 1975, the sobriquet loosely defined the entire southeast side of Fort Worth, bounded by Loop 820 on the south and east and the two interstate highways (30 and 35) that intersect in downtown Fort Worth on the north and west.

Fort Worth gangs were as lethal as any in the country, and they were growing. Members were associated with crimes all over North Texas. Some of these men were outlaws, no less dangerous than the outlaws of Texas's wild-west legendry—Sam Bass, John Wesley Hardin, and Wild Bill Longley. They were not to be crossed. No one dared to stand alone against such an awesome force as the gangs of young men whose recreation was littering the Texas landscape with terror.

The Steppingstone Youth Center was located in Burleson, twenty miles south of the stop six area, but well within the range of Fort Worth gangs. Prior to 1976, about the closest thing to a motorcycle gang in the suburb had been a group of graffitists who rode around in an old Ford spraying symbols that vaguely resembled motorcycles on highway abutments. But in 1977, the influence of gangs touched the families of teenagers who had become active at Steppingstone. Many of them came from East Fort Worth where the Meadowbrook Evangelistic Temple was located.

I held the dubious honor of being well known by the gangs. The sister of a teenage boy who had started attending the Tuesday Bible study lived with a gang member. Sometimes she attended Bible study with her brother. I talked to her about the Lord and about her life. She never had much to say, but she always listened. She came with her brother one Saturday night and turned her life over to the Lord, setting in motion a chain reaction that could have resulted in disaster if not for God's grace.

The girl recruited others from the gang. As a result of her witnessing, one by one almost half of one gang was saved. Most of them lived in Fort Worth, and I encouraged them to attend church at the Evangelistic Temple, where Tony Wise was still pastor. Although I had started attending the Assembly of God church in Burleson, I wanted the young people to go to a church close to their homes. Besides, Tony could relate to those young people in a very special way. He had played saxophone in a band at nightclubs before he was saved and called into the ministry. His lifestyle had not been very different from theirs.

As they began to believe in Jesus Christ, many young women became convinced that they needed to sever ties with the gang. The Jekyll and Hyde contradiction between their new beliefs and their lifestyle was untenable, and they came to me for advice. The young woman and a few of her friends expressed desires to escape the gang culture. I prayed with them and encouraged them to seek the Lord.

Soon, the gang leaders had reason to resent my ministry and me personally. Their girlfriends no longer related to them in the same way. The girls refused to have sex with them, and I, as a personification of the Steppingstone, was a threat to the gang's survival. A gang would not hold together long if members kept breaking away to become Christians and go to regular meetings at the Steppingstone. My ministry was as big a threat as the police or rival gangs, and although no one had ever directly threatened me, rumors floated like an oil slick on wet pavement that the gang had determined that the Steppingstone should be destroyed.

One warm evening I had opened all the windows and doors of the building, which, as usual, was overflowing with young people. As they often did, Bob's Donuts had provided us with snacks. The music seemed especially good that evening. Several teens and young adults with ties to the gang showed up. We were listening to a Christian rock band and singing praises when we heard what could have been the rumble of a prairie storm. The rumble grew louder and became a constant low drone, and soon there was no doubt that what we had heard wasn't thunder. It was the sound of motorcycles trolling the nearby streets until the deafening roar of the Harley-Davidson engines drowned our conversation and the music. When the sound stopped moving, it was as though a tornado had parked right outside the door of the little house.

The sounds outside were deafening. I peeked out a window.

They sat astride their motorcycles, leathered kings upon their individual thrones, and revved the over-powered, under muffled engines. Inside, even in the safety of God's sanctuary, the fear was palpable. Many of the young women who were trying to break away from the gang acted as though they already felt the palms of the gang members closing about their throats. They believed I was about to suffer and that they would be next.

I stepped toward the door. One young man took my arm.

"Don't go," he said.

"Don't go out there, Gloria," others echoed.

"What are you going to do?" one of the ex-gang-members asked.

"Well, I guess I'll just go out and invite them to come in."

Engines revved. The little house could have crumbled from the earthquake force of the sound, but almost miraculously, it held together. The girls especially were afraid. They knew the violence these men were capable of. Most of them had seen it. A few of them had been victimized by it—beaten and abused. It was inconceivable to them that I might actually invite those men inside.

"Don't go." The vote was unanimous, except for the Lord's and mine. I had surrendered veto power over every decision in my life to Him, and He wanted me to confront these men, not in kind—with threats or violence—but with God's love. I knew that to be obedient to Him, I must offer God's peace to them.

I stepped outside. If there were ever young people in danger of stepping off the precipice and dropping straight into hell, they were sitting out there. Leather vested and tattooed, the nearest hoodlum sat astride the huge machine with his arms stretched wide like he was riding a Longhorn and steering it by its horns. One of them revved his engine. The orchestra followed the bass solo, revving engines in a gruesome, guttural chorus. I waited for the engines to vent so that I could be heard. Hatred has a feel, and I knew then that these men hated me. Their silent stares screamed louder than the deafening belches of their engines.

"Would you like to come in?" I smiled at the leader, and then made eye contact with each one of them. They just sat there. It could have been some macho pride that held them back, or better yet, maybe God was actually softening these men who were not permitted by the laws of their culture to show any sign of compassion. Certainly, there could be no bragging rights for killing a small woman who offered them donuts and soft drinks. Or maybe they were a little intimidated by me; though that's unlikely because men of that sort simply destroy those things that intimidate them. Maybe it was the hand of God, physically restraining them, weighing on the back of each man, which kept them in place on their bikes.

Before I had gone outside, I had asked the band to keep playing, and I could still hear it despite the combustive cacophony of the engines.

"Come in and listen. It's really good," I offered. "We would love for you to come in," I said again, and I meant it, too. Anytime we surrender to our fears, we lose a chance to witness. "We've got snacks and something to drink." If Jesus wasn't too good for publicans and sinners, I wasn't too good to invite these men to Cokes and donuts.

I smiled as cheerfully as I could and really wished one of them would get off his bike and come in. While many young people were simply caught in the flow as they drifted to the precipice, these men were speeding toward it like Evel Knievel heading into a jump over the Grand Canyon. I did my best to try to talk them into the house, even though there was little doubt in my mind that some people inside were silently praying that the gang would not take me up on the invitation.

The kids inside told me later they wanted to call the police. I was glad they didn't. At best that would have only led to future confrontations. As it was, the gang sat on their motorcycles and stared at me. I had said all that I had to say and stood there smiling for two minutes. No one else said a word. Finally, there was nothing else to do. I turned and went back into the Steppingstone.

The gang sat outside until a member of the pack gunned his engine a final time, and his motorcycle belched rudely. Then he slowly let out the clutch, and I, with the young people inside the meeting hall, listened as the pack gunned its engines in unison one final time and drove away without ever speaking a word. Other than the guttural utterings of their motorcycles, they had nothing to add to a conversation.

"Well, I guess they're not coming in," I said.

The threat had been real. After one girl had been saved, her boyfriend had beaten her so badly that she had been taken to the hospital. Her friends called her parents, who lived in Abilene. They had to sneak her out of the hospital because the gang was still threatening to kill her.

Most Christians in America today do not have to pay such a high price for their beliefs. Courage is not often counted among the gifts of the spirit, but anyone who has ever had to overcome timidity to speak about Jesus with a stranger or withstood criticism, or worse, because she is a Christian, knows that it is not of ourselves that we are able to bear witness of our Lord's sacrifices for us. While everyone around me was willing to succumb to fear, I confronted the gangsters singly, but not alone. The Holy Spirit was at my side, and whether anyone could see Him or not, they must have known He was there.

The gangsters must have sensed it. At least some of them were impressed enough to believe that there was something in that little building and among those people inside that they wanted, a strength that superseded the power that they derived from being part of a feared organization. Jesus told his disciples, "In the world you face persecution. But take courage. I have conquered the world" (John 16:33, NRSV).

Over the next year, some of the girls talked their gangster boyfriends into coming to the Steppingstone with them. We rejoiced each time one of them was saved.

Danny Bransom, a Burleson native, was among the motorcyclists that were saved over the next few years. He wasn't with the group that had threatened us that Saturday evening, but he was part of the culture of the gangs. He continued to attend the church and often brought some of the former gang members with him until he died in 2006. As time went on more gang members were saved. There were ex-gang members who still attended the church almost forty years later. While I was writing this book, I spoke at the funeral of one of them who died in a motorcycle accident.

Long after that event on a Saturday evening in the summer of 1977, I learned that the gang had come to the Steppingstone with the intent of burning the building to the ground. After that night, we were never bothered by them again.

Chapter 31

700 Club

God was moving through the Steppingstone ministry, and it was being noticed by, no less than, the 700 Club, which notified us they were sending a production crew to Burleson. They had heard about our Operation Blessing and were coming to interview me about it. Soon everybody knew.

Through mutual friends, I was informed that some representatives of the school district were aware of it, too. They were a little apprehensive about the visit. Despite the stated purpose of interviewing me about Operation Blessing, some people were privately concerned that other stories could slip out. A story about the films that the schools had planned to present in the guise of educating our children coupled with the recent embezzlement would have made for hours of salacious television fare. But it wasn't the nature of the 700 Club to turn local issues into national news. Besides, I had no intention of mentioning the episode.

However, the emphasis of the program did change once the producers and crews arrived and started interviewing people in the community. The television crew quickly realized that the Steppingstone was changing lives and that young people were finding Christ through our ministry. Many of them had given up drugs. That was the big news that they would eventually report about Burleson.

They spent two days filming constantly, interviewing dozens, if not hundreds, of people. During those two days, the 700 Club's producers never asked about the things going on in our schools. So either none of the people they interviewed mentioned it, or they simply weren't interested in our local imbroglios. Their story was about salvation and the good work we were doing in Christ's name through the Steppingstone. That may not be what the secular news media would consider newsworthy, but that is the only thing really worth reporting. If you believe that Christ Jesus died on the cross to redeem us from our sins and that we can save others by making them aware of Jesus' sacrifice and God's love for us, how can any other news compete?

If there was excitement about the television crews, it was nothing compared to the energy pulsing through the community when the 700 Club announced that the report about Burleson had been scheduled. The town's population was about 10,000 at that time, and we were going to be on a national television program. There probably wasn't such a media stir in Burleson for another thirty years when Kelly Clarkson became the first American Idol.

I was told there were some people who were not looking forward to the airing of the program. They hadn't been interviewed themselves and didn't know what had been said to the media during the two days of filming. The story of the Steppingstone must have been presented a dozen times during the following year, and eventually gossip circulated back to me that the superintendent of schools had watched one of the airings and had exclaimed how wonderful the report was.

Chapter 32

A New Vision

EVERY MORNING I took the boys to school and then dropped by the Steppingstone to pray. After depositing the boys at school on a bright morning in 1977, I started my drive across town to the Steppingstone. A few blocks before getting to the youth center, I had to cross railroad tracks that ran north and south through Burleson, bisecting the city. Traveling east, into the morning sun, on Eldridge Street and starting up over the tracks, I was overwhelmed by a vision. Jesus appeared before me. He filled the sky, and His hands were outstretched like He was saying, "Come to me." Blood dripped from the cups of his palms. I tried to look at his face but couldn't make out any details, except His eyes. His eyes were pools of love. They were overflowing with tears. He didn't speak. Instead, He looked away from me, and I looked in the same direction, following His gaze.

Even though the sun was up and it was a bright morning, I found myself peering into the same darkness I had seen thirteen years earlier. People were falling into hell. The flow of souls toward the cliff had become a flood. It seemed impossible to stop, and if anyone stepped into the current, they would be swept over the cliff. I knew that the Steppingstone was living up to its name. Like a boulder in the middle of a stream, those who reached for it could crawl out and then step safely onto the banks of eternity. I wasn't sure why I was seeing the vision again. I looked back toward Christ and saw blood flowing from His hands.

He still didn't speak. His mouth didn't move at all, and He never made a sound. In fact, everything was peacefully silent. There were no sounds from cars passing on Renfro, one of the main streets through Burleson. In the absolute silence, I heard my Lord speaking to me, not aloud, but I suppose in much the same way that He must hear our silent prayers: "My blood was shed in vain for all of these who go into eternity without salvation because I died for everyone."

I had never thought about it that way before. God loved the world so much that He died for everyone. But only those who will come to Him are saved. He shed his blood in vain for those who don't come to Him, and He grieves over each soul. I saw his loss. I saw the pain and sorrow in his eyes. David said in the Psalms, "If I make my bed in hell, behold, You *are there*"(Psalm 139:8, NKJV). God loves the world. He died for the sinners, and we are all sinners. Those of us who get saved aren't the only ones He loves. He loves all those that don't get saved just as much. I felt insignificant. The things we could accomplish at the youth center were so miniscule compared to the incomprehensible number of people who needed to be saved.

I guess angels took over the car because I made it to the Steppingstone. I wasn't aware of driving into the parking lot. I had been completely consumed by the vision since the moment it had started, and now that I realized I was still in the car, I prayed for all the lost souls. I sat there and prayed for a long time. The youth center was so small, yet I said, "Oh Lord, I will win as many as I can, and I will do the best I can for You." More than thirty years later, I remember that vision as vividly as I saw it that morning, and each day the message tugs at me. It's my motivation for getting out of bed and for continuing in the ministry. That's why it doesn't matter what I have to go through. I will continue, and I will keep my commitment to the Lord.

I don't know how long the vision lasted. It could have been seconds. It could have been much longer. For me, time was suspended. When it was over, I made a new commitment, and I received His assurance. I know that as long as we are reaching out and preaching the gospel, and as long as we are doing our best to lead people to the Lord, He will bring us through whatever trials or hardships we may encounter.

Chapter 33

A Growing Youth Ministry

AT STEPPINGSTONE, I was in charge of Saturday night, whether it was a concert, a movie, or a Bible study, and I was teaching Sunday school class the following mornings at the Assembly of God. So I was almost like an assistant youth pastor. At the end of 1977, the couple who led the youth ministry was called away.

On hearing the news, the senior pastor didn't hesitate to ask me to take the reins of the youth ministry, and I didn't hesitate to accept. It seemed natural that I should be the youth pastor. As I entered the new phase of my service in December, we had twenty to twenty-five kids. I immediately started making plans for the upcoming year.

Compared to the ministry at Meadowbrook, being youth pastor at the Assembly of God was like a promotion. Even though both were unpaid positions, it was like getting a raise because at Meadowbrook I had financed everything. I bought all the refreshments. I purchased all the supplies. To have the church paying for supplies was almost like getting paid because I didn't have to pay for everything out of my pocket.

We had a youth retreat during spring break. We went to a camp near Glen Rose, and then we had a summer camp. The teenagers loved going to camp. I brought in groups that ministered and entertained. Many of the kids got filled with the Holy Spirit for the first time at the camp meetings. While I was youth pastor at the Assembly, the youth center, still a separate ministry, continued to grow. The little house was always packed. People were getting saved.

Burleson was growing so fast that every school campus strained to hold the inflow of new students. Newcomers to Burleson saw advertisements for the Steppingstone in the Burleson newspaper, and every meeting was crowded.

The Age of Aquarius may still have been speeding toward its apogee in Haight-Ashbury, New York, and even in the large Texas cities of Dallas and Houston, but many young people in small town Texas were already looking for something more in their lives than free love, drugs, gangs, and the ephemeral pleasures that had supplanted religion in a culture of narcissism. The fortunate few found meaning for their lives in places like the Steppingstone.

From the start, the little house on Dobson had hardly been big enough to contain the crowds. Even though I, with help from several adult sponsors and committed teenagers, had stripped out the building's interior walls and converted it to one big room, there wasn't enough space for the throngs of teens who squeezed into the meetings. As the reputation of the Steppingstone grew, young people came from all around. On any given night, teenagers arrived by the carloads from Arlington, Saginaw, Fort Worth, Dallas, Cleburne, and even Mineral Wells. The growing number of kids searching desperately for meaning in their lives overflowed the building regularly.

My vision was being fulfilled. Kids that would have been wandering aimlessly toward an eternal doom were noticing the woman who was waving at them and trying to get them to see where the current of their lives was taking them. Once they were wakened, they reached out desperately for help, and they found a steppingstone. There was no way to get to them all, but I knew I had to reach as many as I could. The ministry, any ministry, must first and foremost be about bringing God's Word to those who need to hear it. It's not about buildings, but we needed more space.

In January 1978, at a service commemorating the second year of the Steppingstone Youth Ministry, I announced that the organization had established a building fund. In addition to donations, the Steppingstone raised funds by sponsoring moneymaking projects, and any money left over after expenses went into the fund. "The building was bulging at the seams Saturday," Mary Cowley observed in a January 19, 1978, *Burleson Star* article titled "Plans for a New Youth Center Revealed." The brief article about the youth center's second anniversary included my announcement about the building fund.

Donations began trickling in from everywhere. I don't know how all the donors heard about it. I found a check in the mail for $500 from somebody in Dallas whom I had never met. Then I started getting $100 bills in the mail. We would get three, four, five letters at a time with bills in them. Despite the occasional check for a hundred dollars or more, the fund was supported mostly by little contributions, fifty here, thirty there. We knew God would have to work many miracles before we could start a building project.

Unless they were accompanied by a note or letter saying that the money was for the building, most of the contributions were used to continue financing concerts and other events. Spreading the gospel to young people, after all, was the principal mission of the Steppingstone, new building plans or not.

Ray Phillips, one of the Steppingstone youth who was taking drafting classes, helped me complete the plans for an eighty by forty foot building, including plumbing and electrical design. The building was nothing fancy, but serviceable. Like Noah's ark, it was to be built for a specific purpose. It didn't need to be a Taj Mahal or a Carnegie Hall.

Over the following months, the donations dwindled until they were drifting in as sparsely as a central Texas autumn snowfall. I split my time between the Steppingstone and my duties as youth pastor at the Assembly of God. John saw that I was spread thinner than the mustard on a nickel hot dog. He knew that something was going to have to change long before I was able to see it for myself. I was a full-time mother, a full-time youth minister, and a full-time administrator of a new ministry. Something had to give. He worked into conversations that I needed to make a decision. "You're working so hard with the church youth and the Steppingstone youth," he told me. "I think you need to concentrate on the Steppingstone because God gave you that ministry." His first suggestion hit with about the same effect as a single snowflake on a hot pancake griddle: barely a sizzle and it's gone.

"I can't do that. I can't give up the ministry at the church. My first love is the church." John already knew that I felt every Christian's first obligation, after telling others about Jesus Christ, is the church. The church is the body of Christ. There may be more than one church building in a town or city, but anyone who is a Christian is a member of the body of Christ. Elders, teachers, evangelists, apostles and pastors—everyone working together has a function in that local body of believers. "For as the body is one, and hath many members, and all the members of that one body, being many, are one body: so also is Christ" (I Corinthians: 12:12).

As I saw it, an individual's function within the church is that person's ministry despite any other works that individual may do for the kingdom outside the body. It was impossible for me to think of the Steppingstone as my full-time ministry. It was just one of many ways of reaching out to the youth in our community. The church came first. If I poured my energy into the church, God would take care of the Steppingstone.

The prospect of giving up the youth ministry at the Assembly of God presented another dilemma. During the year I had been youth pastor, enrollment had swelled to more than seventy-five kids who regularly attended services, and they were so full of life and fire. Everybody loved our youth group; the whole church was proud. On Sundays, a whole section of the church was occupied by young people.

But everything has its season, and I began to see John's point. On a Sunday in February, I presented my Sunday school lesson to the teenagers. I had prepared the lesson as thoroughly as always. I had walked into the classroom with a message that the kids needed to hear. Yet as I shared it with them, I felt awkward. I felt out of the will of God, even though I knew that sharing Christ with young people aligned perfectly with God's will for my life. I began to realize that God had been speaking to me through John, and I hadn't been listening.

John's words had been prophetic. That morning I had an overwhelming impression that God wanted me to devote my efforts to the Steppingstone ministry. God said, "You are to resign. Walk away. Not from the church, but you are not to have any involvement with the youth ministry at the Assembly of God Church." When church was over, I was still confused and couldn't get it off my mind. I knew that I was going to have a hard time resigning, and I didn't want to disappoint the pastor. He had placed such faith in me to run the church's youth outreach that I regretted having to tell him.

If John hadn't spoken to me, I may not have been prepared for the series of events that Sunday. I was about to get further confirmation that God was calling me down a different path and even more confirmation that the Steppingstone would be my life-long ministry.

While I was still lingering indecisively, the pastor said he wanted to speak to me. He led me to his office, and I knew that such a formal meeting meant something serious. He started talking about the youth ministry and complimented the work that had been done. It had made large strides and was continuing to grow. We were both proud of that. I thought his conversation was a prelude to planning what we would do in the future, and I didn't want to have that discussion. I needed to tell him that I had decided to resign. I had no way of knowing that the pastor was trying to find a way to tell me that he had found a replacement for me, and that I would no longer be leading the youth ministry.

"I'm not going to be youth pastor anymore," I stated flatly during a pause, and he thought that I knew that he had already made plans to replace me. He apologized without making it clear why he was apologizing.

We may as well have been speaking two different languages. He thought I was just acknowledging that he had replaced me, but I didn't know anything about that yet. I was trying to resign. The pastor asked if he had offended me, and I thought he was concerned that I was resigning because of some minor peccadillo. He probably suspected that I should be offended, and he believed I was saying that I was resigning because I had found out about his plans to replace me. I was still puzzled as I left his office.

After I got home, however, I found that the pastor's machinations had gone a lot farther. One of the kids from my youth group arrived just after we got home. This young man, at eighteen years old, had come out of drugs and had gotten his life straightened out in our youth group. I told him, "I'm not going to be the youth pastor anymore."

"I was just coming over to talk to you about that," the young man said. "The pastor told us Thursday night that he had gotten someone else to be our new youth pastor, but you didn't say anything about it in Sunday school. I came over to see what was going on."

The young man told me that the pastor had invited the youth council, a group of teenagers and young adults who planned and organized youth activities for the church and the Steppingstone, to his home the previous Thursday. The pastor had told them that I was too busy with the Steppingstone ministry and that he was going to hire a new youth pastor. He implied that the decision had been mine, and that I didn't have time for them.

I didn't harbor any ill will toward the pastor or to the new youth pastor. Our family kept worshipping at the Assembly of God church. It wasn't as though the move had not been God's will. Suddenly, I was free to devote more of my time to Steppingstone, and I received almost daily confirmations that the youth ministry, separate from any particular church or organization, was the first calling on my life. Church was still an important part of my life, but my responsibilities to the Steppingstone's ministry had started to take precedence.

I was saddened to see that the youth ministry at the Assembly of God didn't continue to thrive under the new youth pastor. Its slow demise affected the whole church. People started leaving. The new youth pastor didn't seem to inspire the kids. My children were bored, and I suspected that they were representative of the other youth in the church's congregation, but I kept encouraging them to go and be involved. They continued attending because I asked them to, but if the decision had been left up to them, they probably would have found other places to worship.

Sandy Browning and quite a few of my other friends who had been going to the Assembly were leaving to worship elsewhere, too. The church had been vibrant with the Holy Spirit, but as time went on, when people gave messages in tongues or prophesied, they were discouraged or silenced. They weren't permitted to operate in the gifts. A few months passed while the church continued to disintegrate. Then it was John who made the decision. "I think we are going to go somewhere else to church," he announced.

I simply agreed, "Ok." We joined the growing list of church members who were leaving.

The pastor eventually called and told me that he was sorry for the way he had handled things. He asked for my forgiveness because, he said, he had discouraged the Holy Spirit's work. He told me that I was doing God's work and encouraged me to continue the Steppingstone ministry. He also feared he had diluted the anointing in the church he had been called to lead.

I returned to my roots. John and I took our family back to Bethesda where my parents still attended church. My sons, now teenagers, visited at Crestmont Baptist church and other churches in the area, until they found a church in Fort Worth called Overcoming Faith Center where evangelist Jerry Savelle was pastor.

Although I remained faithful in attendance at Bethesda, it didn't fill my needs. The pastor was a good preacher and a good teacher. He taught adult Sunday school class, and he preached every Sunday. Whatever he was teaching in Sunday school, I wanted to be there. His sermons were great. But for some reason, the spirit never moved during the services. We never entered into worship. We just sang hymns and praise songs.

It was ritual. There was never an altar ministry, and at the end of each service, we simply dismissed, with no opportunity for those who were feeling conviction or who had need of prayer to come forward. There were times that I had things going on in my life or when I felt burdened about something going on at Steppingstone, and I wanted someone to agree with me in prayer. The church never offered an opportunity for it.

Even though the Steppingstone ministry continued growing, I felt an obligation to serve in the church. I was a church pianist at Bethesda, but that wasn't the same as teaching a Sunday school class or leading a Bible study. I needed encouragement in my ministry. I needed a word.

Chapter 34

Building a Ministry with Miracles

By May of 1979, the Steppingstone had earmarked $4,000 for the new building. Looking back now, from the middle of the second decade of a new millennium, that may seem a paltry sum. You could pay that much for a single consultation with an architect, but in 1979, that was a lot of money. Even in those days, though, it wasn't enough to start a building, unless you were acting in faith.

After praying and fasting, I knew that the time to build had come. With or without adequate funding, it was time to get started. I contacted some builders and was finally referred to a cement contractor who said he could do all the preparation and have the foundation poured for $4,000. It would take everything we had raised so far just to lay the foundation.

Faith is the foundation in our relationship with God. Everything else is built on that. Without that foundation, a church cannot grow. I determined that we should move forward with the foundation even if that was all we could afford. The building's foundation would be the step in faith that would lead to the rest of the building.

There's a lot of work that goes into preparing and constructing a foundation, and if it's not done right, a building is worthless. The foundation for a Christian life must be constructed and cared for, too. In and around Burleson, Texas, we're taught that we need to water the foundation of our homes because the soil is dark clay. In the summer, when it's dry and parched, all the moisture in the clay is lost. Large cracks appear in lawns that don't get enough water. If we don't want broken pipes and cracked foundations, we must water them. The Christian life requires constant care, too—a regular watering of Bible study and prayer.

About fifteen people gathered near the small building for the Steppingstone's groundbreaking services on March 4, 1979. I had to put all my weight onto the shovel to turn the first clump of that cold, hard, Texas clay, but that wouldn't be the last physical effort I personally put into the building, far from it.

The groundbreaking ceremony set off a chain of miraculous events. I watched every day while the land was prepared, the pipes were laid, and the frame for the foundation was constructed. On May 23, I was on hand when the first of the cement trucks arrived. I watched as the workers poured and smoothed the foundation until the wet surface glistened like a mirror.

By the time the foundation was poured, we had raised another $800, just enough to buy the lumber for the framing. It didn't even begin to pay for the labor, though. I contacted people who had previously offered to do the framing free of charge. Three different contractors had expressed an interest in helping with the building, but they were all busy with other commitments, and none knew when they would have enough time to fit the Steppingstone in.

"I believe in the youth ministry," they said one by one, "but I'm just too busy."

The youth of the Steppingstone and those who supported them redoubled their prayers. Donations still trickled in. Twenty dollars, thirty, but there wasn't enough to hire a contractor. Pat Shetter and I prayed together about the building then talked about our options. No one was coming forward to help. "I guess we'll just have to do it ourselves," Pat finally suggested. "How hard can it be?"

"It's all hammers and nails and wood," I agreed.

"Yeah, it's just nailing boards together."

The more we thought about it, the more convinced we were that we could do it. But the Master Builder had already set other plans in motion. He was coordinating the construction of his ministry, and he was lining up the best people to complete each phase of the work.

Mark Emmert drove down Dobson Street every morning on his way to work and again every evening. For the past several weeks, he had noted the bare foundation sitting on the lot at the corner of Dobson and Miller streets. He knew what it was. His mother was in a prayer group with me.

While Pat and I prayed and planned a few blocks away, Mark drove past the building and noted once again that the rain had rinsed the cement block, and it glistened in the afternoon sun. His wife wasn't home that evening, and Mark had the house to himself. Like a lot of us, Mark didn't think of himself as irreligious, but he didn't attend a church he considered home either. As he sat there alone, he noticed the family Bible on the coffee table. He picked it up and began reading where it fell open—the Old Testament book of Haggai. As he reached the seventh verse, he found himself reading slower. The words worked their way into his heart.

> Thus saith the LORD of hosts; Consider your ways. Go up to the mountain, and bring wood, and build the house; and I will take pleasure in it, and I will be glorified, saith the LORD.
>
> —HAGGAI 1: 7–8

Haggai admonished the people of Israel to rebuild the temple, and a few blocks away, the Steppingstone was building a temple of sorts, a place where young people could assemble to worship. Mark read on, but he already knew what he had to do. Just as the Lord stirred the spirit of Zerubbabel, He stirred Mark.

Sometimes God speaks to us in that still small voice; sometimes He speaks to us through the advice of others; sometimes He reaches out to us from the pulpit, and sometimes all we have to do is pick up His Word and read a sentence to know what He expects from us. How often are miracles dismissed as coincidence? Sometimes the real miracle isn't that something miraculous happens, but that we recognize the miracle in a momentary and seemingly insignificant event.

As soon as Mark was up and dressed the next morning at six o'clock, he called his mother and told her to call me. I was surprised to hear from him. I hardly knew him. I knew that he was my friend's son. He got the dimensions of the building from a telephone call and then specified the lumber and supplies that would be needed to complete the framing. I paid for the lumber. It took almost all of the money we had saved. The materials were delivered the next afternoon. Mark's crew showed up shortly after the delivery and got started.

During the next few weeks, while Mark's crew was framing the building, Steppingstone held fundraisers to pay for the next step. Roof trusses alone would set the project back by another $6,000. Even when Mark whittled the lumber company down to $4,000, very little more than cost, by explaining the nature of the project to the owners of the lumberyard, we didn't have enough to move forward.

Once again, my parents, who believed that the Steppingstone was important to the Burleson community and that the building was essential for reaching out to young people, placed their money where their faith was. On hearing the sum, Daddy volunteered, saying, "Well, I'll furnish that." I promised that I would pay them back personally, but my parents never let me. I ordered the trusses so that they would be ready as soon as the framing was completed. Once again, I stepped out in faith, not knowing how we would pay for anything beyond framing.

I remembered other words from Haggai 1:14, "And they came and did work in the house of the Lord of hosts, their God."

The high-pitched trusses were expandable to a limit of forty feet. Huge. And they were scheduled to go up on a Saturday morning. I went to the building to watch, and Otis, now a teenager, was already there helping on the roof. Throughout the framing he had pitched in anywhere he was needed, mostly as gopher, but that day he was a member of the construction crew.

Mark needed his entire crew on the roof to set the trusses as soon as they were lifted into place by a crane. A team on each side of the building caught and steadied the truss as it was lowered into place, then immediately braced it and nailed it down. There was no one on the ground to prepare the next truss and hook it to the cable so that it could be hoisted to the roof. Someone from Mark's crew had to climb down from the roof after each truss was placed, hook up the next truss, and then climb back to the roof to help set the new one. That was a lot of extra work, and it was time consuming, too. They needed someone on the ground hooking up the trusses, but it was dangerous work. The cable had a huge steel ball attached to it as a weight, and it swung freely when the hook was lowered back to the ground after a truss had been removed.

"I'll do it," I volunteered.

"Oh, no. If that big steel ball hit you, it would knock you out. It's too dangerous," Mark insisted.

"Who else is going to do it?"

I stepped in and connected the cable to the next truss. It was no problem at all. As soon as I had connected it, I moved back and stayed away from the ball when the hook was lowered back to the ground. When the hook was moved into place above the truss, I hooked it and never had a bit of trouble.

I hooked all the trusses and had a blast. Although I never hammered a nail, I got to help with the framing after all.

The crane operator watched all day as I hooked truss after truss to the cable. He saw that I was working as hard as the men who were nailing the rafters in place. The crane expenses were over and above the costs of the trusses, and the operator was a private contractor, not part of Mark's crew. He presented me with an invoice at the end of the day.

He had itemized the charges for renting the crane, supplies, and the operator's labor. The labor had been calculated at twenty percent of the crane cost. The twenty percent was added to the rental costs for the total bill. But the operator had marked through the labor charge and recalculated the total so that the Steppingstone was only charged for rental of the machine. I couldn't believe it. He was a private contractor. He had no association with the Steppingstone other than his professional relationship with Mark. Yet he was willing to donate his time for the entire day. I asked him about it.

"If you're willing to work that hard, then I'll work for free, too," he told me.

Mark paid his crew for their labor out of his own pocket. Through these men, God had provided the labor for the walls and roof. Neither God nor Mark was finished, though. Mark contacted the siding supplier and finagled a fifty percent discount off the pricing of the pre-painted siding. Then he got ducking for the roof at fifty percent off, too.

The Master Builder saw to it that finances were just enough to complete each phase of the construction. We always had just enough, with nothing to spare.

The world is watching us. Each one of us professes our belief in Christ through our actions as well as our words. You never know who may be watching, whose life might be touched by your actions as a Christian. That's why it's important to live the Christian life in everything we do as well as everything we say. You never know when you're doing more than connecting a truss to a cable. You never know when you may be connecting another person to the will of God through your actions.

David Atwood managed a building supply company. His son participated in Steppingstone youth activities, and David persuaded his company to donate the roof shingles. Once again, the Steppingstone's building finances were exhausted. We had shingles but no roofer.

Greg Parks, my son-in-law, was a roofer, and he volunteered to do the roofing. He started out alone, but before long had help. Several ladies whose children participated in Steppingstone activities volunteered to help. Patsy Martin climbed up on the roof and helped out. Pat Smith, mother of girls who were regulars at the Steppingstone, had been taught the business by her father, who owned a roofing company, and she chipped in. Shanda helped, too. Greg showed them how. He and Pat mentored them, and the mothers of our Steppingstone youth roofed the building. It never leaked either.

Pat Smith has gone home to be with the Lord, but her daughter Margaret still attends the Open Door church. There may be a good Mother's Day sermon in that somewhere.

The outside was finished, and it began to look like the entire project would be completed by the first of September.

Chapter 35

Preparing for the Building Dedication

BEFORE WE KNEW it, it was time to start thinking about a dedication service. I prayed and asked the Lord to lead me in choosing a date. When I looked at the calendar, I saw that the Jewish Feast of the Tabernacles began on October 18. The Lord spoke to me, "That is the date for the dedication." I started lining up speakers and singers to come in and help us celebrate on that weekend.

From the start, it had been a wet summer. Rainfall in May for the Fort Worth area was more than twice the average for every year between 1979 and 2005, not enough to cause extensive flooding but enough to affect construction schedules. With the exception of one week, not three consecutive days passed without rainfall; the ground never had a chance to dry out.

As a result, a lot of the builders who had volunteered to help with sheet rocking, texturing walls, and installing electrical fixtures had gotten behind on other projects—projects that paid. Work was starting to back up on many buildings that had been delayed by the weather. By the time we were ready for them, they were extremely busy catching up. Construction inside our building fell behind.

Weeks passed with no progress. One morning I was praying and at the same time fighting discouragement. I asked God to send workers to finish the building. Suddenly the Holy Spirit spoke to me so strongly it was almost audible, "Let not doubt fill your heart. Only believe!" Assurance and joy filled my heart, and I began to sing and praise the LORD. I looked down at my open Bible, and my eyes fell on Haggai 1:14, "And the LORD stirred up the spirit of Zerubbabel the son of Shealtiel, governor of Judah, and the spirit of Joshua the son of Josedech, the high priest, and the spirit of all the remnant of the people; and they came and did work on the house of the LORD of hosts, their God." It was like a message straight from heaven. I knew God was answering my prayer and would send the workers needed to finish the building.

Later, Mom and Dad called and invited me to lunch. Over our meal, I told them what had happened that morning and that God would be sending workers. They started getting excited. Dad said, "Let's go down to the Steppingstone and see what's going on." When we got there, the parking lot was full of pickups and the building was full of workers!

God is so faithful.

After that, though, we kept getting delayed because of more rain. It began to look as though the building would not be ready in time for the dedication. With only two weeks left before the scheduled opening, there was no sheet-rock on the walls, no paint, and no electrical wiring.

The *Burleson Star* was printed and distributed every Thursday. Announcements and advertisements had to be submitted by Monday after-noon. On Sunday, October 14, it didn't appear there was any way for the building to be ready for occupancy in time for the scheduled opening, but the deadline was approaching. I had to make a decision before Monday's deadline and submit the announcement if it was going to run before the night of the first meeting on Thursday.

In my personal prayers on Monday morning, I asked for guidance. I asked the Lord if I should run the announcement or not. "Lord, should I place the announcement in the paper? Will we have the building complete enough so that we can have an opening on the eighteenth? We have no tape and bedding, no paint on the walls or electricity."

He said, "Yes. Put it in the paper."

So it was a step of faith that I put a little article in the paper. I never gave it another thought. I knew that the building would be as ready as God wanted it to be on the day of the dedication.

Chapter 36

Electrifying Angels

WITH ONE WEEK to go before the scheduled opening, I found myself reading about praising the Lord in almost every verse I came across. Praise the Lord.

The electrician, Rick Roper, had run conduit while the building was being framed, but no wires had been pulled yet. Like other contractors who contributed to the construction of the Steppingstone, he had other commitments. He was working at the Steppingstone when he could spare the time, but there was little of it. He was finishing the new roller rink just south of town. The rink was due to open on the same weekend we planned to dedicate our building.

I appealed to everyone I knew for help. We called everybody who could hold a hammer or a trowel. Greg Parks showed up again and found himself reprising his roles of trainer and foreman to the crews of unskilled volunteers. He was showing them how, and they were nailing sheetrock coming and going. Ladies who had volunteered because they knew me from church or were friends or who had kids who came to the center or who just wanted to lend a hand for the good of the community pitched in with the taping and bedding. None of us had any experience. We didn't know what to do, but somebody showed us, and away we went.

People throughout the community heard about the building. Cars started arriving at the end of the workday every afternoon, and people who didn't know me from Ma Kettle pitched in to help. Sometimes they were professional builders. Many knew how to put up sheet rock or tape and bed. Others didn't know a trowel from a towel, but they all helped in whatever way they could.

"I heard about this, and I wanted to come and help," one after another volunteered.

They were putting up sheetrock in one room, taping and bedding in the next, and texturing walls in rooms down the hall. It was an exciting time, and everyone seemed to understand their role. We were having a great time.

It was apparent that the interior walls would be completed, the doors hung, and painting well under way. Still, though, not one wire had been pulled through conduit. The breaker box was as empty as Jesus' tomb.

I called the electric company on Monday and told them that we planned to dedicate the building the following weekend. "We don't have electricity in our building yet," I explained, "but if you could get service to our building, then when the electricians put the wiring in, we will already have lights."

"Oh, no, we can't do that," the customer service agent responded. "You have to get your wiring in, have the installation approved by the city inspector, and then give us a call. Three or four days later we will get a truck out there and drop a wire to your building." All hope of having electricity in time for the dedication evaporated. By even the most optimistic estimates, we were running three to four days behind.

We didn't have any wiring in the building, but that really didn't bother us. We didn't know much about permits. We didn't understand anything about occupancy or city and county ordinances that governed construction. We kept working hard and figured that we would use oil lamps during the first services in the new building. Many people my age who had grown up in rural Texas had not had electricity in their homes when they were children. It was no hardship to go to a meeting without electrical lighting. When I was very young my father attended co-op meetings to get electricity provided to the rural area just south of Burleson, an area that is part of the city today. Electricity was a luxury, not a necessity.

Besides, the original Jewish tabernacle was lit by candles and oil lamps. We reasoned that if electricity wasn't ready when we were, then it must have been God's will for us to light the building with oil lamps, just like they had in the Tabernacle. We were, after all, dedicating the building during the Feast of Tabernacles. We didn't know that use of oil lamps violated a city ordinance.

We still planned a praise service on Thursday night, October 18. By that morning, we had finished the walls. The last of the acoustic ceiling was blown in, and the walls were spray painted. There was still no carpet. It wasn't due to arrive for another week. The floors would be bare concrete for the first few meetings, but we had a roof, walls, a ceiling, a floor, and chairs. God had provided all the essentials.

The only thing left was clean up. I met a group of volunteers on Thursday morning, brooms ready. Before we got started, I led them in prayer: "Lord, if it is your will that we have electricity tonight, then just send an angel and work a miracle. But if not, we'll enjoy praising you by the light of oil lamps." We never doubted that if God had wanted the building to be lighted by electricity during the dedication, He would have provided it. If oil lamps were enough for Him, then they would suffice for us.

We had worked hard for about an hour when one of the young ladies carrying out trash noticed a man standing at the entrance to the building. He stood there without saying anything until she spoke to him. "May I help you?"

"Is this the Stone?" He stood there looking at her solemnly, as though he were a soldier sent on a one-way mission. His speech was terse and direct. He wasn't there to make small talk. He was all business, absolutely confident, without a hint of pride or ego. His presence was reassuring.

"Yes. It is."

"I want to speak to the person in charge."

With no more conversation between them, the young woman led him to me.

"Gloria, this man asked to see you."

"I've come to give you electricity," he announced.

I was instantly impressed. His blue eyes were striking, a stark contrast with the rest of his dark features: thick black hair, dark complexion, heavy black mustache. He could have passed for a Jew or an Arab. I couldn't help staring at those eyes that matched the color of his short sleeved, knit, golf shirt, and his slacks that had rich veins of various shades of blue thread. They weren't just one solid color. I'm not a person that takes much notice of clothes, but even the smallest details of his clothing were registering with me, probably because there was something so different about him. The threads of his pants weren't just solid blue. It was a shiny, almost metallic looking fabric, and I thought it so unusual. His eyes were so blue you would notice them anyway, but the blue shirt really brought out the color. I assumed the electric company had sent him.

"Well, I called the electric company on Monday, and they said they couldn't put electricity to the building until we got the electrical work done and all the wiring in."

He stared at me and almost seemed a little impatient; although, at the same time, I sensed that time really wasn't important to him. He just expected things to get done. I recounted to him everything that the electric company had told me, and he stood there staring holes through me until I got through talking, just patiently listening, yet all business. "Then it has to be inspected," I finished.

Without responding to my explanation, he said firmly, "Take me to your telephone."

There was no working phone in the building; so I led him over to the little Steppingstone building. The strange man didn't offer any conversation, and I wasn't sure what to say to him.

I directed him to the phone, and he announced: "I'm going to call the electric company." He dialed a number that he obviously knew and got connected directly to the party he asked for. "We need service to the building at 301 South Dobson," I heard him say. He spoke to the Texas Electric employee by name saying, "We need it today." He listened for a minute and then hung up.

"I have to wait for someone to call me back to tell me what time a truck will be here," he explained. It seemed obvious to everyone that the man must be an employee of the electric company, and he appeared to have some clout.

News about the man was spreading quickly through the cleaning crew. Everyone was excited about the prospect of getting electricity. Some were mildly curious and continued with their work, but a few of the ladies set aside their brooms, dust pans, mops, and cleaning cloths and started to the Steppingstone.

When they arrived at the house, they found us sitting quietly waiting for a call back.

"He's checking to see when they can get a truck out," I told them. The ladies gathered around and sat down together, rejoicing that the building might have electricity for its dedication. After his initial appearance, the man never spoke directly to anyone but me.

While we were waiting for the phone to ring, Doris Couch arrived. She had checked for me at the new building and found that half the work crew had followed me over to the little house. She burst into the building brandishing a new copy of the *Burleson Star*. "We're on the front page of the paper," she announced. The *Burleson Star* ran a small article along with my announcement of the Steppingstone's opening.

Everyone gathered around to look at the paper.

"Yes. That's why I came down," the man said.

"What a blessing," one of the ladies said.

"God is good," said someone else.

"Praise the Lord," the man chimed rising from the chair where he had parked himself to silently wait for the call.

Someone whispered to me, "Well, he must be a Christian!"

I was really puzzled and curious about the article. I didn't remember explaining about the electricity problems to the newspaper. I read through the article, and there was no mention that the electricity wasn't working. The article announced all the activities, guest singers, and speakers scheduled for the opening celebration. So how could the man have learned that we didn't have electricity from reading the article?

When the phone finally rang, he answered. He listened briefly then put down the receiver and told me, "a truck will be out here this afternoon to get service to your building, and you will have electricity tonight."

After my conversation with the electric company earlier in the week, I had called Rick Roper. He wouldn't be able to install wiring for another week. It was nice, I thought, that the service would be ready, but it simply wasn't realistic to expect electricity to be ready that night or to have lighting for the meeting. "Oh, I really appreciate what you have done. But I called our electrician last night, and he said there was no way he could get here until Monday."

"You will have electricity tonight," he repeated with authority. He continued staring at me, and then echoed the words that I had said to him when he had first arrived as though they were his own: "Normally you would call the electric company after all the wiring was done and your building was inspected. Then it would take them a few days to get a truck out."

He filled in other details, while I stood there in shock, not fear, because despite his direct and almost curt manner, there was nothing in the man's demeanor that would make someone the least bit uneasy. Then he added, "Tell Bobby Reagan we're doing it different this time." Bob Reagan, whom I had never heard referred to before as Bobby, was the city inspector.

Although it seemed odd that a representative of the electric company would dictate the rules to a city inspector, I wasn't going to argue. My reticence wasn't out of fear but out of an odd mix of awe and confusion.

So I just said, "Thank you so much."

And with that, he was gone. He had been at the building for about thirty minutes. Although the encounter with him had seemed odd, we were excited about the prospect of getting electricity for the opening. He walked out of the house, and the rest of us returned to work. When we began to talk about the man later, no one had seen him arrive. No one saw him leave. No one knew what kind of car he had arrived in. No one knew how he left. Of course, no one was watching to see what kind of transportation he had. It never occurred to anyone to check. Later, as the significance of what the man had done began to seep in, we asked each other what kind of car he had driven and if anyone had seen him arrive or leave.

At 1:30 p.m., a truck arrived from the electric company and a pair of electricians quickly connected electrical service to the building. We didn't have a single electric wire pulled into conduit. We had no inspection. Nothing. But *we had power.*

Not long after the electric company's crew left, Rick stopped by to check on the status. He had been working at the skating rink all day. It was scheduled to open Saturday night, and he was spending most of his time there. He may have thought the idea to stop by the Steppingstone was entirely his own, but I know the Lord put it in his heart to drive by.

As he drove into the parking lot, he noticed the wires running to the building. Right away, he came and found me. "Where did you get that?" he interrogated.

I told him about the mysterious electrician who had stopped by earlier in the day and promised the building would have electricity that night.

Rick was curious, too. He plied me for the name of the electrician, which of course, I didn't know because he had never said. He tried to spur my memory by naming a list of usual electric company suspects.

I knew each of the men he named. They were local employees of Texas Electric.

"No. It was none of them."

"Well, describe him."

I did, right down the blue motif that started with his eyes.

"Well, I don't know anybody at the electric company that looks like that," Rick observed. He got back in his truck and drove straight to the coffee shop six blocks away, where he knew he would find Les Todd, the local Texas Electric representative.

"Do you know Steppingstone has electricity to their building, and I haven't run a single wire in it?" Rick recounted the whole story. "Did you do that?"

"No. I don't know anything about it. Who did it?"

"I don't know," said Rick. He relayed my description of the stranger.

"I don't know anybody at the electric company that looks like that. Nobody, especially no field rep, meets that description," Les countered. "Must have been an angel," he added with a smile.

An angel. There was no other explanation. Burleson was a dry city in dry Johnson county Texas. The coffee shop didn't serve inebriants, but that might have been a little difficult for someone to believe if they had been sitting in a booth listening to the conversation between Rick Roper and Les Todd. Before they left the restaurant, both men were convinced it had been an angel.

Rick returned and told me that the man must have been sent from heaven. That was the only explanation left, and Rick said he wasn't going to buck any plan that God had set in motion. If God had sent an angel, then providence was in charge of the project, and Rick didn't mind the idea that he was subcontracting for the architect of the universe.

"So I'm going to go ahead and get enough wiring for you to have lights tonight," he said. He didn't get wire pulled throughout the building, but he worked until time for the services that evening and got lights in the meeting room.

We had lights just like the angel said. We had electricity for the PA and musical instruments, too. A few weeks later, I was interviewed by the *Burleson Star*. They had gotten wind of the miraculous sequence of events. It wasn't long before my phone was ringing about the article.

One phone call was from an acquaintance at church. "I read about your visitation by an angel," she said. "The Friday night after you got electricity, we had some good friends over for dinner." Her visitor's friend worked for Texas Electric and was one of the two men who installed the meter and completed connection of the electrical service to our building. He described the situation and told everyone at the table that things simply weren't done that way. It was against company rules, electric codes, and city ordinance to connect service without the complete installation of wiring in a building. He had been surprised to arrive at the site and discover there was no wiring in the building, but he had orders to install the service, and that's what he did.

"When I read the newspaper article, I called my friends and told them it had been an angel," the visitor concluded.

There was no disagreement among anyone at the Steppingstone or at the electric company. Like the utility's employee, everyone involved felt like the project was being orchestrated by someone in a higher position of authority. From the volunteers who worked at the building to the city inspectors, each one recognized God's hand in it. They knew that the Chief Inspector had sanctioned the installation despite rules and regulations. They felt God had intervened, and they had better not interfere.

Six years later, in 1985, I called the electric company to get service for a new addition. "We have service at 128 East Miller," I told the representative. The bill, every month for six years, had come to the Miller street address, although the Steppingstone sat on the corner of Miller and Dobson streets. I called to order electricity for our new auditorium based on the address that our bill came to.

The representative couldn't find a record of service. She consulted with her supervisor, and the two of them researched the billing together. They looked and looked, and I waited and waited, until they came back on the line and asked if it could be under another address?

"Look under 301 South Dobson," I told them.

"We have a record that we turned on electricity in 1975 to 301 S. Dobson, but we can't find where we turned on electricity to 128 E. Miller." The only record they had was for the initial service connection when we had first purchased the house and started meeting in it at the Dobson street address. They didn't have a record for the construction of the new building in 1979.

"We have no record that you have electricity at 128 E. Miller."

"But we get a bill every month," I said.

"We have no record of sending electricity to that building."

That became another confirmation that the whole episode was supernatural. Simple obedience in the little things releases God's hand to work. It's amazing how God works through little things. The angel-electrician had said, "That is why I came down."

Inserting the announcement in the paper in obedience to the Lord and despite the appearance that we may not be ready in time was an act of faith. God did the rest. He brought people over to finish out the building and He blessed all our work. We got through, and then God sent an angel to manage the electricity and provide the one thing that we couldn't do ourselves. Boy, did we rejoice. It just made it more exciting that it was so miraculous. God honors every effort we undertake in faith.

An angel intervened to give us light. Jesus is the light of the world, and He said, "You are the light." You are the angel that brings that light to the world. So Arise, Shine!

Chapter 37

This Will Be a Church

THROUGH 1978 AND 1979, while the building was going up, the Steppingstone Youth center continued sponsoring local activities and events for the young people of the surrounding area. It was like a continuous evangelistic crusade, and some area churches put aside their doctrinal differences to support God's work through the non-denominational ministry.

One morning while I was at my Aunt Lorene's Bible study, a woman who was known to speak prophetically had come to visit June Green. They were planning to come to the Bible study together, and June suggested that they drive by the Steppingstone on the way. "I want you to see Gloria's building," she said.

They stopped at the youth center, which at the time was still under construction. It was a very simple structure, just a straight roof over a forty by eighty feet building. It was like a shoebox with a roof. There was nothing ornate about it. Like Noah's ark, it had been built for utility not for aesthetics. There were no columns or arches. No steeple stabbed into the air. Nothing indicated that it was a place of worship.

As they looked at the building, the woman said to June. "I see a church, and I see a cross right up over that door." They didn't linger at the center, and the woman couldn't elaborate on the prophecy. She only knew that the building was destined to be a church.

I was already at the Bible study along with several of the regulars when June and her visitor arrived. We began studying the Bible and praising God. We were having a wonderful time of prayer and Bible study. Then the woman looked at me. She said, "The building you are building is to be a church, and you are to be the pastor. I see a cross right up over that door." She told me that people would come to the cross in that building. They would be saved.

I continued smiling, at least I think I continued smiling, but my head was spinning and my stomach was churning. I was panic-stricken. This woman had prophesied that the Steppingstone would be a church. That wasn't the intent of the building, and that wasn't my ministry. Later, I pulled Pat Shetter aside and rejected the woman's prophecy.

"I just don't receive that," I said. I knew that God would determine the ultimate ministry of the building. I would never go against His will, but I also knew that I had been called to a youth ministry, and I was very confused. How would I be able to serve God in the building if it were converted to a church? The most obvious answer was unthinkable.

That wasn't the first time that someone had suggested the building might someday be a church. June Green had prophesied it would be a church, too. Some people even called it a church when they referred to it in conversation. But this was no casual conversation where someone had conveniently substituted "church" for youth center. This was no case of a friend or neighbor expressing their wishes for the building. This was an outsider, a completely objective person, who drove by the building and immediately saw a church instead of a youth center even though June had told her the building's intent.

"What do you think? I keep getting these prophesies, and I don't receive it, but what do you think?"

Pat looked at me, and whether she agreed with the prophecy or not, she gave very wise advice. "Just put it up on the shelf and leave it there. Don't worry about it," she said. "Let God take care of it. Let God take it off the shelf, and if He never takes it off the shelf, you have nothing to worry about."

I felt a load lifted off me when she said that. Unlike us, God doesn't forget where things get put, and He knows where to find just the right tool exactly when He wants it. The Steppingstone wasn't built like a church. The double doors opened into the middle of the meeting space unlike most churches. When you stepped in, you walked right into the middle of things. The stage was to the right when you entered the room, and a little kitchen was at the back. It was clearly a meeting hall, a place of fellowship, not a church.

I wasn't there the afternoon that Mark Emmert was finishing up the trim on the exterior of the building. Mark looked over the structure and thought that something was missing. There was no porch marking the entry. The double doors were right in the middle of the building facing Miller Street. With no distinguishing characteristics, it resembled a back door more than a main entrance. The least Mark figured he could do was to construct a simple pediment above the portal. It didn't take him long to complete, and as he stepped away from the building once again and looked over his work, he thought it could use one more thing.

I was at home. Otis was helping Mark that summer, and he came home in the middle of the day. "Mom, Mark wants you to come down. He has done something, and he wants to see if you like it." He was excited, and I could tell that whatever surprise he and Mark had cooked up would probably be a thrill.

So I went with him to the youth center, and as we approached my knees turned to jelly. The building had a new false gable. It added a lot to the appearance, and right above the door—a cross. I thought, *Oh, no!* The woman's prophecy that Steppingstone would be a church also declared that there would be a cross above that door.

It was gorgeous. It looked perfect! I was happy the cross was over the door, but it really scared me. The prophecies were hitting a little too close and way too soon. I was not going to have anything to do with that. No sir, I was not going to have a church!

In the next few weeks and months, I was able to put it aside. The idea of a church was up there on a shelf, and I had no intention of taking it down. The youth ministry went on just as it had for the past five years. During that year, the Steppingstone rented the football stadium and had a concert with Dallas Holm and his group. We had youth revivals and rented the high school's gymnasium for special assemblies as we had for the David Wilkerson crusade. Burleson was on the map of evangelists and Christian entertainers, just as it had been on the map of the drug industry.

While the Steppingstone's ministry was flourishing, it seemed at times that some of the community opposed it. Many parents were afraid their children would disappear into the Steppingstone and then resurface speaking in tongues, praising God, and totally transformed. A lot of them did, too. It was a charismatic, spirit-filled ministry.

Others in the community still harbored resentment toward me for the stand I had taken against the introduction of Humanism into the school curriculum. Some just didn't believe that a woman should lead a ministry. It bothered me that there was such resistance to the Steppingstone ministry when it was so obvious that young people were getting saved.

I wasn't actively resisting the idea of converting the Steppingstone to a church. I had put it on the shelf and was content to leave it there. I knew I couldn't resist God's will any more than one of the young people could restrain the expression of the Holy Spirit.

STEPPINGSTONE CHRISTIAN YOUTH CENTER WITH THAT CROSS ABOVE THE DOOR.

Chapter 38

Overcoming Faith Center and a Word from Brother Jerry Savelle

SANDY BROWNING CALLED one Sunday afternoon. She sounded excited. "Oh, you've got to go to church with me tonight. You won't believe it. The pastor's sermon this morning sounded just like your vision." She had started attending the Overcoming Faith Center, a non-denominational church in South Fort Worth at the Seminary South Shopping Center, an outdoor mall. She wasn't the only person who had started going to the Faith Center when they left the Burleson Assembly of God. My sons had migrated to the Faith Center, too. They hadn't gone to Bethesda with John and me.

Several members of my prayer group attended the church where Jerry Savelle was pastor. I had heard some of his radio messages and knew that he taught the Word. My parents were still members of the Bethesda church, and although I knew they might be disappointed if I started attending church somewhere else, I really wanted to go with Sandy that night.

I told the boys I was thinking about attending the service.

"Mom, if you go up there, you won't want to go anywhere else," Stuart told me.

John wasn't able to go to church with me on Sunday nights. He had been transferred to the night shift, and he left for work at 10:30 each night and got back home at about breakfast time the next morning. Since church didn't start until seven o'clock, he was seldom able to go with me on Sunday nights. I wanted his opinion about which church I should attend that night even if he couldn't go.

He said, "I think you ought to go with Sandy." Even his recommendation wasn't enough to sway me, but it was one more coin in the bank. As the day wore on, I slowly decided that a break from the Bethesda services might be exactly what I needed. So I called Sandy and told her I would go with her. I looked at the clock. It was four.

When I walked into the praise center, it was as refreshing to my spirit as plunging into a swimming pool on an August afternoon. It was filled with lively music. Then they started worship, and I knew I had found an oasis.

Prior to that evening, I didn't know what Jerry Savelle looked like. I had heard him on the radio but had never seen him. There were several men on the platform, and I didn't know which one the pastor was. That didn't matter. Lord, I thought, I really need a word from you.

After the songs had stopped, Pastor Savelle stepped to the podium. He paused for a minute before speaking, and when he spoke, it was as though he was having a private conversation with each person in the room. "I was in my study this afternoon about four p.m. Instead of bringing you a message tonight, God told me he has some words for some people who are here this evening."

I froze. That was the exact time I had decided to attend. I silently prayed that at least one word would be for me.

The Reverend Savelle looked out across the audience. "The lady back there in the pink dress," he said, "come forward; God has a word for you."

He had called me first. I didn't know whether to walk, run, or fly to the altar. I stepped out into the aisle and tried not to look too jubilant. God had already acknowledged my concerns just by placing a thought in the mind of the pastor. As Pastor Savelle prophesied over me, it was as though he had been listening in on my prayers. It was very encouraging and faith building, especially the concluding sentences.

"There are people who are watching you," he said. "They are watching you because they want you to fail. They would regard your failure as a confirmation of their belief that you are wrong and they are right. But it is my word coming out of your mouth that will prevail, and their words will be to no avail."

That has helped me through the years. At times, there have been people who wanted the Steppingstone ministry to fail, and remembering those words always helped.

It is important to understand. When God calls us to a ministry, there will always be spiritual battles to fight, but if we stand strong in the Word, it will be His word coming out of our mouths that will prevail over the enemy. "Be strong in the Lord and in his mighty power. Put on the full armor of God, so that you can take your stand against the devil's schemes" (Ephesians 6:10–11, niv).

Stuart was right. I didn't go anywhere else until the Overcoming Faith Center merged with another church in November 1981. It was evident I had been led by the Holy Spirit to the Overcoming Faith Center. Over the years that I went there, I realized that this was a model for how God wanted church to be conducted. The music and worship was so uplifting, and the preaching of the Word by Pastor Savelle was faith building and empowering—just what I needed!

The praise and worship was like taking a drink of refreshing water of the Spirit, and the Word was like partaking of the bread of life that makes us strong and healthy spiritually. Every service was communion. This produces a well-balanced Christian, empowered to produce fruit for God's Kingdom.

Meanwhile, the Steppingstone was growing. In January 1980, Joe Montana, a former actor who also worked with James Robison's ministry in Fort Worth, became director of Saturday night activities. When the youth center announced Joe's new affiliation, he reiterated the youth center's goals and once again tried to garner community support.

"The Steppingstone is working to fill a need in the community," he said. "There are not that many places for Christian kids to go on Friday and Saturday nights to find wholesome entertainment. The Steppingstone provides that. A youth council is being formed to work to accomplish new goals and be involved as teenagers reaching teenagers. Young people need a purpose: many are lonely, have idle time, and many problems. I believe the Steppingstone can help. The Steppingstone is not to take the place of church or to promote a doctrine of denomination, but to be a supplement to and work together with all churches in their efforts to reach youth with the gospel of Jesus Christ. Our theme is Jesus is Lord of all. We need the support of the community in the enormous task of trying to help teenagers overcome the serious problems they face in today's world."

Chapter 39

End Times

HARDLY ANYONE IN 1980 was teaching that the end times would be ushered in by a great revival. But that's what I believed, and I began to tell the young people to expect a great outpouring. Today, it isn't uncommon for pastors to deliver messages about the great outpouring, but in 1980, it was a new concept. In fact, most pastors and evangelists disagreed with me.

One prominent pastor in Burleson rebuked me saying, "I don't agree with you," when he found out what I was teaching about the end times. "The Bible says in the last days evil will become worse and worse, and men's hearts will be turned away from God. It doesn't say people will turn to God," he insisted.

But I continued to preach my revelation of the glory of God, aware that it is possible for both to occur simultaneously, as the Lord showed me in Isaiah 60.

> Arise, shine; For your light has come! And the glory of the LORD is risen upon you. For behold, the darkness shall cover the earth, And deep darkness the people; But the LORD will arise over you, And His glory will be seen upon you.
>
> —ISAIAH 60:1–2, NKJV.

Those who are not part of the outpouring will be violently opposed to it and will persecute those who are. Their hearts will be turned away. That is the great darkness that will cover the earth while the light of the Lord will shine forth from those who love him.

I started teaching that God will show his glory in a great revival. He is going to pour out His glory in the same way He did on the day of Pentecost: "All of them were filled with the Holy Spirit and began to speak in other tongues as the Spirit enabled them" (Acts 2:4, NIV).

In that same meeting Peter quoted the prophet Joel saying, "In the last days,

God says, I will pour out my Spirit on all people. Your sons and daughters will prophesy, your young men will see visions, your old men will dream dreams" (Acts 2:17, NIV). I knew in my heart that there will be a great outpouring of the Holy Spirit, and a great revival will come.

I continued to work and study in the Word, and eventually God sent me another vision. In the vision, I had gone into the grocery store and was shopping in fresh produce. It was significant where I was. I was picking out tomatoes, and a woman standing at the apples suddenly began to weep. Another who was looking for bananas started crying, too.

I looked around and asked them what was wrong. And each one said, "I need to be saved. I am a sinner." Everyone in the store was being convicted of their sins.

Then I found myself standing in a large office with several women sitting at desks. Two or three put their heads down on their desk and began to weep and said, "I need to be saved. I'm a sinner."

I was transported again and found myself standing in a church. I looked out from the pulpit and saw three sets of double doors standing wide open and leading to a glass-walled foyer, and beyond that, I saw a parking lot. People were waiting to get inside. They filled the parking lot. Inside the church, seats were packed with people waiting to hear the good news and to worship.

Suddenly, I found myself standing outside the building on the front porch. I looked out across the parking lot and saw that people filled the field beyond. The Lord spoke to me and said, "People will feel the conviction of the Holy Spirit, and they will go to a church looking for salvation. When the revival comes, the churches will fill. The churches won't be big enough to hold all the people." When the conviction of the Holy Spirit falls, much like the Holy Spirit fell on the believers at Pentecost, it is going to be a sovereign move of God. It will be precipitated by prayer, fasting, and commitment of believers holding forth their light. I believe that is our part in the end time. We must continue to hold forth the light of the Word so that others can see it and be drawn to it. Jesus is coming soon. So arise, shine.

When people enter many churches, they won't feel God's presence. They won't hear a word that gives them answers for their lives. They will search until they find churches where they feel the presence of the Holy Spirit, places where God touches them the moment they walk through the door and they hear anointed music and preaching of the Word.

When I had the vision, I had no idea I would someday be pastor of a church or that I would be thinking in terms of building a church myself, but the reality became apparent within a few days.

The youth pastor of Crestmont Baptist Church and his wife sang in the Steppingstone's concerts and often volunteered to help with outreach and youth revivals. Their church had been trying to decide if they should build a new auditorium. When the pastor and his wife heard me speak about my vision, they agreed that it was a prophetic word about the end time. My brother attended church at Crestmont, and knowledge of my vision influenced the church to move forward with plans for expansion. They built their auditorium.

The great end time revival may not be here yet, but Burleson has grown, and many congregations have had to add space just to accommodate the city's expansion. Someday, perhaps not very far in the future, all churches will need space for the crowds. There are a lot more people in the community than the churches can hold, and even though the churches in our city have tried to prepare for the coming revival, we still won't have enough room to hold all the people who will be seeking the Lord during those last days.

The Steppingstone moved into its new youth building in 1979 and had great services. Many people were saved that year, and in 1980, the whole year was one continuous revival. God blessed all our efforts. It was an exciting time. It's always an exciting time if you're serving the Lord.

Arise! Shine!

Chapter 40

Prayer

I HAVE NEVER BEEN one to underestimate the power of prayer. My direct experience with the healing available to us through faith has led me to believe that anything is possible. Mountains will move on a command uttered in faith. Prayer is the catalyst that God uses to work miracles. It exercises our faith. Prayer releases the Holy Spirit to perform God's work.

In 1977, I recruited members from my church to participate in a prayer team at the Steppingstone Youth Center every Thursday night. Anyone who heard about the meeting was welcome to participate, but I built the prayer group around a core of twelve people who were committed to attending the meetings and praying each week.

The group prayed for the youth of Burleson. We prayed that God would move and that the Holy Spirit would draw in young people and change their lives. We got a lot of answers to our prayers, and when news got around that we were having a regular prayer group meeting, people began calling in their prayer requests.

When the group started, Jimmy Carter, the submarining, peanut farming, Georgia governing, nuclear propulsion engineer was the first-term president of the United States. The crisis of Jimmy Carter's presidency had hit in September of 1979 when sixty-six American citizens were taken hostage by government-sanctioned terrorists in Iran.

The terrorists flooded past the marine guards at the gates of the American embassy in Teheran. The guards were quickly overwhelmed by a mob. Once inside the compound, the terrorists stepped out of the horde brandishing their guns.

The marines fell back to more defensible positions within the embassy, but the battle was already lost. They surrendered the compound after a few hours and immediately became hostages. The scourge of radical Islam had opened a new front in its war against civilization.

The hostages had been interned for almost six months when the United

States attempted to rescue them. During the mission, a Marine helicopter wandered into the path of a C-130, and both aircraft exploded in flames killing five crewmen on the airplane and the three-man flight crew of the helicopter. Eight American soldiers died in the unsuccessful mission, and fifty-three hostages remained in captivity. We prayed for them in our weekly prayer group. We disagreed with many of President Carter's liberal policies, but we still prayed for him and for the captive Americans. It's important that we pray for our national leaders, especially when we disagree with them.

Ronald Reagan was the Republican Party's candidate for president. We prayed for him to be elected because of the things he stood for. Carter may have been a devout Christian in his personal life, but Reagan stood for Christian principles in his politics. He was pro-life. He honored prayer and Bible reading for children in schools. We believed he would stand for the values upon which our nation was founded. So we prayed earnestly for the election, and we were thrilled when he won. It didn't matter if the president was Democrat or Republican, a peanut farmer, a nuclear engineer or even an actor, the group prayed for him and that God would bless his presidency, guide his decisions, and keep him safe.

Neither Reagan's election nor the release of the hostages on the day he was sworn into office in January, 1981 meant that the prayer group could take the president off the prayer board, a dry-erase board where we listed the topics of prayer. We prayed for the president in every meeting.

Chapter 41

The President's Night

O N WEDNESDAY, MARCH 25, 1981, David and Diane Atwood, members of our prayer group, entertained out-of-town guests. David was the plant manager for Manville in Cleburne, and one of the executives from the home office in Denver was visiting the Cleburne plant. He went to dinner with David and Diane on the last night of his visit, and Diane told him about her personal ministry counseling women. David and Diane also told him about their participation in and support of the Steppingstone's ministry and the wonderful things that were happening in the lives of young people in Burleson because of it.

Their visitor told them about the prayer group at his church in Colorado. He told the couple about his group's intercession for a particular young man. He wished aloud that Diane could counsel the young man: "I have a neighbor who is a really good friend of mine, and they have a son that they have had a lot of trouble with."

"I would need to talk to him and get directions from the Holy Spirit," Diane explained.

They talked more about the young man. His parents had sent him to psychiatrists in Denver who had not been able to help. They ejected him from their household on the advice of a psychiatrist who told them that forcing the young man to leave home would make him less dependent on them. The psychiatrist didn't believe the young man was dangerous. He had never said or done anything to indicate he was. The boy's father, Jack, would later remark that following the advice of the psychiatrist was "the greatest mistake of my life" (Hinckley, Jack, Jo Ann Hinckley, and Elizabeth Sherrill, *Breaking Points* [Grand Rapids: Chosen Books, 1985], 295).

The prayer group met as usual at seven in the evening on Thursday, March 26. More than eighteen requests had been listed on the prayer board. That was a large number for us because we took turns praying for each topic. A long list of subjects led to very long prayer meetings. Because of the size of the list that evening, the Atwoods decided they would not add the disturbed young man. They had been praying for him at home, and they would continue to do so.

We prayed individually. Each of us prayed through all of the requests on the list, and usually, as we prayed and interceded for one thing, the Lord revealed how the enemy might be attacking that person, group, or ministry. We got very specific in our prayers, including as much information as we had about the person or subject. Normally we reserved the president and the nation until the end of the session. Although nine o'clock had come and gone, we would not conclude the meeting until we had covered our nation's leaders with prayer.

Early in the meeting, David Atwood began experiencing chest pains. He didn't tell the rest of the group about it at first. A few minutes after we began praying for the president David spoke up. "Ever since we began to pray for the president, I have been having severe chest pains. I thought it was my heart. I thought I was having some sort of physical problem, but God said it was for the president."

When we began to pray for Reagan, each of us struggled for the right words. It was as though we had been pushed against a wall and were pinned there. Just uttering a simple prayer was a struggle. We were fighting to get the words out. Nobody was saying anything, but all of us were thinking the same thing—something was terribly wrong.

With the burden for the president and the realization that there were forces that seemed to be working against saying a single word of prayer, the group could not let go. Since David had pain in his chest, we thought President Reagan might suffer a heart attack, and we prayed that he would be spared. We prayed that if he had a heart attack, he would survive it.

As we were praying for Reagan and the nation, Diane had a vision of the map of the United States. At first, the entire continent was dark, and then she saw a light like a candle almost where we were in Texas. It got brighter and brighter until it covered the entire nation, and the darkness went away.

Diane asked the Lord, "What does this mean?"

He answered her. "Without intercession, there will be darkness, gross darkness."

We became convinced that the devil was going to try to kill President

Reagan either with a heart attack or by some other means. And we knew if the attack was successful, our nation would be plunged into chaos.

Reagan had barely gotten started. He had been president for only two months, but it was clear he would turn things around. Over the last several years, the entire globe seemed to have adopted an anti-American sentiment, but Reagan had begun to make everybody believe in America again.

One of the devil's devices is distraction. Not long after the group had started praying for the president, we were nearly thrown off topic. While we were praying, the phone rang. Someone answered the phone, and the caller asked for Sandy. It was a prank call, but a threatening one. The caller told Sandy that she was doomed. She was about to die. She returned to the group visibly shaken. "I didn't know whether to take it seriously or not," she said. She didn't know why they had asked for her.

That reminded each of us of the scripture in Proverbs. We made an effort to read chapters in Proverbs that coincided with the same day of the month. Our scripture that day, the twenty-sixth day of March, had been from Proverbs 26. "As a mad man who casteth firebrands, arrows, and death, so is the man that deceiveth his neighbour, and saith, 'Am not I in sport?'" (Proverbs 26:18–19). That's the Bible's description of the malicious practical joker.

We didn't let the distraction throw us off topic. I realized this was a clue for how we needed to pray. I said, "We must bind the spirit of death," and everybody began to intercede for President Reagan. The feeling of the Holy Spirit was powerful, but it was still a lot of work to pray. I have never labored in prayer like I did that night. Even though we were inspired to do it, it was as if we were pressing through an invisible wall.

Then I suggested that we should proclaim Isaiah 54:17. "Let's say it out loud, and send that word to President Reagan. And no weapon formed against President Reagan shall prosper." We repeated the scripture-based proclamation three times in unison. The group had no idea how literal our prayer was. We pleaded the blood of Jesus over President Reagan. It was about 11:00 p.m. when we finished praying, and we had started at 7:00. We had spent an hour or more praying for President Reagan, and when we left, we felt like we had done a day at hard labor. Each of us was exhausted.

The following Monday, March 30, Reagan was shot outside the Hilton Hotel in Washington D.C. John Hinckley, the disturbed young man who waited outside the hotel, fired his .22 caliber Rohm revolver six times. His bullets found four human marks. At first reported as dead, James Brady, the president's press secretary was hit in the head. He would never fully recover from his wounds.

A Secret Service agent, Timothy McCarthy, was shot in the stomach.

One bullet entered the neck and ricocheted off the spine of a Washington, D.C. police officer, Thomas Delahanty, who had been working crowd control at the VIP entrance of the Washington Hilton that day. He would be forced to retire within the next few years at the age of forty-five with permanent nerve damage in his left arm.

A fourth bullet found the intended target after ricocheting off the side of the car. It struck President Reagan puncturing a lung and stopping within an inch of his heart. At first neither Reagan nor his secret service team realized he had been hit. Secret service agent Jerry Parr, pushed the president into the limousine and covered him as the car sped away from the scene, heading for the safety of the White House. Although he was wounded, it took Reagan a few minutes to realize that the secret service agent's manhandling wasn't responsible for his pain. When Parr saw the president coughing up blood, he directed the driver to head for George Washington University Hospital.

Back in Texas, members of the Burleson prayer group got word of the attempted assassination, and each of us immediately thought of the preceding Thursday. We contacted other members of the team. We prayed for President Reagan's life and for his full recovery. That may have been true all over the nation, but it was especially true of the Steppingstone's prayer warriors. We knew the events of the day were related to our Thursday night prayers. God had wanted us to pray, and the enemy had tried to stop us. It was unbelievable. No one who had been in that meeting could have doubted that we had been led to pray for President Reagan. There was no doubt that the enemy, not John Hinckley, who was merely the tool, but the enemy of God and of mankind had plotted against the president.

When reports began to surface that Reagan was dead, I said "Oh, Lord," and immediately I felt God responding powerfully. "No, he is not dead. You bound the spirit of death." So I knew what we had been praying about Thursday night was death. We had bound the spirit of death and had proclaimed, "No weapon formed against President Reagan will prosper." None of the Devastator bullets designed to explode on impact had worked.

News reports later said the bullet was supposed to explode, but it didn't. So, it didn't prosper. Although impaired for the rest of their lives, Delahanty and Brady had been spared the worst that the bullets could have done.

Reagan would later credit God with saving him in his book *An American Life*: "It wasn't Jerry's weight I felt; according to the doctors, the flattened bullet had hit my rib edgewise, then turned over like a coin, tumbling down through my lung and stopping less than an inch from my heart. Someone was looking out for me that day."

Reagan was a religious man. Just how deeply he believed becomes obvious when you read through the diary of his presidency. As many other people would, he said a prayer for the man who had shot him after he saw Brady wheeled past on his way to the operating room. "I silently asked God to help him deal with whatever demons had led him to shoot us," the president wrote.

When they first heard the name of the young man who had shot the president, the Atwoods were stunned. Hinckley had been in their prayers daily since they had met with the visiting Manville executive. However, already knowing the name of the shooter somehow was a sign confirming that God had supernaturally visited us in intercessory prayer that would affect the future of America.

There were many people that seemed to think it was important to remind us, "Well, you weren't the only ones praying for the president." That's true. There were a lot of different people who felt a special urgency to pray for the president on the day of the shooting. I heard that a teacher in a Christian school stopped in the middle of third grade class and said, "Class, I feel like we need to pray for our president right now," and they did.

I know that ours was not the only intercession on behalf of the president, but I believe that the combined prayers, including ours, protected the president. You break through with combined prayers. In the Bible, God guarantees that when we gather together in His name, He is there with us.

The combined intercessory prayers of God's people stand against the enemy and release the Holy Spirit to do battle. Faith moves mountains, but that's not all of it. The exercise of faith moves mountains. Until you speak or act on your faith the Holy Spirit can't do anything with it. Prayer is our way of freeing

God's will to be done in earth as it is in heaven (Matthew 6:10). It is a way of declaring that our faith is in concert with His will. It's how we participate in the battle that God is constantly waging against the devil. It is warfare against the schemes of the devil, the plots he is trying to bring about. Whatever plan the devil has can be defeated with prayer. God is ready to act, but He requires us to ask. "The effectual, fervent prayer of a righteous availeth much" (James 5:16). I know in my heart that if prayers had not been offered for President Reagan, he would not have survived. The bullet may have traveled that extra inch. The bullets may have exploded as they were designed to do. The police officer and the secret service agent who took bullets for the president may not have been in position to protect him, or the bullet that struck President Reagan may not have hit the limousine first.

When we were walking out at the end of our prayer meeting on Thursday night, we were looking at each other asking, "What is this? What can this mean?" We knew that God was moving. He was motivating us to pray, and we in turn were motivating the Holy Spirit to move in a miraculous way, even though we had no idea exactly what we were praying for.

When God lays a prayer on your heart, a concern for someone or some event, it's time to get down on your knees and pray for them, at that moment. As we found out, it could very well be a matter of life and death.

This was in 1981, the year prior to Steppingstone becoming a church. We really laid the foundation of our church in prayer. We referred to that Thursday as "President's Night" for a long time."

Chapter 42

This will be my Church

O N THE AFTERNOON of Mother's Day in 1981, the phone rang. A baby had fallen into a swimming pool. The emergency medical technicians had arrived on the scene and were able to get the child breathing again, but it was still on life support and in critical condition. The family had requested the prayers of the community, and Christians throughout Burleson encouraged each other to pray for the tot's life. I normally went to church on Sunday night, but instead of going to church that afternoon, I drove to the Steppingstone. I decided I would pray there privately, not just for the baby but also for the entire community. I felt heaviness for the city.

I expected to be alone. No one ever went to the Steppingstone on Sundays. Teens were encouraged to go to church with their parents, and everyone involved with the Steppingstone ministry attended one of the various churches in the area. Most were actively involved in their churches. As I drove my car into the parking lot and started opening the door, other members of the prayer group arrived.

"What happened?" I called.

"The Lord told us to come and pray," one said. "What are you doing here?

"The Lord told me to come, too."

The small group started into the building while yet another car wheeled into the small parking lot. By the time we got inside, about eight of our normal prayer group members had shown up to pray. Each of us had been summoned to the Steppingstone individually. We prayed for the baby, but soon we found ourselves praying for God to deliver Burleson. While we prayed, one of the men began to prophesy over us.

"God is very pleased with this group," he stated. "Because each one of us heard His call and responded to it. We answered Him when He called. He called us to prayer, and He wanted to speak to us. I'm very pleased with you because of your faith and intercession. I am pleased with you because you are standing in the gap." It was as though God were telling us He was pleased with all that we had been doing through the prayer group and through Steppingstone ministry. We were all beginning to feel very pleased that God had found us worthy of recognition.

The tone of the speaker's voice suddenly changed. He started prophesying about churches in the city. He said God was not pleased with churches for the way they had treated the Holy Spirit. Some of the churches in Burleson had been opposed to the Steppingstone from the outset because they did not believe in the baptism of the Holy Spirit or the expression of spiritual gifts. For the first year or two, some churches fought the ministry. They didn't want their kids attending. They were telling people not to have anything to do with the Steppingstone "because they speak in tongues down there." Burleson had become a battlefield between charismatics and non-charismatics.

The prophecy was saying that God wasn't pleased that the Holy Spirit was being rejected by some of the churches in Burleson. Some churches were waging war against the Holy Spirit through their condemnation of its expression.

Chapter 43

My Fire-of-God Experience

FELT THE AWESOME presence of God fill the room. The fear of the Lord came over me because I knew He was judging churches in Burleson. Then I heard the prophesier say, "And though I am pleased that you came when I called, still I have trouble with you." I knew that was to me personally. I felt as though I were alone in the room. In that moment, I knew God had been calling me to start a church and become its pastor. I had rejected His call despite some very specific prophecies. I had wanted Steppingstone to be a youth ministry.

I had been convinced that the Steppingstone could never be a church with me as the pastor. I was a youth minister. That's all I had a desire to be. But that afternoon I realized God had been calling me, and I had been rejecting His call.

This was my fire of God experience. It was as if I was standing in front of the burning bush. My eyes were closed in prayer, and I felt that if I opened them I would be consumed. I could feel warmth on my face, and I started feeling like I was standing before God's judgment. Even though I am secure in my Christianity, I began to feel distanced from the Lord, so I said to him, "Lord, your word says I'm righteous in Christ." I was calling on His righteousness because I didn't feel right with Him, and I didn't know why.

He answered, "Your righteousness is filthy rags." In my experience, when God answers you, there is always a revelation with it. All of a sudden, you just know stuff. When He said, "Your righteousness is as filthy rags," I knew He was saying that my work for Him out of my own flesh and motivations didn't mean a thing. What matters is His righteousness, His will. The Holy Spirit spoke to me. "Nothing matters but My will. Nothing else matters on this earth." I was immediately reminded of the scripture: "Not everyone that says to me Lord, Lord, will enter in, but the one that does the will of my Father who is in heaven" (Matthew 7:21, ESV). He spoke to me again and said, "You want to do my work, but you want to do it your way."

I had once asked God to make me worthy of persecution in His name, worthy to suffer shame for His name, and God had answered my prayer. I had not wanted to go through that again. I was comfortable with the youth ministry. I had a desire to lead young people to the Lord. Becoming pastor of a church was beyond my desires. I had refused to permit the thought, even when God had sent me one signal after another. Now He was speaking directly and powerfully to me, not only telling me that the Steppingstone should be a church, but that I should be its pastor. He had taken it off the shelf and there was no putting it back again.

I didn't think I could bear the rejection and persecution that being a woman pastor would bring. If I became pastor of a church, resistance to my ministry would start all over again. By 1981, the Steppingstone was tolerated by most in the community. It was accepted and even respected by many. A charismatic church, especially with a woman pastor, would have to suffer the same birth pains all over again.

I had convinced myself that the youth ministry had become so fruitful that it was God's permanent will for my life. Churches weren't fighting the youth ministry as much anymore. People in the city seemed to accept the ministry and my role in it. They treated me graciously, and I received compliments for myself and the ministry from various people and organizations. Despite all that He had said about the churches in Burleson through the prophecy, I wanted the approval of many of those same people who rejected the Holy Spirit.

He said, "Nothing matters but my approval." I suddenly saw this, and I realized the wickedness in my heart. I have taught many messages out of what I learned in that brief encounter. Scripture says that the fear of man will bring a snare (Proverbs 29:25). I was trapped in that snare, but that afternoon I stood in shock and awe of the Lord. He had dropped a bomb on my serenity and reduced my pride to rubble. I felt His presence and His rebuke as powerfully as I had ever felt Him in my life before. The fire of God was burning all pride out of me. I hardly heard a word of the prophecy after the words were spoken, "but still I have trouble with you."

While I was being convicted, one of the women in the group started crying and saying, "I just don't feel right with God." The conviction swept across the group as powerfully as a tornado's whisper. I knew it was His Holy presence and felt like Job who hid himself saying "my eye sees You;

therefore I abhor myself, and repent in dust and ashes" (Job 42:6, NKJV). You can feel pretty good about yourself until you get in the holy presence of God.

I ministered to the woman who had cried out, and afterward I told the rest of the group what happened to me. For the first time, I publicly confessed that God was calling me to be a pastor and that the Steppingstone was to be a church. I didn't matter anymore. I didn't care what anybody said. I didn't care if they threw rocks at me. Nothing else mattered. I just wanted to do the will of God. In my heart, I understood that we can't serve God doing just those things we like to do. I think a lot of people feel they can serve God in the way they choose, but it's not enough to serve Him out of our will and our desires. We need to submit our will to Him whenever He reveals His will to us.

Doing the will of God almost inevitably requires sacrifice. While it is infinitely rewarding, it's not always pleasant. Remember what Christ said to the disciples: "If anyone desires to come after Me, let him deny himself…" Jesus' disciples were told that they must deny their own will. When you do the will of God and know that you have done what He wants you to do, there is no deeper satisfaction. It's the greatest fulfillment you can have when you know you are in God's will. When you're working within His will then you don't measure your success by outward results. You measure your success by being in His will. Deeds and accomplishments do not matter. My confidence is in knowing that God will produce the fruit and bring forth the harvest.

If crowds are not very large on Sunday mornings or something distracting is going on in the community, I immediately say, "Lord, am I missing your will? Is there anything I'm doing to miss your will?" I open myself up for His correction, and if He needs to correct me, He does. If He says I want you to start doing this thing or that, I just do it. And then it doesn't matter what the crowd says. All that really matters is doing the will of God.

I take my example from Jesus. John 5:19 states, "The Son can do nothing of himself, but what he sees the Father do; for whatever He does the Son also does in like manner" (NKJV), and in John 6:38, He says, "For I have come down from heaven not to do My own will but the will of Him who sent Me" (NKJV).

When other things get in the way or hold me back I remember these verses to put things in perspective. Even Jesus, our Lord, was here to do the will of the Father. Who am I to question God's will? God expects me to pursue His will with courage and conviction. Speaking up boldly for the Lord is another form of worship.

Look at Paul. He was boldly doing the will of God, and the Jews of Iconium and Antioch stoned him and left him for dead. That didn't discourage him from proclaiming God's word wherever he went. Comfort, wealth, or any other outward results were not his gauges of success. Success was simply being in God's will. This has sustained me through many hardships as a pastor.

During the next two weeks, I told the entire prayer team about my experience. Each of them told me that they always knew the Steppingstone would be a church someday. That was God's intent for the building and the property. They were just waiting for me to see God's will. We became a church in God's timing.

Chapter 44

God's Covering

THE NEXT STEP was John. I needed his permission and blessing. Women were not readily accepted as pastors, and I knew God would have to put it in people's hearts to attend a church with a woman pastor. If He was going to lead others to follow my teaching, then surely He would speak to my husband. Until John gave his OK, I could not accept the call, and that was a biblically sound attitude because the husband is the spiritual leader of the family. Before I took the proposal to the board, I broke the word to John by saying that our prayer group was thinking that the Steppingstone was meant to be a church.

"I was thinking that it needs to be a church," he said.

I knew God had put that into his heart, and I asked him who he thought should be the pastor.

"Well, you're the pastor, and if anybody doesn't like it, they can talk to me."

If God wants to do something, He'll make His will apparent in a lot of different ways. I knew God had called me, but I also knew that when God calls, He has everything in line. John's endorsement was the first step. The acceptance of the board of directors for the Steppingstone Youth Ministry was the second hurdle. I proposed to convert the Steppingstone to a church at the next meeting in June. I told them that I wanted to hold the first meeting as a church on September 1. I didn't tell them about the fire of God experience, although some of them were the same people in the prayer group. I wanted God to speak to them and confirm the word He had given me.

As discussion began, one board member after another endorsed the decision. It quickly became clear that if it were put to a vote, the board would overwhelmingly support a new direction for the ministry.

Only one person dissented, but it was the one person in the world whose opinion I revered above all others: my father. He felt that the Steppingstone had a unique ministry. "There are plenty of churches in Burleson," he argued, "but there is only one youth center." He was adamant and couldn't be swayed.

After my father voiced his objection, my brother, also a board member, followed. Both of them had contributed to the development of the youth center and both had witnessed first-hand the wonderful things the Steppingstone ministry had accomplished in Burleson. They argued that the unique ministry should remain centered on youth.

Despite the acceptance of the majority, I respected my father's wishes. I did not call for a formal vote. It was clear that there were enough votes to overrule him, but as far as I was concerned, my father had vetoed it. He was a respected member of the Burleson community. He served six years on the board of the Burleson Independent School District while I was in school and continued serving another three years after I had graduated. He was on the board when a high school was built in the early sixties, and he was president when an auditorium was added in the mid-sixties. There was always a lot of controversy over school expansion, and he took the bickering in stride. Dad handled complaints from both sides of every argument with equanimity. On one hand, many voters believed that the community couldn't afford the construction; others lamented that it would be negligent if the school district failed to provide its children with adequate educational facilities including a teacher's lounge, which was the addition that most people opposed.

In the early 1960s, Dad had presided over the dedication of the Mound Elementary School. I took Shanda to the ceremony. She was two-years-old, and when Daddy got up to speak to the semi-formal gathering, she called out, "Look. There's Grandpa!" disrupting the solemnity of the occasion. Dad just smiled, and the crowd had a good laugh.

Later he served on the Board of the Bethesda Water Supply. He did all these things while maintaining a full time job at the paper company. He was a man to be reckoned with, a man to be respected, but most of all, he was my father. It was inconceivable to me to violate his will.

I went back to my intercessory prayer group and told them that each of the seven board members, except for my father, was in favor of converting Steppingstone to a church. They told me that I should go ahead with the change because six out of seven were for it.

I answered, "If it was anybody else, six out of seven would be fine, but if that one person is my father, I'm not going to do it. God will have to change his heart." He had given so much to the youth ministry. He had purchased the property, and he had provided constant financial support. I felt that I would be betraying him if we moved forward without his blessing and full consent. God's word establishes our parents as the spiritual authorities over our lives.

I told the prayer group that we were putting plans for a church on hold. It was a real dilemma for me, and most of the prayer team members were puzzled. More than one noted, "Gloria, you said that nothing matters but the will of God."

I answered, "It is the will of God to show respect to my dad, too. If it is God's will, He will change Dad's heart. I am going to wait on the Lord." As a group, we decided we would wait at least through the end of the year before revisiting the change in the ministry. During that time, I believed, God would make his will known to my father.

The Sunday when we had met at the Steppingstone because God had called us together soldered the loosely knit prayer group into a powerful network. All of us started going to the Steppingstone on Sunday evenings to pray. Soon, every Sunday evening we were having a prayer meeting. Everyone brought their Bibles and often referred to them as we prayed. Someone would recite a passage of scripture that was pertinent to the situation we were praying about whether it was healing or guidance or answering God's call.

Slowly the prayer meeting evolved into Bible study. By September, the group was meeting every Sunday for prayer, and I was leading a Bible study. Not officially a church, the little group had already started worshipping together.

More people started coming to the Sunday prayer meetings. Many of them were members of the Overcoming Faith Center. Most of us really loved that church, but we felt we were being led to our Sunday evening worship at the Steppingstone.

People who were musically talented and who wanted to have music began attending. Before we knew what was happening, we had added a praise service. We were having Sunday night church services. We only met on Sunday nights, and all of us continued to go to the churches where we were officially members on Sunday mornings and Wednesdays.

I got up with John early every morning when he got ready for work. Often I prayed during the morning between his departure and time to start breakfast for the children. One October morning I was up early, praying, after John had left. I prayed for about an hour, and the Lord gave me a plan for the church. He instructed me to show it to my father. As soon as the kids had left for school, I called my parents.

My father hadn't left for work yet. They were getting ready to eat breakfast.

"I'm coming out," I told my mother.

"Come on," she said.

As Frances lowered the phone back into its cradle, Clyde looked up from his coffee. "I know why she's coming," he told my mother. "She's coming to talk to me about the Steppingstone being a church." There may have been a brief pause before he went on. "I was going to tell her the Lord has spoken to me."

The day before, my father had been driving between customer calls when the Lord had revealed that Steppingstone was supposed to be a church. As simply as glancing up to see a car in the rear view mirror, Clyde saw God's purpose in the Steppingstone. Dad had been making it complex, and God showed him that it really was simple. The message of Jesus Christ's sacrifice isn't for one demographic group. It's not just for teenagers or one race or one gender or one political party. One age group doesn't need or deserve the word more than another. So when I got there, Daddy told me his mind had been changed. He seemed joyful and excited about it. I shared my vision for the church, and he gave his blessing.

That evening I received another word. The Lord said the church was supposed to open the first Sunday in January. The delay while waiting for my father's consent made the first Sunday of the new year the perfect time to hold our first service. I told my father that God had given me a date, and my earthly father bending to the will of our Father gave his OK. As it had been when we had started the Steppingstone youth ministry, and as it had been when we had constructed the new building, God pulled things together. I was by no means a spectator. It was more like I was a receiver, and God, the quarterback and coach, had complete control of the game. Somehow, even if I had fumbled the ball, Jesus would have completed the play; only, he may have delivered the ball to someone else.

The praise team was already set. The members were meeting with the prayer group each Sunday evening. Right after I got my father's approval, a couple asked if they could lead the children's ministry. They had visited our prayer group one Sunday night. They were going to Calvary Bible College in Fort Worth where they were studying to be children's ministers. They felt led to our ministry, and they were wonderful. From the outset, we had top-notch children's pastors. So the youth ministry benefitted from the delay. My father had feared it would be weakened, and I shared his sentiment to a small degree, but everything was coming together perfectly.

In retrospect, I can see that we were able to proceed in God's timing because my father held back. God brought together all the necessary workers during that period. The master organizer lined up all the people and resources to launch the new church and make it a success. He had rounded up a core group of dedicated Christian warriors who would lead the church.

The Overcoming Faith Center closed its doors in November of 1981, just two months before we started meeting as a church. The Lord led the Faith Center to merge with another church in Fort Worth. Jerry Savelle became a traveling minister and later did a lot of TV ministry. Some members of the Faith Center had already started attending our Sunday evening services. Other people who sought a new church home when the Faith Center closed found their way to the little church in Burleson. Our congregation was growing fast, and we still had not officially started meeting as a church.

Over the years, the Lord had always provided my family with the right church at the right time, and God used each of the churches and ministers in my life to instruct me and prepare me for my ministry as pastor at the Lighthouse Church. In my years at the Overcoming Faith Center, I saw how to conduct a church service that blends praise, worship, teaching, and personal ministry in one weekly meeting. That ministry showed me how church services should be conducted. Before the Lord told me I was to be pastor, that is before I had my fire of God experience, I became convinced that the format followed at the OFC was exactly how God wanted services conducted.

The uplifting choruses of their praise music washed out any misery and left the congregation basking in the glory of the Lord. Then Pastor Jerry Savelle dug into the Word when he preached. He usually preached about an hour and fifteen minutes, sometimes a little longer, and if it wasn't in the Bible, the pastor didn't preach it. Praise and worship is the spiritual drink to fill the thirst in your soul, and the Word is the bread of life. You have to have both. There should always be a balance.

Praise and worship were sometimes so good that people said, "I think we ought to just have praise and worship."

I had to remind them, "No, God said we have got to balance it with the Word."

That doesn't mean we never varied from the routine. We let the Holy Spirit dictate that, and occasionally we went straight to ministering to people after the praise service and continued healing and praise until we dismissed, but that was rare. Usually, we balanced praise, worship, and the Word. It was our goal to have anointed praise and worship, then preaching the Word, and finally signs and wonders.

I continued to organize the church team as God brought others forward. From November until our first service as the Steppingstone church, people continued to come forward and volunteer. With Sunday school teachers, children's ministers, and our praise team, everything was in place for the first official service in the Steppingstone church on January 8, 1982, but in a lot of ways the ministry was born on Mother's Day in 1981, when a small group of believers met in direct response to a command from their Master.

Answering the call of pastor, Gloria began leading worship at Steppingstone Church.

Chapter 45

Mac Gober

EFORE LONG, THE building was full every Sunday. Between 120 and 150 people attended almost every service. The church ran advertisements in the *Burleson Star*, but most people came because they had heard about the wonderful things going on at the Steppingstone from others who visited. One of the first things we had to do was buy new chairs.

I preached at the services on Sunday mornings and evenings, but at least once a month another speaker led the service. That pattern continued throughout the life of the Steppingstone church. I spoke most often, but we frequently had a visiting pastor, especially pastors of the many missions that the Steppingstone supported over the years. Otis, who eventually became an associate pastor, and Cory, who served as associate pastor for many years, were regulars in the pulpit, too.

Regardless of who was bringing the message on Sunday morning, people were getting saved, and that was what mattered. We still had youth events, and the Sunday morning crowds were good, but I always wanted to see more people saved. Shortly after our first worship service, I decided a revival meeting would be just the thing to launch the new ministry. I invited Mac Gober to be our speaker. Mac was a Vietnam veteran turned motorcycle hoodlum turned evangelist whose powerful testimony riveted young audiences. Everybody loved Mac. He was a dynamic speaker and was on TV a lot. He had preached one weekend at the high school gym when Steppingstone was a youth center, and one hundred twenty people were saved.

The revival weekend targeted youth. Of course, we wanted to reach out to everyone but particularly to young people. We promoted the revival that way. I told everyone, "Let's believe God for one hundred souls to be saved." I believed it, too. Planning for a revival was a new thing for me, but I believed that one hundred was a good number. After all, more than that many had been saved in Mac's previous visit to Burleson.

As we sat waiting for the crowds to fill the church on Friday night, it became clear that we would fall short of one hundred. By the time we started the praise service, only about twenty-five church members showed up. That was it. I knew everyone. They were all Christians, most of whom you would have to drive away from a revival service with a stick, and if you tried that they would just stand there and pray for you.

Then, a lady who had seen the advertisement came in. She had a teenage son, and she brought him and all of his friends. Altogether, there were about a dozen of them. I already knew the woman. I had talked with her about her son. He had become dependent on drugs, and she was worried that he might overdose.

I was so disappointed that more people hadn't come that I was a little distracted during the praise service. I had great expectations, and they were disintegrating right before my eyes. Mac, however, was unfazed by the small turn out. His message and enthusiasm would have been the same regardless of the size of the audience. He preached a sermon like he was preaching to a thousand people, and the glory of God and the anointing of the Holy Spirit were on him. When the invitation was given, the woman's son and all of those kids who had come with him came down to the front. They lined up across the room in front of the pulpit, and they were weeping and getting saved.

I can't describe what I felt. Twelve maybe even fourteen kids were saved that evening, it was a bunch. I was repentant because of my disappointment. One soul, I realized, is enough to exult over. I had been disappointed in the numbers, but if the revival weekend just reached one young person, that was reason enough to shout, "Victory." The kids who were saved in that meeting were enough. That was God's will. That was the whole purpose for what we were doing.

That night I learned to prepare for the large crowds, be ready to reach out to thousands, but trust in the Lord, and if only one person walks through the door or if only one person looks to the cross out of the hordes who are wandering toward the cliff, then we should celebrate that one as if he were a thousand because that is the one person God wanted us to reach at that moment.

"Lord," I said. "I want your will and your purpose to be done." We must leave the rest to Him. So many times we have expectations, and we want to see a specific result from our labors. What we should be saying is, "Thy will be done." That little lesson at the beginning of my preaching ministry served me well through the years. It keeps me from getting discouraged.

Prepare for thousands, but rejoice for one. You never know whether that one person you reach out to and stop will become another Mac Gober who turns around and reaches out to thousands of others, pointing them toward the cross.

Chapter 46

Go and Tell my Brethren

PEOPLE WERE BEING saved at Steppingstone church. Since I had surrendered to be a pastor, I felt if people didn't want to listen to what a woman had to say, they would simply choose to worship elsewhere. It may be that there are always people who are unhappy with the minister and rather than finding another church, they try to replace the preacher, and from the outset, some church members, even some church leaders, began conspiring to replace me with a male pastor. How much of the behind the scenes manipulations had to do with my gender is hard to say, but gender was a factor.

Although I had experienced rejection and resistance to the Steppingstone ministry for years, I had never understood it. I never became inured to it. It was inconceivable that some members of the fledgling church, in some cases people who had endorsed the conversion of the youth center into a church and who had even agreed with my role as the church's chief administrator, undermined my role as pastor. Some members of the Steppingstone told outsiders that I was only the acting pastor until the church found a man who would come in to take over. That was never my intent, and it certainly wasn't consistent with God's call on my life. Once I had accepted that call, I knew that He had commissioned my work.

Even today, many people feel that women should not pastor churches even though wives of pastors often play prominent roles as teachers and praise leaders. Jesus, after all, didn't select a woman as one of the twelve disciples. The most frequent arguments against women in the pulpit come from I Corinthians 14:34–35. Often, the first reaction from people on learning that I am a pastor is, "What about the scripture that says women are to be silent in the church?"

Jesus commissions women just as he commissions men to preach the good news of Christ's resurrection. As a woman, I have had to make that a recurring theme in my ministry, but it seems to me that it should be apparent. Women teach, sing, testify, and pray at church. They aren't silent. Yet preaching the gospel is placed in a different category. Women sat apart from their husbands at meetings in the early days of the church. If they had questions or needed to converse with their husbands, they had to call out. That caused a disturbance. One way of explaining Paul's instructions to the Corinthians is in this context. When he instructs women to learn in silence, he's simply telling them not to interrupt the civility of the meeting.

The passage also refers to the *law*. "Let your women keep silence in the churches: for it is not permitted unto them to speak; but they are commanded to be under obedience, as also saith the law" (I Cor. 14:34). However, no law exists in the Old Testament mandating women's silence, so there is some confusion about Paul's reference. Some Bible scholars believe he was referring to social mores. The international standard version of the Bible translates the phrase referring to the law as "as the oral law also says."

The social law of that time went so far as to proscribe men and women from conversing in public at all. Paul could have been referring to that law. Given Paul's background in Hebrew law, it may have been common for him to refer to oral tradition as the law. However, Jesus not only spoke with women in public, but allowed the woman at the well (John 4) to go into the city and preach about him to the men of the city. Verse 39 relates, "And many of the Samaritans of that city believed on [Jesus] for the saying of the woman."

Some Bible scholars believe that I Corinthians 14:36, which follows immediately after the statement for women to remain silent, shows that Paul was actually rebuking the church for forcing women to keep silent. "What, came the word of God out from you? Or came it from you only?"

If Paul intended to forbid women to teach, preach, or prophesy, he was ignoring a lot of temple history. Anna was a prophetess in the temple at the time of Jesus' birth. Luke 2:36–38 records that "she...departed not from the temple...and spake of him [Jesus] to all them that looked for redemption in Jerusalem."

The Holy Spirit doesn't discriminate. Jesus instructed us to receive the Holy Spirit in order that we have power to be witnesses to him in all the world (Acts 1:8). And on the day of Pentecost, the Holy Spirit was poured out on women as well as men. Acts 1:14 states: "These all continued with one accord in prayer and supplication, with the women, and Mary the mother of Jesus, and with his brothers."

In the next chapter, verse four tells us that "they were all filled with the Holy Ghost, and began to speak with other tongues, as the Spirit gave them utterance." Acts 2:16–18 explains that the Holy Spirit isn't restricted to men, "this is that which was spoken by the prophet Joel; and it shall come to pass in the last days, saith God, I will pour out my spirit upon all flesh: and your sons and your daughters shall prophesy...and on my servants and on my handmaidens I will pour out in those days of my spirit; and they shall prophesy."

The Greek word translated "prophesy" means "to foretell events, divine, speak under inspiration, exercise of prophetic office." This same word is translated in I Corinthians 14:1 in the Amplified Bible as to interpret the divine will and purpose in inspired teaching and preaching. Acts 21:8–9 says that Phillip, an evangelist, had four daughters, each gifted with prophecy. Paul speaks of the women who labored with him in the gospel in Philippians 4:3. The word, gospel, is from the Greek word meaning to evangelize.

Jesus gave the first message of his resurrection to a woman with the instructions, "Do not be afraid. Go *and* tell My brethren to go to Galilee, and there they will see Me" (Matthew 28:10, NKJV). They believed not, and Jesus later reproved them for not believing her (Mark 16:14), refuting the notion that women should not be allowed to teach, preach, and instruct men and other women. In a sense, Mary was the first evangelist as *evangelize* means *announce God's news.*

Some denominations prohibit women from holding any position of authority in the church. The doctrine is usually based on a single passage: I Timothy 2:11–12 says women were not to teach or usurp authority over the man. Most Christian doctrine is based on clearly defined and repeated themes, not on single lines or isolated passages that are subject to interpretation. There are many other scriptures that refute a doctrine based on this single passage. For example, many women recorded in scriptures (Old and New Testament) held the office of prophetess, which is a position of authority. God spoke to the nation and the church through them. Miriam, Moses' sister, was a prophetess (Exodus 15:20). Deborah was not only a prophetess but also a judge, the chief authority over the whole nation of Israel for forty years. Her commands to Barak, captain over the army, led Israel to a great victory over their enemies (Judges 4). God spoke a message to the nation of Israel through Huldah, a prophetess, when she was consulted by Israel's priest (II

Kings 22:14–20). If God intended that women should not hold positions of authority, He wouldn't have violated His own law by appointing a woman to be in authority over a nation or prophetic office.

The passage from Timothy is misinterpreted by those who base church doctrine on it. It says for women not to 'usurp' authority. Women should not place themselves into positions, but must be sure they are called by God, nor should they use any office to dominate others. First Peter 5:5 states, "Yea, all of you be subject one to another."

Paul assigned women to positions of authority. In the letter of introduction and recommendation for Phoebe, he wrote, "I commend unto you Phebe our sister, which is a servant of the church which is at Cenchrea: That ye receive her in the Lord, as becometh saints, and that ye assist her in whatsoever business she hath need of you: for she hath been a succourer of many, and of myself also" (Romans 16:1–2).

Paul's introduction in the original Greek makes it clear that Phoebe wasn't merely a servant. Paul "commends" Phoebe, which means to *approve, stand with*. The word used for servant is "diakonas," an attendant, waiter, but especially a teacher, pastor, deacon, or minister. Almost everywhere else in the New Testament, this word is translated minister and is used in regards to the ministry of the gospel. Three times it is translated deacon. The words more literally translated as servant are the Greek words "doulos" meaning a slave or "oiketes" meaning a domestic or household servant. This is not the type of servant Paul is referring to in regards to Phoebe. She is a servant in ministry at the church at Cenchrea. Paul is asking them to receive or accept her as a pastor, a teacher, or a minister. She is a leader. Paul is requesting that the people stand beside her in the work, affairs, and all matters of the church. The word succourer also implies leadership. It is translated from "prostatis," a feminine form of a Greek word for guardian. It is defined in *Strong's Concordance* as a "woman set over others." Paul said that Phoebe had held this position before. Some translations call Phoebe a deaconess. However, deacons and especially deaconesses are not sent from one church to another to serve. Pastors and teachers are.

There is a God-ordained order in the home: the husband is the head or authority over the household. The wife is subject to her husband, and the children are to be in obedience to both parents (Ephesians 5:22, 6:1–2). It is an error to extend this doctrine to church organization. Galatians 3:28 states,

"There is neither male nor female; for ye are all one in Christ Jesus." Acts 10:34 explains that, "God is no respecter of persons." II Corinthians 5:16–17 says, "Know we no man after the flesh…Therefore if any man be in Christ, he is a new creature.…" The word translated "man" in the preceding (and many other) scriptures is "oudeis" which means "no one (man, woman or thing)."

Our new creature in Christ is neither male nor female. Another word translated as man which means men or women is "anthropos," meaning a human being.

Many use Genesis 3:16, which says the husband shall rule over the wife, referring to the curse that came with the fall, to postulate that men, in general, should rule over women, in general. But the passage in Genesis is addressing the marital relationship. Galatians 3:13 declares, "Christ has redeemed us from the curse of the law, being made a curse for us." Any curse that came upon women in the fall was taken care of at Calvary.

· In the body of Christ—His church—we are all to be in obedience to Him. Then He commands us, "Yea, all of you be subject one to another, and be clothed with humility: for God resisteth the proud, and giveth grace to the humble. Humble yourselves, therefore, under the mighty hand of God, that He may exalt you in due time (1 Peter 5:5–6)."

It is God who places the call upon our lives, and our response must be, whether male or female, "Here am I, Lord, send me."

The Steppingstone ministry couldn't have existed without the support of (l-r) Shanda, Stuart, Otis, Richelle, and John (front-center with Gloria)

Chapter 47

God Speaks in an Audible Voice

AT THE BEGINNING of my pastoral ministry, God miraculously directed people to the Steppingstone church. In the early eighties, before the Steppingstone became a church, several Burleson churches united to sponsor a series of presentations by Peter Marshall, author of *The Light and the Glory*. Arlene Wohlgemuth, wife of a prominent doctor in the Burleson community, contacted me and asked if the Steppingstone would help sponsor the series. I was pleased to help and participated as member of the committee that organized Mr. Marshall's visit. Over the next several months, Arlene and I became friends.

On a Saturday after the Steppingstone had converted to a church, we ran into each other at the grocery store. From our conversations, I knew that she and Mikeal were looking for a spirit-filled church. In fact, she told me that four families were looking for a new place to worship. The group had agreed that they would visit various churches in the Burleson area, and they occasionally met to compare notes and discuss their feelings about the churches they had attended. I invited her to visit.

Of course, I had no way of knowing that the group had ruled out the Steppingstone primarily because it had a woman pastor. The church wasn't even on their list.

Mikeal was on a mission trip that weekend, and Arlene decided to attend our services bringing along her two daughters, Sarah and Cristen. I greeted Arlene following the service, and she said that she had enjoyed it. The girls had loved children's church. After their father returned from his mission trip, they begged him to let them go back to Steppingstone. Mikeal conceded, despite the search group's agreement that they wouldn't consider the Steppingstone. Mikeal enjoyed the service, too. Soon, to the chagrin of their friends, the Wohlgemuths were regulars.

None of their friends was more upset than Joe Ed Spencer. Joe Ed, the bursar for the Tarrant County Junior Colleges, couldn't believe that Mikeal had allowed himself to be so deceived. Joe Ed railed that his close friend had been duped just like Adam had been deceived by Eve, and now they were worshipping at that church where a woman was pastor.

The next Saturday, Joe Ed was home by himself in his daily devotional. Carolyn, his wife, had gone shopping. He was dumbfounded when heard someone speak his name.

"What?" Joe Ed asked reflexively. He started looking around to see who was in the house. The voice came again, and then he knew he had heard the Lord. If that wasn't disconcerting enough, Joe Ed was even more taken aback when he learned the reason for the Lord's calling him out. In an audible voice, the Lord said, "You are to go to Steppingstone and help the pastor raise up that church."

When Carolyn got home, she found Joe Ed sitting in a state near shock. He was pale. "Carolyn, we've got a problem," he announced sincerely. "God spoke to me in an audible voice. We have to go to Steppingstone. We have to help that woman pastor raise up that church." They were in church the next day.

Joe Ed and Carolyn owned property near El Dorado, but locally they had leased some land where they raised sheep. Coincidentally, my message that Sunday was about Jesus as a shepherd. In fact, I was in the middle of a series of lessons on shepherds and sheep. After one of the services, I spoke with Joe Ed about the sermons. I asked if my descriptions of shepherds and caring for sheep were accurate, and he confirmed each one. Soon Joe Ed was involved in every aspect of the Steppingstone ministry.

He became an elder and a member of the church board. For over twenty years he served as the church's business administrator. He told the story of God speaking to him at a Rotary meeting in later years, adding that he had eaten crow and found that it tasted good.

I can't imagine our church flourishing as it did or the ministry being as strong as it was if it hadn't been for Joe Ed and Carolyn who assumed leadership roles, and for the Wohlgemuths, too. God had promised that He would bring the people into the church, and He had done just that. He didn't just bring people to the church; He recruited warriors.

During the first year after converting the youth ministry to a church, I received some "fan mail" from people who vehemently opposed a woman's leadership, even though they had never once stepped through the doors of the little building or met me or listened to me teach. I received letters quoting scriptures to support the writers' arguments that I should not be a pastor. People were saying that I was leading people to hell because I was out of the will of God. If anyone was curious, they could have asked Joe Ed about it. He was always happy to tell about hearing directly from God on the subject.

After Mother's Day in 1981, my focus was on pleasing God. I look forward to hearing Him say someday, "Well done." I finally accepted that if God approved of what I was doing, it didn't matter what people said.

Chapter 48

The Sound Room

OUTSIDE OPPOSITION TO my ministry didn't bother me. I had never expected that there wouldn't be any. I had been through too many experiences where I had been blessed with shame for His name to believe that every soul in the Burleson community would accept me as a pastor without hesitation. What I hadn't been prepared for was the opposition to my ministry that rose up within the church. Many of the same people who had encouraged and helped me convert the youth ministry to a church opposed, though seldom openly, a woman in the position of pastor. Despite God's ordination of the Steppingstone ministry, there was a series of surreptitious movements to remove me. More than once, a man within the church decided that it was time to replace me and lead the church himself. The movement would start in casual conversations when someone would say, "Well, she's just pastor until somebody comes in that can take it over."

In one instance, a man who had become a leader had a vision for organizing men in the same way that I had already organized the women. The man was very active in the church. He was a good man. He seemed thoroughly dedicated to its ministry. He ran the sound system during each service. As he organized the men, they began to meet separately, and the men's movement at Steppingstone began to thrive due, in no small part, to his contribution. At first, he didn't directly assault my authority as pastor, but he undermined it in a number of small ways. Starting subtly, he worked on the minds of the men, continually implying that I was not fit to be pastor.

"She's a good teacher," he said in one meeting of the men or to an individual.

"She's just a teacher," he modified it at another time.

"She's not really a preacher, she's a teacher," he would say in another.

Then finally, at another time he added, "Well you know she's just a teacher, and she doesn't have any authority over us."

Over a period of weeks and months, the seeds grew into weeds that choked out God's message. Men's meetings assumed a different tone, and he started having private meetings with those men who were receptive to his goals for re-organizing the church.

I wasn't aware of any of this, but I had noticed that the men were acting funny. They responded differently to my requests for assistance. I noticed that if I asked some men, who in the past may have volunteered before I asked, for their assistance with a task, they ignored me. If I asked them to do something or said, "Would you help me move this over here?" they hesitated or made excuses. They wouldn't budge unless some woman came over to help me, and then they would help as a courtesy to the woman assisting me, not because I had asked for help. I knew something was wrong.

After the Steppingstone had become a church, we added an entry outside the doors leading into the building. It was little more than a mudroom, a vestibule about six by six feet. But people entered the building through it, and they often left umbrellas there or paused there if they were running late before entering the service. Without that room, when someone opened the door they stepped right into the middle of the meeting hall.

The vestibule had been added in July. The carpentry work had been completed, and some men in the church had started trimming it out with decorative rock on the exterior, but the work wasn't finished. The rocks had been placed, but they weren't secured with mortar around them. I expected the men in the church to complete the work, but I noticed that construction was slowing down.

I didn't mention it to the man who had assumed responsibility for all the men's activities. I had turned that responsibility over to him, and I didn't want to interfere. I had just stayed out of it, but weeks passed and still they had not cemented around those rocks. If they did not have time, I was more than willing to accept that. I didn't want the work on the church to be a burden for anyone.

On a Wednesday night in August, as people were coming into church, one of the rocks above the front door fell. Although the mini-avalanche had come at a time when people were going into the church for the weekday service, no one was injured. The boulder crashed onto the sidewalk in front of the church without doing any physical damage. Someone ran in and told us that the rock fell, and we were all alarmed. Many of us praised God that one of the children hadn't been around at the time.

"We have got to get cement around those rocks before church next Sunday, especially over the entry way," I announced. Cars were often parked right next to the building. Some people would pull their cars up so close that their bumpers were almost touching the brick. Others parked a little farther away leaving room between their vehicle and the building for them to walk. Until the rocks were securely in place, there was danger of damage to automobiles even when there wasn't a direct safety concern. I thought everybody would want to be at the church on Saturday ready to finish the mortaring.

No volunteers spoke up in the service, but I wasn't too anxious about that. God had always provided workers for the church, and He, no doubt, would select the best man for the job. Some women came down and cleaned the church on Saturday and got it ready for Sunday. I thought it was likely that a man or two would show up, too. But when I got to the church on Saturday, not one man was there. Pat Shetter was there to vacuum and clean the church.

Since none of the men came, Pat and I got the bags of cement from storage. They were heavy. We mixed the mortar and squeezed it out between the rocks. It was work, really hard work. This was in August, too, and it was in the upper nineties, maybe even one hundred degrees or more in the afternoon. Pat and I worked all day, and we got it done, except up over the doors where the cement was needed the most. We didn't have a ladder, and we couldn't reach that high.

One of the men finally showed up. It was about four o'clock in the afternoon, and he had just gotten off work. He thought other men would be there, and he came by to see if they needed any help. When he saw us, he started helping right away. He went home and got a ladder and brought it, and then he helped finish mortaring in the rocks that were high up on the wall.

At that point I still didn't suspect that a move to replace me was in progress. The man who helped with the mortaring didn't seem to know why others hadn't shown up either. Well, I know how things are, I thought. Perhaps none of the men could come because they were working or had other duties at home that had to be attended to. After all, it was August— yard work, the last fling of summer vacation, or getting kids ready for school were the usual suspects at this time of year. I credited it as a possible miscommunication, too. A lot of times someone will assume that others will get the work done. If everyone is thinking the same thing, nobody comes.

I thought that could be what had happened. I didn't think anything more about it.

I had no idea that what had started simmering with conspiratorial whispers had slowly bubbled into subterfuge and was about to boil over into rebellion. The pot would boil out long before I would learn that the men's leader was planning to take over administration of the church and eliminate me, but I had slowly begun to see that something was wrong. I found myself alone during my sermons. The praise leader abandoned his post as soon as praise and worship was finished. Soon the elder in charge of worship was missing in action during the sermon, too.

I began to notice that many of the men headed to the sound room shortly after I started preaching in each service. The first time I realized it, it was of no great concern. I thought that there may be issues with the sound system, and they were consulting with each other. But more and more men were disappearing into the sound room week after week. I had noticed that six or more men that served as ushers, or others who assisted with the service, vanished after I started speaking. When the offering was taken, the worship leader left the platform and joined the others in the sound room.

There was a window that they could open so they could hear the service and adjust the audio, but when they met, they closed that window, and they visited and caroused throughout the service. Their disappearance must have been obvious to others, and it must have been recognized by everyone in the church as a challenge to me as pastor. They couldn't have been more insulting if they had heckled me.

That didn't keep God from working in people's lives, though. With its recent conversion from a youth center, the church was still attracting a lot of young people. Many of them were in bondage to drugs, and I couldn't disrupt the service and teaching to go hunting for the lieutenants of the church. People were still getting saved, and that was my main concern, but it worried me that the men in leadership positions were abandoning their posts during the message. I was so busy with a frontal attack of the devil that I knew I had to rely on the General to make sure the enemy wasn't penetrating the flanks. I pushed ahead with my sermons and left the rest for God to sort out.

Each week, I got to the invitation, and people were ready to come forward. New converts were getting their friends to come. A lot of people were getting healed, too. Some of the people who came forward were into drugs and alcohol; a lot of times there would be demonic manifestations, or a new Christian would start crying as she was being delivered. They repented and cried out very loudly because the power of God was there. People being ministered to sometimes dropped to the floor as hands were laid on them. I needed a lot of altar help. But when I looked around for the men, the song and worship leaders were in the sound room or just outside it casually talking and passing the time of day. They didn't even know what was going on in the service. I had to interrupt the invitation and ask somebody to go tell them that I needed them.

I prayed about it. I wasn't sure what was going on, but I knew that something was terribly wrong. I prayed one Saturday and said, "Lord, this isn't right. Speak to them." I wanted God to do everything. I didn't want to have to say anything to anybody, especially because it was apparent that these men were resisting my attempts to get anything done.

The next day the men, once again, assembled in the sound booth. I spoke out, "All of you back in the sound room." The soundman heard me and opened the window. "Tell all of the men to come out here. Only you stay in the sound room." Now, that was God because I was really meek. I was used to working with young people and handling them with kid gloves by encouraging them. I prefer to relate to others as a servant with respect for them, and if prodding becomes necessary, it usually appears as gentle cajoling. You can't reach people by ordering them around. You ask them to do things. But at that moment, I felt God cover me with a mantle of authority. The soundman closed the window, and I started reading my text and launched into my sermon. They didn't come out, and I was forced to acknowledge that they may have decided to remove me as pastor. Their refusal to come out undermined the little authority I had. I didn't believe it was God's will for me to be removed from the Steppingstone ministry, but I was forced to accept the possibility that my time as pastor may have ended.

I determined right then, *if they do not come out of that sound room, I can accept it. I can walk out at the end of the service and not come back.* I made that decision in my heart. I didn't know that I had just fired the first salvo in a spiritual campaign taking place in the sound room. The men hadn't ignored me, far from it. As a result, of my challenge, God was putting each of them in the position of making a decision about the church and my authority as its pastor.

"You don't have to do what she says," the soundman told the others packed into the crowded room.

Up until that moment, the worship leader had been complicit in the conspiracy. He suddenly realized that he was making a mistake and laid the case before the others, "Either she is our pastor or she is not. I am making the decision right now that she is my pastor, and I'm going out there," he announced to the group. The tall man was highly respected among the men camping in the sound booth. He was easy going and likeable. "I am going out there, and whoever wants to follow me can, but I am taking my stand with the pastor." He pushed his way through the small, crowded room to the doorway while the soundman encouraged the others not to listen. The conspiracy was about to erupt into a coup if he had his way. The time had come.

Each man was forced to decide for himself whether he would follow the sound man's advice or return to the congregation and accept me as the pastor of the Steppingstone church. The worship leader came out, and one-by-one the rest, every one of them, followed him, and they sat down in the congregation. I went on and preached. I thought, well, I guess I will still be pastor. There is nothing like God's wisdom. God used the potentially devastating situation to force each man to decide for himself whether he could and would support a woman pastor. That laid the groundwork for the next episode.

I arrived early for praise team practice a few weeks after the Saturday when Pat Shetter and I had mortared the entry. I was the pianist for the praise team, and I always attended the Saturday practice. I came early because I had to get the music ready. I walked into the sound room, and the leader of the rebellion was over by the soundboard. He turned when I walked in and greeted him, but when he looked at me, it wasn't his face I saw. I saw a demon. It was like his face had turned into this grotesque, awful thing that looked like a bird face. If evil has a look, that's it. Instantly, I knew that was where the trouble was coming from, and I got out of the office as fast as I could. Later I wondered how I reacted because I had been so stunned by what I had seen that I didn't remember. I didn't say anything to him about it, but I left the room and started praying. "Lord, help me know what to do." Then I said, "Lord, I am going to call my elders and tell them."

The Lord told me not to do that. I didn't know how God would expose him, but I knew that He had told me that I was to take no action. As He had so many times, God would display His power and authority by personally taking control of the situation. All I had to do was turn it over to Him. God himself would take the battlefield, and I knew that the best thing I could do was stay out of His way. Once again a small action in response to God's command released the power of the Holy Spirit to complete a greater act. When I called on the men to come out of the sound room, without even realizing it, I was calling on the Holy Spirit to take charge. God wants us to assume authority in his name. That releases the Holy Spirit to act.

One of the deacons of our church was a singer for Jerry Savelle's revivals. He had practiced a song at the end of the praise team's rehearsal, and he planned to perform a solo in Sunday's service. In the sound room, he had plugged his microphone into a channel that wasn't being used. He had set up that channel so that it would be ready for taping his performance. That was the only channel on the soundboard that he touched. He didn't interfere with the sound board's settings.

On Sunday mornings, the men met before church for a sunrise continental breakfast and a prayer meeting. The regular attendees had arrived. Many of them were sitting down for breakfast when the soundman walked into the sound room to confirm that everything was ready for the Sunday service. He saw the microphone plugged into a channel that he had left empty the day before, and suddenly furious, he stormed back into the hall.

"Who touched the sound board?" he snarled rhetorically. He ranted about the audacity of anyone who dared to change his set up. He wasn't interested in an answer. He didn't really want to know. Before the soloist had a chance to confess, the soundman pulled the keys to the church out of his pocket. As the organizer of many activities and the church's media manager, he had keys to the front door, the sound room, and a supply room where tapes were stored. The men of the church had no time to respond. Whether in shock or awe, they could only watch as the sound man hurled his keys at the worship leader. Still ranting, he slammed the door open as he exited the breakfast, leaving the men of the church staring after him.

When I got to church, a man met me at the door and apologized to me.

After I entered the building, others greeted me with apologies. At first, I didn't know what they were apologizing for. As far as I knew, none of them had done anything that should have offended me. I tend to have a short emotional memory of offenses against me, and I didn't think to associate the men's apologies with their tendency to haunt the sound room every Sunday instead of attending to the lost. I had long ago dismissed the falling rock episode and would never have connected that and the rebellious attitude of the men on Sundays anyway.

"We really saw what he was and how much he has influenced us, and now we see it was just the devil," they chorused.

They saw the light, but I was still confused. Slowly other people and events focused the picture for me. Within a couple of weeks, the sound man had left his wife, and she came to me with a spiral notebook. She allowed me to leaf through the pages of his plan for church reorganization, and she told me that many of the men from the church had been visiting their home regularly and meeting with her husband. She showed me an elaborate reorganization plan. "They have been reorganizing the church, and you were not included," she explained as I turned the pages and saw the hierarchical structure that the soundman had planned to install with himself as the alpha male.

Several men had been designated for leadership positions, but he had elevated himself to the pinnacle position in the church. My name was not listed as a member of his bureaucracy. He had been within weeks, days, or possibly even hours of instituting the reorganization, and the thing about it that was most disturbing was that the men assigned to positions of responsibility in the new hierarchy represented the majority of the families of our church. If all the men who were conspiring together had decided to leave and start a different church, there wouldn't have been enough families left to sustain the Steppingstone.

The devil was trying to destroy this church from the very beginning. If I had walked away, it would have folded because the devil was behind the man's work. But as it was, God took care of it. We were standing in the fiery furnace, but I had barely smelled the smoke.

The church was still in its infancy. It's not as though the people, whom the soundman was stirring, didn't like me, but they were vulnerable to the man's misguided attempt to usurp the authority that God had put in place. No women's names could be found anywhere in his organizational plan, even though women had organized the Steppingstone and helped in its construction. Even though I had invested myself in the church, I was excluded from all positions of leadership. There wasn't a place for me as Sunday school superintendent, praise leader, elder, or even teacher or pianist, and certainly not as a pastor, assistant pastor, or assistant to the assistant pastor.

That's the way the devil works. Ultimately, the devil is fighting God, and he does that by influencing us, by slowly eroding our relationships, and you can bet he's got an elaborately calculated plan. In the devil's way of thinking, a victory over us is a victory over God because that is as close as he can get to experiencing true victory. If God has a purpose for me, the way the devil can fight God is to try to get me out of God's will and out of His purpose. When he does that, he really only defeats me, not God. He tries to defeat us by assaulting us directly using our health, finances, or relationships. He will try to defeat us by influencing the people around us.

The man never returned to Steppingstone, but I was told that he had inspired the men's rebellion. He had convinced others to stay away on the day that the walls were to be completed. He had persuaded them that they needed to make a unified show of strength because I had no right to make work assignments or to interfere with the men's ministry in any way.

God took care of it. He showed me that He was faithful. He was watching my back. And miraculously, at the same time, He was point man. In early attempts to ignore God's call for my life, I had used the excuses that people would not come to hear a woman preach and that they would not submit to the authority of a woman pastor. I had said to the Lord, "I do not want to be a pastor because people will not come." Then I argued that people would not submit to the authority of a woman pastor, and they wouldn't respect me as a leader. God didn't pay any attention to my excuses. He reassured me that He had called me, and He would take care of everything because the Steppingstone was His church. After the church survived the episode with the soundman, my leadership solidified. It turned out for the good. I praise God that I have not been involved in any more direct or more traumatic confrontations.

The church's reputation grew. People all over the Fort Worth area heard about the movement of the Holy Spirit in the Steppingstone's services and wanted to be part of it. Many of them joined the church even though they didn't feel that women were accepted by God as pastors. There was always an undercurrent. It continued throughout my ministry. I couldn't worry about what people think about me personally or about women in ministry. I chose to think about and praise God for the many hundreds of people He brought to Steppingstone/Lighthouse who stood loyally with me, worked so hard alongside me, and who devoted so much of their lives in service to our Lord. There are too many people blindly walking toward that cliff. There's no time to worry about such trivia. We have work to do.

Arise! Shine!

Chapter 49

ACE

THE STEPPINGSTONE'S MINISTRY, as it had before becoming a church, emphasized the importance of reaching young people for Christ. So, it only seemed natural that the leaders of the church considered creating a source for Christian education, an alternative to public schools for parents who wanted their children to be educated with Christian values. We began looking at ways to sponsor a school through the Steppingstone church.

Accelerated Christian Education (ACE) was introduced in the early seventies, and by 1985, several Bible-based schools using the ACE curriculum had been started in Texas. The Steppingstone's leaders began looking at the possibility of hosting an ACE school. Children in the ACE program would be able to learn at their own pace. Our small church could not have afforded to hire teachers, but with the ACE program, we didn't need them. Teachers weren't required because the student was responsible. It only required one person to administer the system and monitor students' progress.

At first glance, an ACE school appeared to be a good fit for the church. It wouldn't cost a fortune to sponsor the faith centric curriculum, and a married couple stepped forward and volunteered to organize the school and to serve as program administrators. They went to the orientation and training, which lasted a week, and returned to the Steppingstone and reported to the board, "The pastor has to be the principal, so Pastor Gloria is going to have to go through this orientation if we are to have a school with her as pastor." That's the way the presentation began, with an assumption that I would be the principal, but instead of filling in my name at the top of the organizational chart that they began drawing on a blackboard, they put their names as the co-principals and de-facto pastors of the church.

Instead of saying it, they just wrote up at the top of the blackboard. They appointed themselves pastors. I still had an evening service to conduct so there wasn't time for discussion after the couple's presentation, but each member of the board sat silently as if waiting for someone else to speak first. I glanced at one board member then another. Some of them looked at me questioningly. Others remained transfixed on the chalkboard where the couple had laid out their plan. As we dismissed, no one had anything to say.

As I was leaving the room, I almost audibly mouthed a prayer. "Oh Lord, I do not want to go through one of these things again."

God spoke back. "You are not ready to start a school." I had a brief vision. It was like a little tree that has recently been planted, and it was maybe ten feet tall. It didn't cast much of a shade. It was just a sapling really, just beginning to take root and grow. It wouldn't be big enough to shade a yard for several years. At first it stood alone. Then I saw the sapling being crowded by other plants. They grew into huge shrubs surrounding the tree and consuming all the nutrients from the soil. The little tree shrank down. A school would sap the life out of the church.

I was relieved.

I have always believed that a Christian education is important. The ministry to young people has never been far from my mind, and I knew that a Christian school would provide another way for God to do his work in Burleson. The Steppingstone had been a church for about three years, and we were still in the forty by eighty foot building that was little more than a meeting space. We were too small to sponsor a school.

As I called the board and told them what the Lord had spoken to me, each member expressed relief. They feared that the school would overwhelm us. One board member later commented, "Well, did you get that? They were saying they would be pastor." Other than that, almost no one mentioned the presentation by the couple who would be pastors again. We never talked about it.

Chapter 50

The Mantle of Leadership

IT MAY BE that pastors of all churches have to deal with threats to their ministry from time to time, but I think that is especially true for a woman. Through the years since I assumed the role of pastor, movements to replace me with a male pastor came and went. From the beginning, I left those concerns in God's hands. There was a lesson with each episode. I had to go through it, but God always brought me through victoriously. Sometimes I never suspected there was an effort to supplant me until the entire thing had ended.

Some of the movements originated outside the little church. Some of them, usually the more lethal ones, slithered through the church, silent and unseen except to those who colluded in the subversions. Sometimes, you could say the conspiracies were almost innocent.

In the eighties, at about the same time that we were looking at the feasibility of hosting a school, there were some Baptist ladies who had gotten filled with the good news of Christ. They had visited the Steppingstone and had been baptized in the Holy Spirit. They began meeting at homes of various members of the group because their tendencies to praise without inhibition weren't exactly encouraged by the church they attended.

They invited the Steppingstone's assistant minister to their home meetings. They had heard him preach and they particularly liked the way that he presented the word. Unwilling to leave their church for a charismatic church led by a woman, they remained members of the Baptist church, but they were hungry for more of the Holy Spirit. Soon their home meetings weren't enough. They began to encourage the spirit-filled minister to organize a movement to replace me as the Steppingstone's pastor.

He was flattered at first. He was tempted, too. Like most assistant pastors, he hoped and planned to lead a church someday, and maybe as a middle-aged man he was beginning to feel like that possibility was slipping away. Like many Christians, he wasn't completely convinced that the

Bible licensed women to fill the pinnacle position of church leadership, but one of the things that had drawn him to Steppingstone was the activity of the Holy Spirit. He recognized the anointing on our ministry. He devoutly served as my assistant, and he brought his family to the worship with him because he recognized the anointing for exactly what it was.

He couldn't help lending an ear to the encouragement from the Baptist ladies, and he seriously considered their suggestion. Praise God that he was less ambitious than he was willing to accept God's call and God's timing in all things. For weeks, he prayed for God's will to be done. He walked in one day and resigned.

"I am leaving here. We are packing up and moving to Florida," he told me. He described the conspiracy in which he had become unwittingly and now unwillingly complicit, telling me about it and how the women in the group were encouraging him to depose me.

He said, "I left the meeting Friday, and God spoke to me, saying, 'You make one move against that lady, and you are a dead man.'" He said the Lord just came over him, and he asked, "Lord, what do I do?"

God's answer to him was, "Leave. I have a place for you in Florida." And he did. He went down and became pastor of a church. God told him that He wanted him to dissolve that conspiracy and, I guess, make a clean break of it.

"I have never felt the fear of the Lord like this before," he told me. "God's hand is on you." He felt really badly about it and was so apologetic that I felt sorry for him, but it was a wonderful reminder that God was taking care of me. "Nobody had better try to remove you," he summed up. "They are going to be in big trouble if they do."

Chapter 51

The Medium and the Message

THE STEPPINGSTONE'S NASCENT ministry was one of the most progressive and socially active in the Burleson area. In 1982, I presented the BISD and the Burleson library with copies of Peter Marshall's history, *The Light and the Glory*. Marshall had visited Burleson and spoken over a period of several days at a seminar sponsored by local churches. Dr. Bernard Erickson, the president of Burleson ISD's school board, accepted the donation for the school district, and Sherry Warren, Librarian, accepted for the library.

We used technology, too. I believe that each Christian has a responsibility to reach out to as many people as possible and to use any means available. Since the beginning of the Steppingstone, I tried to extend the church's reach using electronic media. Before the end of our first year, we had bought a satellite dish and a TV beam projector capable of showing a ten-foot wide television picture. Big screens and high definition are commonplace now. Low definition projection TV is arcane, but in 1982, projecting images for a church audience was an ambitious enterprise. That's the kind of thing we were trying to do to reach out to a community that was growing more technologically savvy by the day.

The Steppingstone "will be trying out [the satellite receiver and screen] this week with a Sunday-through-Wednesday seminar featuring nationally known Christian speaker Norvel Hayes," the *Burleson Star* reported in an anonymously authored article titled "Seminar by Satellite" on November 8, 1982. The article was accompanied by my picture. "Pastor Gloria Gillaspie and Minister of Music Don Reeves are expecting 250 people for the series, which they hope will be the first of many," the caption stated.

"A number of special weekend events have been scheduled at Steppingstone church and Youth Outreach," the newspaper reported almost a year later on July 8, 1983, in another un-authored article, "Special Events at Steppingstone." The write-up announced that my brother, Ercel, would be guest speaker for Sunday morning services and that Youth W.A.V. 83 would be presented via satellite.

The brief description of Ercel's ministry in the *Burleson Star* didn't begin to tell his story. "Lewis is a missionary to Mexico and the brother of Gloria Gillaspie," the article began. "A native Burlesonite and BHS graduate, he is the son of Mr. & Mrs. Clyde Lewis of Burleson. He began his ministry in Mexico eleven years ago by establishing churches in villages outside Ciudad Victoria."

I guess that was Ercel's fifteen minutes of fame. Actually, the history of Ercel's ministry could fill a book, and many of its chapters would describe the danger of delivering God's word to the people of Mexico. God has miraculously intervened and saved his life or the life of one of his family members on several occasions. Today, the dangers of living in Mexico are greater than ever, but Ercel's ministry is still growing. Souls are being saved by the hundreds.

At the time, though, the newspaper seemed just as interested in Ercel's extra-ministerial activities. "Lewis continued to minister in about fifty villages around Victoria until September, 1981, at which time he accepted the position as head football coach at the University of Agronomy in Ciudad Victoria. Since that time, his ministry has taken a new direction. His position at the university opened doors for his ministry and enabled him to hold meetings in most of the area schools."

Ercel is still pastor of a church in Ciudad Victoria. The church has more than a thousand members, but his life and the lives of his family and church members are in constant danger. They have felt death's breath on the back of their necks many times over the last few years. He refuses to abandon his ministry in Mexico, even though many family members in Texas wish that he would return, but God peppers his apostles over the globe, and only He and they understand the call on their lives. Please pray for Ercel, his ministry, his family, his church, and God's continuing movement in Mexico.

Chapter 52

Angels in the Outfield

THE DEVIL IS not an adherent to the adage, "if you can't beat 'em, join 'em." He attacks on many fronts at the same time. If he can't get a foothold in our lives and destroy our fellowship with God, then he will devise circumstances that can lead to our physical harm.

In the winter of 1983, an interdenominational organization sponsored a conference at the Radisson, one of the large hotels in the Dallas Market district. The conference was open to anyone who was concerned about America's spiritual direction.

Still a neophyte pastor, I decided to attend the conference. There is no such thing as being over prepared for God's work. I had gotten into the ministry because I was concerned about the direction that so many young people were taking in their lives, and I was equally concerned about the course of the nation. God was being banished incrementally from the very nation that had been built for Him by the Pilgrims who fled to a new world where they could worship freely. His name was banned from schools and stricken from public edifices by the pharaohs of agnosticism and intellectualism. His name was being erased from every monument, every book, while every form of reprobation was exalted in literature, television, and film. The goal of government seemed to be to deny that God exists. History was conveniently revised as though the founding fathers had no concept of a God, and Christians who are taught to turn the other cheek allowed the effete mob to slap them seventy times seven times, and we go on allowing them to debase us, drawing us down into their depravity by making laws that force the rest of us to share in it. God was banished from the classroom, the courtroom, public meeting halls, and even from the womb.

I really wanted to go to the conference, but I had no one to go with me. I drove by myself. The drive was cold. A series of days with temperatures in the teens had confounded north central Texans, who often don't quite know how to dress for a cold morning because all signs of an overnight blizzard usually melt away by noon of the following day's glorious sunshine.

When I got to the hotel, the free parking lot was full. I didn't want to park in a separate garage with paid parking, and I noticed that people were parking in a graveled area across the street from the hotel. There was no attendant, but cars were lined up at the entrance, and it seemed as good a place as any. It wasn't far from the hotel, and it was obvious that others who were attending the conference were parking there. They had their Bibles with them as they made their way toward the hotel.

I drove into the parking lot, and although there were no striped parking spaces, the cars were parked at an angle just as though the slots were clearly defined. I got out and stood up in the blustering cold. I pulled the collar of my full-length coat up around my cheeks to keep the cold from nipping at them.

I still measured my career as pastor in terms of months, not years. I wasn't acquainted with most of the church leaders in the Dallas-Fort Worth metroplex. I didn't know anyone at the conference and sat alone through the seminar, taking notes and paying close attention to the speakers rather than striking up conversations with other attendees. This was important stuff, and I didn't want to miss a syllable. When the program had ended, I noticed that other people were visiting and talking. I would have enjoyed listening to some of the discussions, but it was getting late, and I had a long drive ahead of me.

I dreaded the drive home. The cold was such a concern that I hadn't given much thought to the creatures that swarm the streets of Dallas after dusk. It hadn't occurred to me that at about this hour they would be scurrying out of their diurnal haunts. I just got my things together and put on my coat, buttoning it up because I knew it would be so cold outside that once the chill had crept inside, it could be a miserable walk back to the car.

I was not accustomed to fear, but as soon as I stepped out of the building into the darkness, something like fear gripped me, not fear exactly, but an almost tangible sense of foreboding. I started to turn back into the lighted warmth of the hotel and ask one of the ministers if they would mind walking me to my car, but I was already outside and decided to go on alone. The farther I got from the light and safety of the conference, the stronger that feeling of fear grew. I had never experienced that kind of fear before, but I'm not going to have someone come out into this cold and walk with me, I chided myself. Besides, it was so bitterly cold that I couldn't talk myself into retracing my steps. With every step, I was closer to the car. I figured that I would be warm within minutes, as soon as the car heated up. I kept walking and began a prayer for my safety.

When I reached the street, I waited for cars to pass so that I could cross to the graveled parking lot. As I stood at the curb, I heard the grind of a starter and the rumble of an engine. The sound startled me. My sense of danger heightened. I felt weak. I saw the ominous car idling at the curb.

Instantly, I knew there was something evil there. That was what was making me feel so fearful. I could feel an evil. The figure silhouetted against the streetlights had a massive nest of hair. I thought it must be a woman. It was impossible to make out her features except that she seemed very large. I admonished myself again for being afraid, but then I realized she was following me into the parking lot. Again, I felt the presence of evil.

I had only owned my car for two months and still couldn't easily tell the difference between the key that operated the ignition and the one that opened the door, especially in the dark. I debated which key to try first as I pulled them from my purse. The sense of foreboding was so strong that I doubted I might have a chance to try a second key if the first one didn't work. I needed to be ready to get in the car quickly.

I whispered prayerfully, "Oh, which one of these unlocks it?" as I stood outside my car and reached for the door. At the same moment, the sinister car came to a stop behind mine, blocking my exit. I can't describe the feeling of danger. The evil exuding from the car was more noxious than the billowing exhaust. I was trying to put the key in but couldn't help looking back. I couldn't see the person in the car at all now. There were no lights anywhere behind the car, and I could no longer make out the silhouette. I heard a latch, but wasn't sure if it was mine or the car's blocking mine. At least if I could get into my car before the door of the predatory car swung open, I thought, I might be safer.

Suddenly two men rose from the ground at the far side of my car. They were huge, each at least six feet, eight inches tall, and even in the dark I could tell they were wearing suits. Despite their size and the way they had risen from nowhere, the trepidation, dissolved instantly. I thought I heard them mention the conference in their casual conversation. Oh, they must have been fixing a tire, I told myself. My fears dissipated faster than the puffs of breath, which slowed to a more *normal* rate. As soon as they stood up, I was completely at peace and knew I was totally safe. I calmly unlocked my car.

I heard a clunk as the transmission of the sinister car slammed into gear. The car jerked, and the tires spun through the loose gravel as it backed out of the lot and sped away. I got into my car and started the engine. I looked back, but there was no sign of the two men who had been changing the tire. I couldn't tell if they had gotten into a car. I told myself that since they weren't in the parking lot anymore, they had probably headed back to the hotel, but I couldn't see anyone. Those two, massive men would have stood out like twin Goliaths as they passed through the parking lot. I glanced back as I drove away. The car they had been next to still sat there. There was no sign of two men outside the car. As I drove to the parking lot's exit and stopped before turning onto the street, I strained again to see if they were walking toward the hotel, but I could only see a few dark figures under the street lamps in the distance making their way toward the parking lot. None of them stood out as exceptionally tall. No one was walking opposite the flow of exiting conference attendees. I was certain I would have been able to see them passing under the street lights and heading toward the lighted hotel. There was no one.

I started driving home and singing praise songs. I laughed and praised the Lord for delivering me. I was sorry that someone had a flat tire and had to change it in that cold and darkness, but just the same, I praised the Lord for the appearance of the two men. "Lord, you just had these men right there, and I hate for anybody to have a flat tire, but thank you." All the way home, I praised God. And all the way home my memory played through the scene again and again. I remembered I hadn't seen anyone near the adjacent car as I walked across the parking lot. It seemed that I should have seen at least one of the two huge men changing a tire because I had seen between cars as I approached. Why hadn't I heard them talking? Walking toward my car, I had been convinced that I was alone in the parking lot, and my senses were so heightened that I surely should have noticed them. I should have heard something, but it had been eerily quiet until the phantom car pulled up to block my exit.

Then I realized what had happened. There was only one explanation: they weren't there when I left the hotel, or when I crossed the street, or when I made my way toward the car. They weren't there at all, at least not visibly, until the sinister car had pulled up. They seemed to have materialized out of the cold, dry air. And that's exactly what they did. I began to praise the Lord.

The following Sunday, I sat in the safety and comfort of my living room watching the evening news at 10:00 p.m. Church had ended hours before. The television news reporter described a man that had been arrested in Dallas. He had attempted to rape a girl who had fortunately escaped. The intended victim described a huge, ratted hairstyle, and chills sprinted down my spine. The man had used a huge red wig to disguise himself. A police officer displayed the replaceable coiffure for television reporters. If I hadn't already known, that would have been enough to convince me: it had been the same man. I remembered that I had looked at the silhouette thinking it was a woman but that the shoulders and other features seemed very large, not feminine looking at all. I had argued to myself that some women do have big features, but sitting in front of the television, I realized it was a man—that man. The Lord confirmed it to me. "Yes. You were his target that night, but I sent angels to deliver you."

I told the story in the next Sunday's service, and we had a time of rejoicing. After the service, my son-in-law remarked, "I thought I was going to have a heart attack when you told everything."

"Why? You see me," I replied laughing. "You know I'm safe."

You can feel the presence of evil. Sometimes even though there is no reason for it, those prickly hairs on the nape of your neck rise, and you can sense that something isn't right. I felt it that night in the parking lot. The man was possessed, and I could feel his evil presence.

Jesus could sense the goodness and the evil of all the people He came in contact with. He knew beforehand of Judas's and Peter's betrayals. He knew that his life had been sold for thirty pieces of silver. He stood under the judgment of Caiaphas who mocked and scorned him and knew absolutely that He was going to be crucified that very day. He was surrounded by evil and He knew what was coming. We know that in the hours before Jesus was arrested, He sweated blood, dreading the moment when He would take upon himself the sins, diseases, and sufferings of all mankind. He could have called for angels, but He stood alone and chose to die holding the key to mankind's redemption. He didn't call angels to save Him, although He could have. God sent an angel, but only to strengthen Him for the journey to the cross (Luke 22:43).

Who knows how many times He may have sent an angel for each of us? We are delivered, strengthened, and enabled to go through trials and sufferings in order to fulfill His purpose for our lives and bring glory to Him. Oh, how He must love us to send angels when we're in danger when He wouldn't summon them for Himself.

Chapter 53

Hats

THE TERRORS OF the parking lot were a Sunday walk in the park compared to the responsibilities of a pastor. The leader of a church must be preacher, builder-contractor, confidant, teacher, political activist, accountant, and attorney. I've never been much of one for hats (although high-heeled shoes are a completely different subject). If I had been, there would have been no room in my closet for anything else, and adding the hat of businesswoman would no doubt have burst the door off its hinges. Income statements and balance sheets were becoming part of my daily life. I was responsible for the finances of a growing church that by 1984 was once again too large for its building. We began raising funds for a new building. This time, the church had little trouble securing a loan from the Farmers and Merchants State Bank, one of the mainstay businesses in Burleson since 1913, according to an article published by Robert Griffeth on the website, "A History of Burleson Online" at Burlesonhistory.com.

By the time the new sanctuary was dedicated on April 20, 1986, the church had come a long way. The fledgling church was now recognized as a force to be reckoned with. I began to enjoy the respect and appreciation of the community. Political figures courted the church's influence. Joe Barton, US Congressman for a district that included much of Burleson, was on hand for the new building's dedication ceremony and delivered the address. Barton said that he didn't believe in the separation of church and state. He said it was important for church members to be involved in politics. "One person does make a difference," Congressman Barton concluded.

The dedication of the new sanctuary was a lot more than a political whistle stop for the freshman representative. It was a homecoming. In the week before the November elections in 1984, Joe had been counted out. The experts who litter the national media like the Wall Street Journal with their biased punditry had predicted that all congressional races in Texas were unpredictable, except for one. It was a foregone conclusion that Joe Barton didn't stand a chance.

Joe had barely survived a run off for the Republican nomination for the seat that was vacated by Phil Gramm, who had left the house to run for the senate. In the general election, Joe was pitted against the popular democrat Dan Kubiak, a long time state representative who had been named one of the top ten legislators in Texas by *Texas Monthly* magazine in 1972.

Although he was still campaigning valiantly, by the Sunday before the election, Joe was feeling discouraged. He had been scheduled to speak somewhere that evening, and at the last minute, the engagement was cancelled. That couldn't have boosted his spirits. Arlene, one of our church members who was a pilot and owned her own plane, had been flying him to his campaign destinations. Although it was a last minute engagement, she asked if Joe could drop by Steppingstone and speak to our congregation.

He gave a short address stressing the responsibility each of us has to vote. As the young candidate wrapped up, I felt like we were supposed to pray for him. I asked if he minded, although I don't think Joe fully appreciated what his assent meant in a spirit-filled church. I called for the elders, and we gathered around him. He wasn't used to being the center of a prayer circle with everyone gathering around and stretching their hands toward him. He later admitted that as people started laying hands on him he noted the location of each exit. But he didn't bolt. He was really nice about it and let us pray for him.

The Holy Spirit moved in the prayer, and the words became prophetic. People began speaking about the things Joe was going to do when he got to Washington. Often when a politician speaks at a church, he is out the door and running for the next lectern before his words have registered. I figured Mr. Barton would be the same, and before I took the podium I gave him an out. I told him that our congregation understood if he couldn't remain for the rest of the service. We knew that he was tired and nearing the end of a long campaign. We were happy to excuse him if he needed to go.

He said, "Well, I think I'd kind of like to stay." He stayed for the whole service. I preached about Joshua leading the people of Israel and taking the Promised Land. I related it to Christians taking America for God. When I finished my message, one of the members of our church asked if he could read a prophecy that God had given him during my sermon. He had written it down. The prophecy was related to Joe and the work that God had called him to do. Congress, according to the prophecy, was God's call on Mr. Barton's life.

Immediately after the service was over, we made an audio copy and gave it to Joe to carry home with him. He said he had a really good feeling after he left our church that night, and he listened to the tape as he drove to Ennis. He felt very encouraged.

On Tuesday, Joe Barton was elected to represent the sixth congressional district, a post at which he has stood steadfastly for conservative and Christian values ever since. He has cast many pro-life votes.

The congressman's topic on the night of the dedication of the new sanctuary, the separation of church and state, was close to my heart. I had completed a study of religion in early America, especially of the religious leanings of the founding fathers, and I knew that the first Amendment to the Constitution of the United States did not dictate that Christ has no place in government. It forbade the Congress from making any laws establishing a religion or prohibiting the free exercise thereof, which our modern courts have unrelentingly done since the 1960s by forbidding prayer in public places and promoting a godless religion with man as the only deity. The first amendment declared that there shall be no state church, but our national government has created a state religion, albeit a godless one. The Bill of Rights never intended to eliminate Christian participation in government or a single individual's right to religious freedom and expression or an individual's right and responsibility to base personal political decisions on religious or moral principles.

Approximately 350 people attended the dedication of a building that was designed to seat a little more than 400. So, it was filled almost to capacity from the start.

THE NEW SANCTUARY WAS FILLED EVERY SUNDAY, BUT
THERE WAS NO ROOM TO SPARE ON EASTER, 1987.

Chapter 54

Flying High

SOME MIRACLES ARE private matters. The miracle in the parking lot was a private miracle. It was just for me, and I continued to build my faith on it. Others, just like the gifts of the spirit, are as much for other believers and for non-believers as they are for us.

Three years after I became pastor of the Steppingstone, a team of optometrists, dentists, and volunteer carpenters from the Burleson area asked me to accompany them to Mexico for a weekend mission. The medical professionals, who included Mikeal Wohlgemuth, were providing glasses and dental services to the people in a Mexican village. Other volunteers were building a small church in a nearby mountain village. The team felt that a pastor should act as chaplain for the mission.

I accepted with excitement, and at first, I looked forward to the trip, but on the Tuesday before our scheduled departure, I had a sense of dread. Then the weather began to turn bad. I started to question that the trip was in God's will, and I called Arlene Wohlgemuth, one of the pilots and my primary contact with the mission team. I almost hoped that they were going to cancel the excursion. Instead, Arlene said that a group had met and decided to go forward with the trip despite the weather conditions. I prayed about the trip for the next three days. The weather didn't improve. The clouds hung around like a sick, morose roommate.

Even as I drove to the small airport and joined three other missionaries on the single engine plane that would carry us more than a thousand miles, I continued praying. I was catching a flight piloted by a friend who was a member of the Assembly of God church in Burleson, and I climbed into the back seat next to an optometrist friend. The man occupying the co-pilot's seat was a member of the Disciples of Christ church in Weatherford.

Mikeal and Arlene were on a separate plane. While we all flew down on the same day, several small, private planes were making the trip. My silent prayers continued as the plane lifted off the runway and headed into the gloomy clouds that crowded us like masked surgeons and nurses standing fuzzily unfocused around the operating table above a drowsy patient.

Once we were on our way, the sense that something wasn't quite right never left me. It hovered like a recurring flu. Every time I shook the notion off, it returned a few minutes later even worse than before. The monotonous drone of the airplane engine would have had a soporific effect if the weather had been calmer, but with the looming clouds, the plane seemed to be uttering a prayerful mantra. Monotony would have been preferable to what happened next. The engine sputtered. It started up again almost immediately, but I was already praying. It wasn't time to panic, but a shriek of terror might have lightened the mood.

The pilot seemed to accept the sputtering engine with equanimity. Still, not much was said while the engine took hold, started back up for a moment, and then sputtered again. Then the engine fell silent. We glided along at an altitude where the angels could have reached out and touched the wings, and it must have been angels that were keeping us aloft, because the engine had apparently crossed into heaven, and it seemed for a moment like we might be destined to follow.

The pilot hurriedly worked the ignition switch, and I could tell by the reaction of the co-pilot, who was also a licensed pilot, that we were in trouble. I helped in the only way I knew how: "In the name of Jesus, I command the devil to get off this plane and the engine to start now." Immediately, the engine took hold. We were flying again instead of gliding. My fellow back seat passenger stared at me aghast, like he wasn't sure whether he should be more afraid of plummeting into the ground or surviving and finishing the trip with a crazy woman. I tried to explain, "We have all this power. Why shouldn't we use it?" The copilot was the most surprised. I don't think he was very familiar with miracles or someone exercising their authority in Jesus' name. There were no more problems with the engine, and we landed in Mexico a few hours later. After we were safely on the ground, our co-pilot told Arlene that he was rededicating his life to the Lord. The flight had changed his life.

I was told later that some of the team had met on the Tuesday before the trip, the same night that I had a strong sense of foreboding and had called to check on the trip's status. They had discussed canceling the trip, not just because of the weather but because some of them had forebodings like mine. Two of the doctors had even decided they would not make the trip.

The four people on my flight hadn't been on the ground long before another plane full of volunteers arrived. Their flight had run into bad weather, and without instruments, the pilot had been forced to pick his way through the clouds, much like a game show contestant choosing life or death hidden behind door number one, two, or three. It was an ominous beginning to our trip, but we agreed God had already performed miracles. He had delivered the entire team safely despite the bad weather and the engine problems. We praised God for getting us there. We prayed for the umbrella of God's protection for the rest of the trip, and the team completed its mission, not without other miracles though.

As chaplain, I was scheduled to speak to the people in the village that night, but once a resident missionary found out the speaker was a woman, he pulled me aside and suggested that I shouldn't speak, at least not to a mixed group. He recommended that we find someone else to preach. "The men of this village will not respond to a woman. This is a different culture," he told me. I didn't explain that those attitudes didn't necessarily distinguish the Latin American culture from the North's, but I decided to bring a message to the community anyway. The doctors had asked me along as chaplain, God had brought us to Mexico safely, and although I was physically and emotionally exhausted after the trip, I was determined to fulfill the mission that God had given me.

When I got up before the small gathering, I talked about a miracle Jesus had performed that wasn't far from my mind after the problems with the airplane. I told the story of Jesus walking on water, coming to the disciples during a storm when they feared their boat was about to sink. He calmed the storm and got them to shore. I told them that when God directs you to do something, He will get you there. He will supply all that you need. It was a message about faith. When we opened the altar call at the end of the service, every man in the village gave his life to the Lord. That was the biggest miracle of the day.

I witnessed to men and women for the rest of the trip. What a victory. While we were there, we built a church, literally and spiritually. Many of the men had come to erect a church building, and God had used me to make sure the building would be filled.

Chapter 55

India Connection

N 1987, NEHULIE Angami, president of Kohima Bible College in North-eastern India, toured the United States educating Americans about the struggle for religious and political freedom in his home state, Nagaland, a thin peninsular appendage of mountainous terrain on the Northeast border of India. Geographically, culturally, politically, and religiously, Nagaland is an orphan. Predominantly a Christian state, it belongs in neither India, Burma, nor China.

The tiny state with four million inhabitants was more than 90 percent Christian. The predominance of Christians in Nagaland was the state's most glaring contrast to the rest of Hindi dominated India. In the eighties, it was referred to by some as the most Baptist state in the world. They were starving for the word of God. A large percentage of the population attended church regularly. Many made frequent pilgrimages to the state capital and other major cities just to worship. They didn't go by car, plane, or train. They trekked the alpine miles on foot and sometimes took days or even weeks to hike to and from Christian rallies.

Nagaland's believers were isolated from the rest of Christianity, not just geographically, but politically. At least in part due to the area's radical religious differences with the rest of the country, the Nagas have sought independence from India for decades. On March 22, 1956, the tiny state virtually declared independence by establishing the Naga Federal Republic. Nagaland's secessionist declaration was regarded as open revolt by India's central government, which quickly isolated the Christian state by passing The Foreigners Act. The law required that anyone who traveled to India for the purpose of proselytizing must obtain a special Missionary Visa. Any foreigner who traveled to Nagaland had to obtain a special travel permit, and they were not easy to come by. They were granted primarily to foreign travelers of Indian origin with relatives who lived in the restricted areas.

Of course, applying for the visa didn't guarantee that you would ever get one, much less that your request would navigate the bureaucratic minefields in time for you to attend the meeting or event that you had intended. The US state department advised that US citizens planning a visit to India and intending to engage in missionary activity may wish to seek legal advice regarding the legislation. It was very difficult for missionaries from foreign countries to gain access, and when they did, they were under constant surveillance.

Nehulie wasn't visiting the states only to educate Americans about the church in Nagaland. His primary mission was to locate three people that had been selected to fulfill a twenty-year-old prophecy that three foreigners would visit Nagaland, and they would bring a great revival with healing and a great movement of God.

Toward the end of 1986, Christian organizers of the annual prayer conference in Nagaland prayed for God's guidance. As they were praying, a prophetic word was given that the 1987 conference would be the fulfillment of the old prophecy. The three foreign missionaries would attend the conference and perform great miracles in Christ's name. Because of the prophecy, people were planning to come to the three-day conference from all over Nagaland.

Educated at Southwestern Assembly of God College in Waxahachie, Texas, Angamie was the president of the organization of churches in Nagaland. He had accepted the mission to recruit the three American speakers at the urging of church leaders, and he recognized the awesome responsibility to find the three foreigners as a great honor.

Nehulie knew many giants of Christian faith. He was familiar with leaders in the healing ministries of Oral Roberts and Kenneth Hagin. He knew David Nunn, a Fort Worth-Dallas area evangelist, who had founded the Kohima Bible College in 1970. His association with these leaders may be one of the reasons that he was commissioned to find the three missionaries of prophecy. But as Nehulie prayed for guidance, God didn't direct him toward any of those great evangelists and men of God.

Instead, he thought about will and Pat Thomasson, a couple with whom he had attended college in Texas. Although Will worked at the General Motors plant in Grand Prairie, Texas, he had been pastor of a church and was very involved in the ministry of the Steppingstone church in Burleson.

Will was on the music team, and he and his wife led Steppingstone's singles in Sunday school.

Nehulie and I met during his 1986 tour when he was a guest speaker at the Steppingstone. Immediately he felt that I was the one destined to bring the word to the Nagas. He prayed about it, but he knew as soon as the thought first struck that it was God's will for the Thomassons and me to go to Nagaland.

I was humbled when he asked me to be the main speaker. He said the Thomassons were to go and also speak at one of the day services, but I had been selected to lead the revival. I knew instantly it was God's will for me to go. I thought the trip would be an exciting adventure, too, and as Nehulie described the circumstances—the prophecy and Nagaland's isolation from the rest of the world—I felt an awesome responsibility. I had no idea how much of an adventure it would become. I knew it would give me an opportunity to serve God, and that was enticement enough.

I still had to get John's permission. Although he was hesitant to let me travel around the world, he could see God's will in it. He wasn't about to stand in the way. The Thomassons were excited about going, too. They believed the prophecy meant that we had been singled out and our service had been recognized. We're all chosen by Christ, but it was awesome to think that God may have commissioned the three of us for the Nagaland mission twenty years earlier, before I had even started the Steppingstone ministry. The Thomassons were as convinced as I that the opportunity was both a blessing and a mission from God. We accepted the challenge eagerly.

Nehulie told us he would coordinate the Visas and special permission. Once we got our passports and plane tickets, we were all set.

A few weeks later, we boarded a flight at DFW airport and set out on an adventure that would rival a spy novel for action, intrigue, and danger. First to London, where we changed planes, then we touched down in New Delhi and changed planes again to fly to Calcutta. During the layover in Delhi, I got my first glimpses of India. The living conditions appalled us. As the plane landed, I looked out the window and saw what appeared to be dead bodies lying everywhere. People were scattered over the landscape like diced onions on a hot dog. Nehulie explained that they weren't dead. They had no other place to sleep, he said, and they came to the airport each night to sleep on the grass.

The political hurdles for missionary trips to Nagaland may have changed in the intervening thirty years, but I doubt the physical toll of the journey is radically different or that the milieu that we stepped into when we carried our bags down the jet way of the international Airport in Calcutta, almost thirty-six hours after our plane had lifted off the runway in DFW, has changed much.

We had slept a little on the trans-Atlantic and trans-Europe flights, but we were tired. My legs wobbled when I walked. We expected to get a good night's sleep in the Calcutta hotel. It was going to be nice to sleep in a bed instead of an airplane seat or a chair in an airport lounge. Nehulie met us at the airport and took us to the hotel. On the way, he delivered some discouraging news.

"I was not able to get the travel permit," Nehulie admitted. "I'm so sorry. You've come all this way." He had applied for the permits in New Delhi, but still hadn't received a response. Nagaland was under martial law because its citizens wanted to secede from India, but neither the Thomassons nor I had realized how difficult it was to get permits or how dangerous it was to travel there. We still didn't have the permits for us to travel into Nagaland, and we had no idea that we needed special missionary Visas required of anyone who intended to speak at a religious gathering.

A plane ride from Calcutta to Nagaland takes about an hour. It's a short hop over Bangladesh. So here we were, stuck in Calcutta, 98 percent of our journey completed. It felt like running into an invisible wall with only one more step to take to cross the finish line.

"We have been calling, and they are saying we don't have the permit yet," Nehulie reported. "They can't tell us anything more. No one knows if it is approved or not."

We three weary travelers retired to our rooms wondering if our expedition had ended before our mission had begun. I had to rest. Even so, as I got to my room I couldn't help thinking of all the miracles God had worked in my life. God works miracles of all sorts, and arranging a travel permit seemed no more miraculous than healing twisted feet, giving sight to the blind, sending angels to protect me, or changing an unbeliever's heart. It couldn't be much different from the miracle of providing electricity to a building that had not yet passed the local building codes. Despite that, I was willing to accept that our trip might end in Calcutta because God had ordained for us to serve Him there instead of in Nagaland.

When in doubt, pray. That's what I did. "Lord, before I go to sleep, I want to know if we are going on. Do you have another plan for us here, in Calcutta? I know there is plenty you want to do here, too. Here we are, Lord. What is it we are supposed to do while we're here?" I had my Bible. I was so tired that I was almost a zombie, but I couldn't sleep until I had prayed. I mechanically opened my Bible and stared blankly down at the page. It was open at Psalms 118. I was so tired I didn't know if I had opened it there or if it had just fallen open to that passage. I started reading at verse 19. "Open to me the gates of righteousness: I will go into them, and I will praise the Lord."

When your body is as tired as mine was and your mind has almost shut down, I think your spirit must be extra receptive to God's will. In my spirit, I suddenly knew that God was going to open the gates, and we were going on to Nagaland despite the setbacks of the day. I started praising the Lord and said, "Thank you Lord." I don't even remember turning the pages, but the next thing I knew I was looking down at Isaiah 62. "Go through the gates. Prepare the way for the people..."(Isaiah 62:10). There was another reference to going through the gates. As I read the passage in Isaiah, in an instant the Lord gave me a song. I scribbled down some notes so that I would remember it the next day.

I finished my prayer and almost immediately fell asleep, confident we would continue to Nagaland. It was God's will, and in the morning, we would take the next step to complete the mission for which God had brought us around the world.

When I awoke, I was just as tired as I had been when I lay down. I dressed and went down for breakfast anyway. Nehulie and the Thomassons were already in the restaurant. I walked to the table and announced, "Nehulie, God told me we are going to go in." I recited the scriptures to the group and told them about the song God had given me. I knew it had to be the Lord talking through me because I barely had the strength to exhale much less to make my lips move and form a complete sentence.

A broad grin stretched across Nehulie's face showing a string of pearls that appeared to never have been touched by a dentist's drill bit. "Let me go make a phone call," he said with sudden energy as if he had just been baptized in a tub of ice water. He called a local commissioner. "I want to bring some American friends over to meet you," he said, careful not to divulge the purpose of his visit in advance. He knew that to say too much would doom the project. We hurried through a breakfast that consisted mostly of fruit, and then Nehulie drove us through the streets of Calcutta to the commissioner's office. The trip through the city was a different view of Calcutta than most tourists saw.

The commissioner seemed impressed with our group and our mission. He was eager to help. "How were the accommodations at the hotel?" he asked. Although he was conducting an official interview, he visited with us as casually as if we were in his living room. He seemed genuinely interested in our dilemma. Nehulie brokered a translation for the commissioner who spoke English, of sorts. I had difficulty deciphering the accent and was only able to grab an occasional word.

I recounted my prophecy while the commissioner listened politely. It was difficult to tell whether he believed a word I said or not. We didn't know if he was a Christian either, but we talked to him like he was. We assumed that he agreed with our point of view and our mission. I was telling him about the Lord giving me the verses, and he pulled a form from a drawer and began filling out a permit.

"Take this to the airport in the morning," he said. "I will send my deputy with you so there will be no problems."

All the way back to the hotel, I silently sang the song I had written the night before, while as a group, we praised God for the victory.

Later that day, Nehulie took us on a brief tour of the city. I had never seen such poverty. I took lots of pictures that showed how bad things were. As we drove, we saw a field that had big tiles lying on it. They stretched to the horizon like autumn's leaves. Each one was as big around as an office desk. Nehulie said there is a whole city of people that live among and beneath them. They slept out there because they felt safe, Nehulie said. Many were wrapped in blankets, but it was pitiful. Knowing that they were Hindu, I thought, oh, my goodness, look what their god has not done for them.

In another area, small patchwork houses, each barely more than a parking space in width and length, obliterated the natural landscape. They seemed to have been constructed from whatever materials were available. Two vertical poles connected by a solitary, flimsy, horizontal beam supported the front of a dwelling. The façade may have been pieced together from a sheet of tin and a frame with shingles nailed to it, and every joist was supported by that two-by-four beam. It was a city of lean-tos crammed together with no more than two or three feet between them. All the roofs were thatch, and if you were able to get high enough to see, the waves of thatch rolled on endlessly like a quietly turbulent ocean of reeds. If a shelter's occupants were fortunate, a smokestack might extend upward out of the thatch like the disappearing mast of a sinking ship. The floors, as far as I could tell, were earth, and the stream of trash flowing from one house washed about the base like sea foam.

In the downtown area, the streets teemed with activity and a hodgepodge of every conveyance short of a Cadillac—mostly bicycles, mopeds and rickshaws, some pieced together from wood and bicycle wheels. Traffic rules, if there were any, only seemed to apply to quadruped, motorized vehicles. The streets were teeming with people stampeding in every direction. A woman made her way across the street lugging two, four-gallon buckets hanging from leather tethers that connected to opposite ends of a spar that balanced across her shoulders. A taxi, a three-wheeled bicycle with a covered passenger seat on back, inched along in the opposite direction. It might have been a town out of the old west if not for the absence of work animals and the broad, paved roads.

The next morning the commissioner's armed deputy met us at the hotel and accompanied our little group of nomads to the airport and to the gate for our departing flight. The gate attendant demanded to see a travel permit, and when Nehulie presented him with the slip of paper the commissioner had signed, he glanced at it and snarled, "This is no good. It's not valid."

The commissioner's deputy didn't even try to reason with the attendant. He immediately drew his revolver. "Move out of the way and let them in," he commanded.

The attendant shrugged and relented as casually as though the gun were a perfectly acceptable writ of passage. Maybe we were in the Old West. Of course, the Thomassons and I had no way of knowing if the permit was valid. We didn't know what was going on. Nehulie didn't translate during the exchange, but it was obvious that the permit was written in lead, not ink, and it was only as valid to the attendant as the deputy's resolve to use the weapon. Apparently, he was convinced.

We boarded the plane a little apprehensively. It seemed at any moment that our permit could be revoked by someone with a bigger gun, but that didn't happen. We were only slightly relieved as we found our seats. We knew we wouldn't really feel safe until the small commuter plane was in the air. As the plane prepared to taxi to the runway, we realized our relief was to be short lived.

As soon as we had squeezed into our seats, an elderly Indian sprang from his and began ranting. He paced the aisles jabbering loudly until the pilot came into the cabin to calm him. Spitting demands into the pilot's face, he pointed at me and at Pat. We asked Nehulie what the man's problem was.

"He doesn't want to sit by you. He thinks you will defile him," Nehulie explained. The Hindu demanded that the pilot eject all the Americans from the plane immediately and stomped up and down the aisle of the small aircraft.

Finally, the pilot sternly told him, "Either sit there or get off the plane."

Still in a rage, the man returned to his seat, but throughout the flight, he chanted the same phrases over and over. He raised his hands and made symbolic repetitive gestures, starting low and slow and gradually building to a furious high-pitched crescendo. "Woo." Then he started all over again.

I got tickled. I tried hard not to laugh aloud. He looked so funny. It probably didn't help that I was sitting there almost convulsing trying to keep from laughing, but I couldn't help it. Of course, even though it was amusing, it was a scary situation. He seemed so out of control that he could have done anything. I was never afraid, though. Fortunately, it wasn't a long flight, or the man's continuous rants could have become tiresome. Later that evening, after we were safe in Kohima, Nagaland, Nehulie explained to us that the man was calling curses down on Pat and me throughout the flight. If I had known that, it may have seemed even funnier.

When the plane touched down again, we still weren't in Kohima, not even in Nagaland yet. It was only another relay layover. As the plane taxied toward the terminal, Mr. Thomasson pointed out the window at the armed guards lining the taxiway. We were forced to exit the plane, and the thought passed through my mind that we could be arrested for hijacking the airplane after the deputy's performance in Calcutta. Neither soldiers nor police accosted us as we exited and walked across the tarmac. We were greeted by much worse. Hatred. I had no idea what city we were in, but I could feel the loathing radiating from the eyes of other passengers in the terminal. They glared at my uncovered, blond hair as though that, of itself, was a sin. The Thomassons had darker hair, but their blue eyes merited the same disgust as my hair. It was like a whole terminal full of the elderly man who had flown into a rage at the sight of us.

Nehulie guided us through the airport. "I'm going to take you to the VIP room. I don't want you sitting out here. It could be very dangerous." He paid a fee and ushered us into the VIP lounge, a small cubicle with a few old sofas, the fabric of which was so worn that VIPs sat as much on cotton covered springs or bare foam as on the upholstery. A small window air-conditioner wheezed, struggling to maintain the room temperature at a sub-Saharan level. Nehulie paid for a meal, and we, still lagging from our transatlantic, trans-Europe, trans-India series of flights, ate quietly. Nehulie continuously checked the status of our connecting flight's arrival. He was more concerned for the well-being of his guests than we were ourselves, but then perhaps he had more insight into just how precarious our situation was. He seemed to relax a little when boarding for our flight to Demipur was announced.

We boarded the plane without further incident and arrived in Nagaland after another short flight. We were met by a disconcerting detail of armed guards. They surrounded us but never pointed their guns at us or threatened us. Not much was said, and we weren't certain that they weren't going to march us straight to the stockade. They didn't. They were there to escort us, although we were never quite sure if they were assigned to protect us or to protect the people of Nagaland from us. It started to rain just after our arrival as though the elements spurned our arrival as vehemently as the people in the penultimate leg of our trip.

The conference was already underway, and Nehulie guided his three American guests encapsulated in an envelope of uniforms to the prayer center that night in a heavy downpour. The guards seldom spoke to Nehulie or to the three Americans, but they were courteous, polite, and professional throughout the trip.

If the weather was souring, the people of Nagaland made up for it. Eleven thousand waited for us at the prayer center. Most had walked to get there, some from as far away as Nagaland's border with Myanmar. The contrast between Nagaland and the rest of India was striking. The day before it was as though we were surrounded by wolves, but the people of Nagaland greeted us like puppies delighted to see a human face.

The prayer center in Demipur had been established in the 1960s. Built like a brush arbor, there was a stage and a podium with tents, lean-tos really, that had huge poles holding up tarps. The prophecy about the three American missionaries had been delivered there during the dedication thirty years earlier.

People arriving at the conference told us over and over to tell Americans how much they loved our country for sending the gospel to them. They seemed to think that everyone in the United States is Christian and prays all the time.

The thing that impressed me the most was the religious commitment of the Naga people. Many had traveled for miles, and automobiles were almost unheard of. They walked, often carrying heavy packs or pulling loads. They braved weather conditions that could change as fast as a thunderstorm can roll across the Texas prairie. Despite the hazards and their limited resources, they entered the grounds with excitement and enthusiasm. They had faced brutal conditions just to make it to the assembly so that they could worship with other believers, and they were genuinely happy to be there. They did not come to the annual meeting out of some sense of religious obligation. They came because they wanted to be there. They wanted to worship the Lord God. They came and stayed there those four nights without any shelter and no chairs. They brought blankets, spread them, and sat on the ground. They attended morning, noon, and afternoon services and prayed between the meetings.

God performed miracles during those four days. I was interviewed by Carla Pommert from the *Burleson Star* after our return. Her report printed in the June 15, 1987 edition, summarizes the trip very well.

> Interpreters translated their words to the four fifths of the audience that could not understand English. In addition, they played instruments, sang, and prayed. "We prayed for God to heal people. One girl's hand had been clenched in a fist for ten years, and God opened her hand while we were praying," Gillaspie related. The twelve year old was brought on the platform and the people started praising God for the miracle. A group of people near the stage became overwhelmed and fell over after hearing of the miracle...It was like

a wave. People just started falling over. It looked like a giant hand pushed them down. Other people ran over and put blankets on them. Although they were escorted on and off the platform, the Nagas wanted to touch and talk to Gillaspie and the Thomassons. "We just couldn't resist."

The girl described in the newspaper article had come forward with a paralyzed hand. It was stiff and as immobile as it if it were frozen. It had been that way all her life. She had never been able to open it. It was withered. When I prayed for her, it opened up, right then. The other believers went wild at the sight of the girl's healing because many had known her all her life. Suddenly, everyone wanted even more to be prayed for by the American team. We probably laid hands on thousands of people that first night. For hours they came, just to have us lay hands on them and pray for them.

The young girl's hand was one of the more dramatic miracles that evening, but it wasn't the only one. Nehulie reported that there were thousands. We could feel the presence of God everywhere we went.

I prayed for a woman who had huge tumors in her stomach. I didn't see the tumors, but her stomach protruded. I didn't see a change while I prayed, but she believed that she was healed. After the conference, Nehulie passed on word that the woman had confirmed that the stomach tumors had disappeared over the next three days. Everyone pressed in on us, and the sense of responsibility to them was only surpassed by awe at the faith expressed by this crowd. They believed strongly that the Thomassons and I were the three Americans that had been prophesied about. They wanted to touch us. I think they thought we were angels. I fell in love with the Naga people because they were so hungry for the Word.

We stayed until late in the night laying hands on the sick, witnessing, and receiving the blessings of the Holy Spirit. Then emotionally, physically, and mentally exhausted we returned to the hotel and caught a few hours of rest before we started all over again the next morning.

GLORIA WITH THE CHILDREN OF NAGALAND.

Never leaving us, the armed guards accompanied us back to the hotel at the end of the service. We were as nice to them as we could be under the circumstances. We talked to them and praised the Lord. They seemed to enjoy us. They seemed to think we were nice people. They never interfered with our ministry, although we never got a sense that they either believed or disbelieved. It is difficult to think that anyone who witnessed the miracles we saw over those three days could be unaffected. These men were not oblivious to all that was happening, but they never said a word. They simply observed, although it was never clear if they were there to protect us from harm or to prevent us from going somewhere or saying something that could be considered incendiary to the audience, which I am sure they suspected was filled with insurrectionists.

On the drive back to the prayer conference the next morning, I held my stomach as the car bolted, jolted, and bounced over the rough road just as it had on the drive out and back the night before. We drove what seemed a long time, and although we really didn't cover more than a few miles, it took us forty-five minutes to get there. I had ridden across many unimproved roads and tractor paths in my childhood in rural Texas, but nothing matched the severity of the mountain road to the conference in Nagaland. We went out that morning and back again to the night service. Then the next morning we went back and ministered all day and that night, too.

With more than 11,000 people attending each service, I had never spoken to groups that large. At lunchtime, we took a break. There was a picnic area; we walked up steps and entered a pavilion with a thatched roof. There the

Nagas treated us like royalty. It was sometimes hard to tell who was ministering to whom. Here were these people serving us, and we thought we had
come to serve them. Everybody served, and they bowed low and spoke to us
like we were important. Four nice, comparatively well-dressed men served
our food. They bowed as they served us, showing tremendous respect.
Nehulie explained they were congressmen. They represented Nagaland at
the national government in Delhi. They were some of the highest elected
officials in the state, and they were serving us because we were held in such
high esteem. The people of Nagaland would have considered it an insult to
allow anyone of a lower rank to wait on somebody of high esteem. You have
to have somebody of equal stature, or at least as close to the same rank as
your guest as you can find. That's why the congressmen were waiting on us.
The Nagas obviously held us in very high esteem.

We were amazed. In a state that has been in quiet rebellion for a generation and that is as isolated as Nagaland, a reasonable person would expect
the horrible living conditions in Delhi and Calcutta to be idyllic by comparison. But you could see the difference in people that serve the living God.
God had blessed these people. They weren't wealthy by any means, but
the people of Nagaland were not living in squalor. There was no apparent
reason why the rest of India couldn't be like Nagaland. The Nagas were as
poor as the people of other states, but it was like you went into a different
country rather than a different state when you arrived. They lived in houses
or at least permanent structures.

Of course, one of the tenets of Hindu is that they don't kill any insects
or rodents even when the rats eat and contaminate the grain supplies. They
don't eat beef because cows are considered sacred. The people of Nagaland,
a Christian state in a Hindu country, didn't have the same restrictions on
their diet or their lifestyle. They loved chicken, and we were fed chicken
for most meals during our stay. Nevertheless, the Christians in Nagaland
were bound by the laws of a Hindu dominated, virtual theocracy. Like most
Christians, the Nagas believe that it's all right to eat meat, but the practice
was discouraged throughout the country. If we had killed a cow, I suspect
our armed escort would have hauled us straight to the hoosegow or maybe
even have summarily shot us on the spot.

God worked miracles for three nights, and the team did far more healing
than preaching. At the end of the third day, the Thomassons and I packed our

belongings. We were tired and wished we could lay hands on the airplane and find ourselves instantly at home. We weren't looking forward to the trip back. We knew it would be long, arduous, and at times unpleasant. We suspected it might even be dangerous. Until we were in Delhi, we couldn't feel safe.

EVERY SERVICE IN NAGALAND WAS PACKED. THOUSANDS OF PEOPLE HAD TREKKED FOR HOURS OR EVEN DAYS TO ATTEND.

When we arrived at the airport, Nehulie was not permitted to enter the terminal. He had already been out of Nagaland twice that year, and the authorities would not permit him to leave again, even to fly to Calcutta. Since passengers with plane tickets or residents with permits were the only people allowed into the terminal, we had to say goodbye outside.

"These are my friends, I've got to get them back to Calcutta," Nehulie argued with the airport authorities. He had done all the organization and scheduling for the group during our visit. We had never worried about tickets or boarding passes or security or meals. Nehulie had seen to all of it. Nehulie wasn't concerned because they wouldn't let him leave. He had no desire to leave Nagaland for a third time in the year, but he felt it was his duty to take care of us. He was concerned for our safety, and he tried to cram a lifetime of understanding about travel in India into the few minutes we had before our flight. He admonished us with some key instructions and cautioned us not to forget them. "Now when you get to the airport, go immediately to the VIP room," he stressed, as we stood outside the airport and said our last goodbyes. "VIP room," Nehulie reminded us before we turned away for the last time. I could almost hear him saying it again as I exited the baggage check and the three of us walked toward our plane. "Go to the VIP room."

"Oh, he was so worried," I said to the Thomassons, "but he didn't need to be." I wasn't afraid, and I don't think they were either. We knew the Lord was taking care of us. Especially after the miracles of the last three days, we knew that we would be watched over.

On arriving at the small intermediate airport, we weren't sure where the VIP room was.

"Do we go over there to pay?" Pat asked. We slowly made our way through the airport. Suddenly a man was standing in front of us. He carried himself with the confidence and authority of an armed deputy although neither the Thomassons nor I ever saw a weapon.

"May I help you?"

"Well, we were trying to find the VIP room," I explained.

"Follow me."

He led us to the VIP room, and as we got settled in, he got us something to eat. "Stay here. Don't leave this room, and you'll be alright," he instructed us. We smiled at each other and commented how much like Nehulie he sounded.

While we snacked, a storm blew in, and airport traffic became unpredictable. After an hour or so, our new guardian returned.

"The plane from Calcutta has been delayed," he explained. He told us it wouldn't arrive until after the storm had passed through. He checked back with us every half hour or so, making sure we were comfortable, updating us on the flight status, and assuring us that the plane was still coming. During one update, Will pushed a bill toward him.

"Here, I want to give you a tip," he said. The man had not asked for a gratuity. That itself was odd because everybody in the airport seemed to have only one hand for work, the other was a permanently outstretched palm.

"Tip. Tip. Tip." They constantly called, but Nehulie's proxy hadn't asked for a cent, and he looked confused.

"Tip?"

"Yes, we want to give you a tip," I added.

"We want to give you some money for helping us," explained Pat.

But it was as though he didn't know what we were trying to do.

"Well, at least let us pay for the VIP room," Will said.

"Pay?"

"Yes, we know the room is not free. You shouldn't pay for it. We will be happy to pay ourselves," I tried again. It was so strange. He spoke English fluently, but he seemed absolutely uneducated about money and tipping. He didn't expect anything from us, and we didn't know if he had paid for the VIP room or not.

Finally, he announced that our plane had arrived. "Get your things. Go straight to the gate and get on the plane, and you'll be safe," he instructed us.

We gathered our luggage and made our way to the gate looking back to acknowledge the man who had been so helpful. He was nowhere to be seen. We looked around for him again before boarding the plane. We wanted to express our gratitude, but there was no sign of him.

A few years later when Nehulie returned to the states for a visit, I told him about the strange man in the airport. "Oh, God sent an angel," he exclaimed matter-of-factly. "Nobody who works for the airport will do that. There's nobody to wait on people. God sent an angel," he laughed, delighted. That made him remember something else, "Oh yes, two weeks after you left, we received notification that your travel permit to Nagaland was denied." We were there illegally during our entire trip. Even when we were being escorted by government troops, we had been in Nagaland illegally. I supposed the worst they would have done was deport us if our denial had come through during our visit, but it's hard to know for sure.

All the contrivances of man are insignificant when God's hand is in the work. He had determined that the Thomassons and I would go to Nagaland. It was exciting and one of the greatest blessings in my life to be included in the fulfillment of a prophecy. There is an incomparable feeling about knowing that you are walking along the path of God's perfect will for your life.

Chapter 56

And Change To Spare

URING THE TRIP back to the United States, we had a layover in England. Setting down in London's Gatwick International airport after a six-hour flight from Calcutta, my first thoughts were of a hot shower and getting my hair done. I found a small boutique near the hotel and made an appointment.

As I took a seat in the chair and the stylist started to work, the conversation turned from the standard niceties—the weather, hair styles, and fashion—to my trip and the reason for it. The young lady shampooed while I told her all about it. When the story was done, the girl told me she had recently gotten married. She was not a Christian, she confessed, but she and her husband had discussed how they should raise their children in an increasingly godless world. While she trimmed my hair, I told her about Jesus Christ, and by the time the young woman told me to look into the mirror for a final inspection, we were both looking at our new make-overs. I left a tip, but the money had no value in comparison to the gift that she had received from Jesus Christ. As she was kneeling in prayer, the Thomassons walked into the boutique. I had been gone longer than expected, and they had started looking for me so that we could go sightseeing together. When they saw us, they knew what was happening. The missionary couple waved at me and without a word turned and left.

She was one more person whom I had gotten the attention of as they blindly followed the crowd over the cliff, one more who had listened and looked toward the cross. If we had flown to India and hadn't seen one miracle, if not one person had shown up to listen, this one soul would have made the trip worthwhile. I praised God for saving her no less than I praised him for delivering us through the dangers of the trip or for healing a young girl's hand or the tumors in a woman's stomach. This, the miracle of salvation, is God's greatest miracle.

The next day, the missionary trio planned to ride a tour bus and take in as many sights in London as we could during our brief visit. While we waited for the bus to arrive, the tour coordinator proudly told me that they had managed to seat me next to my husband. I wasn't sure what to expect. If John had come to London, it would certainly be one of the biggest surprises of the trip. I was thrilled at the prospect, and at the same time, I suspected that something else was afoot. John would have surprised me earlier if he had come to London, and we would have stayed together in the hotel. It wouldn't make any sense for him to join me only for the tour. I didn't let my hopes get the best of me.

I anxiously scanned the faces of the other passengers as I made my way through the bus and took my assigned seat next to a man about my age. Soon the two of us were laughing together like old friends. His last name was Gillespie. Later, as I must confess many of my conversations do, we turned to the subject of God. While I'm regarded as outspoken by many, I don't normally assault others with my Christian witness. I speak to them during the normal course of human commerce and communication, and eventually God enters the conversation on His own, often as the topic of conversation moves to occupations.

The man confessed he had been trained in the ministry, but he had traveled to the end of the road with God. He had pledged his service to God as a pastor several years earlier when he had been sick. He told God in his prayers that he would preach if God would save his life. He survived, and he kept his promise. He attended the Southwestern Baptist Theological Seminary in Fort Worth, Texas, a few miles from my home. While in the seminary, he sold insurance to support himself. He wasn't home much. The early years of a ministry often test the commitment of a marriage. When you're trying to start a ministry and maintain a full time job, it can be especially difficult. Eventually, his wife left him. Because he was divorced, the church had rescinded his ordination. His life was falling apart, and he felt that he no longer had a ministry to offer the Lord.

He had no idea where to go from there. He still felt that he should be in the ministry, but the choice had been taken away from him. I told him that people had tried to tell me all my life that I had nothing to offer as a pastor. If I had listened to them instead of the Lord, I never would have taken that first step. It's just a matter of taking the first step and believing that God will guide you to the next. It's just like the first step toward salvation. The first step toward ministry is making the decision that you will do it. That takes you out of the world's flow and sets you on a different path. Make the decision and then let that decision guide your steps. I finally told him, "Look at me. I'm a woman pastor."

He had to confess I was right. None of us really has anything that the Lord needs. He's God. He already has everything He wants, except for one thing: you. He's the voice in the unconsumed burning bush. He didn't need Moses to lead the people of Israel out of Egypt. He had established the prophecy, His contract with the people of Israel, and He fulfilled it using Moses. Moses only had to be willing. I explained that I would have been very content to serve God as a youth minister and leader of the Steppingstone. I had loved that ministry. I never wanted to be a preacher. In fact, I had repeatedly refused to acknowledge God's call to preach. The Steppingstone was my will, but God had led me through that ministry as part of my training for leadership of a church. The youth ministry was a steppingstone that God placed in the stream so that I could step into His ultimate will for my life. Once I acknowledged that, I realized how silly my protestations and procrastinations were.

When we know we are out of His will, nothing seems to go right, even if we are financially or professionally successful. When we know that we are walking in His will, even if life appears to be falling apart and we're poor, we are happy because we know that we are serving Him. I tried to help him see some of his alternatives. There are a lot of denominations and organizations of churches that do not disqualify ministers because they are divorced. What mattered most was his relationship with the Lord, not his relationship with any denomination or group of people.

He was grateful for the advice that the Thomassons and I offered, and we all praised God together when Mr. Gillespie revealed that he had gone to England in search of an answer to his dilemma. He had taken the trip to seek an answer from God about his life and ministry. We were the answer to his prayer. That day Mr. Gillespie decided to return to the ministry. God had him and us on the trip at the right place and the right time.

God works so many different angles to show us His will for our lives. It's always a blessing to see the pieces fit into place.

He was still using me in people's lives even after we had left Nagaland. And he's using me today, every day. That's one thing that each of us as a Christian must remember. Our Christian witness and responsibility doesn't stop when we take a seat on a site-seeing bus. We are not spectators who passively accept things as they are. We, who bear His name, have changed the world in His name. Too many of us seem to think that the Great Commission is a thing of the past. While it's not our job to beat people over the head with the Bible, we can open it in front of them, show it to them if they ask, and if they are willing, we can lead them in the sinner's prayer.

The song that God had given me in the hotel room in Calcutta became a routine part of the Sunday services for several years. We continued to sing it sometimes in services at the Lighthouse church until we merged with Open Door ministries in 2013. So many blessings that came out of that trip are still part of my life today, and I pray that the cosmetologist and the man on the bus also have songs for Jesus Christ that they are still singing today.

After we got back home, the *Burleson Star's* reporter interviewed me about the trip. It was a good article, but how could any news account or this book convey the glorious experience of seeing people healed, leading the lost to Jesus Christ, or counseling someone back onto the path for his life. If you want to know how those things feel, all you have to do is take that first step and share Jesus with someone you know, or maybe someone you don't yet know.

My first Sunday back in Burleson was a stark contrast to Nagaland. It rained, but the similarity ended there. We had a good crowd, but attendance was down. In our suburban area, most of us have garages, cars, and umbrellas. The people of Nagaland, if they were fortunate, had clothing or newspapers to hold over their heads. Some of us have trouble getting to church one day a week in our late model automobiles. The people of Nagaland walked in some cases for days to attend a four-day event. Many of us drive through rain, sleet, ice, and snow to go to work, but when it comes to worship, well, let's just say the people of Nagaland are committed to worship. It's first with them. They were so impressed that American Christians had come to visit. They thought they would benefit from our messages and from our faith, but the truth is, the blessings were all ours.

Although things have improved for Nagaland in the intervening years since our trip, Christians everywhere should remember to include the people of this isolated territory in their prayers. Only God has the power to protect them from the oppression and idolatry that surrounds them. Don't think for a minute that oppression is a thing of the past. There are many countries where sharing the message of Jesus Christ can get you arrested or killed. There are many countries where a baptism will earn a new believer a death sentence.

Chapter 57

Stone

As soon as the church was financially able, we once again started emphasizing the youth ministry. On February 6, 1988, we opened the Stone in Wood Shopping Center, a small strip a few blocks away from the church. The Stone was a place for young people to meet and praise God together. It was a way of continuing a ministry devoted exclusively to the young people in our community. As Otis described it to the *Burleson Star* reporter in April, the Stone was a "cross between a Christian coffee house and a youth center." As we had originally planned for the Steppingstone, the Stone offered music by mostly local bands; movies; games, including table tennis and foosball; and Bible studies.

A lot of young people participated. Many of them had lost a regular meeting place with the closing of Dalton's Corner, a very popular, although secular, attraction in old, downtown Burleson. For several years, it had drawn young people from all over the metroplex.

There were sixty to seventy-five young people at the Stone on Wednesday and Saturday nights. The young people painted the wall of the building with the image of a huge hand reaching out to the earth and the words, "God's love reaching out." Every time I looked at it, I was reminded of my vision for a youth ministry in Burleson.

"We go out on Friday night and talk to kids on the street and familiarize those kids with the Stone. It's another place to go with a different atmosphere," Otis told the reporter.

While our emphasis was on the older teenagers, young people from six to twenty found their way to the Stone. Like the original Steppingstone, the organization did not exist to promote the teachings of any particular denomination. If families of the kids who came to us during the week had a regular church home, we encouraged them to go to church with their parents. Although the Steppingstone had established the Stone, other churches helped support it, Otis told the reporter.

Music groups from the Steppingstone and First Baptist Church played at the center regularly on "band night," every Saturday. Groups including LaFe, the John Cox band, and Heir Force, performed frequently.

Tuesday was Bible study night with a youth encounter group that started at 7:30. The thirty to forty young people, mostly eighth and ninth graders, discussed the problems they faced in the modern world and sought answers for those problems in the Bible. Secular counseling services often pop up after a major disaster or a tragedy that affects the youth in a community and then disappear quietly after the immediate crisis is over, but young people need a place and people they can go to for guidance and counseling all the time. That's the kind of service the Stone tried to provide. Our attendance increased when there was some kind of local crisis, but there was always a need for our services.

It's hard to estimate the number of lives that were affected by the ministry of the Stone. Each person saved through its efforts will live with God through eternity. How can you measure that? There is no way to measure the effect of the counseling services either. A twenty-year-old Burleson man came for counseling one night. His arms were covered with scars from his attempted suicides, and he was once again contemplating throwing his life away. On another night, Otis said he sensed that a seventeen-year-old Burleson woman, sitting in the parking lot outside the Stone, was thinking about suicide. He talked with her and invited her in.

Chapter 58

Conquering Cancer

I N THE SUMMER of 1987, not long after we had returned from India, I conducted funerals for two women who had died from breast cancer. At times, it seemed as though death was the only prognosis for the disease that affects more than ten percent of all women. In my position as pastor, I was acutely aware of its prevalence and its devastating effects. It seemed there was always a family wrestling with cancer of a loved one, even though cancer treatment had come a long way in the last few decades.

I believe in healing. God healed Richelle's foot, and He saved my unborn baby. He has always been with me. He has guided my family and the Lighthouse church through illness and pain. There is nothing He cannot do.

I also know that sometimes people don't get healed when they ask for it. I don't understand why, but I believe that God would play no part in the healing of someone who never asks, who hasn't prayed for it, and who doesn't have faith. Healing, like the salvation miracle itself, requires us to believe and trust in God, and it requires that we ask. Almost every one of the Bible's accounts of healing by Jesus described an act of faith by the sick person or by someone who cared for them. The woman who touched the hem of Jesus's garment was healed because of her faith; a man lowered through the roof of a house received healing because of his faith and that of his friends; a little girl was raised from death because of her father's faith.

I had exercised that faith five years earlier, in 1982, when I found a lump in my left side. I hadn't gone to the doctor. Instead, I prayed for healing. I didn't tell anyone in the congregation about the lump. One Sunday morning we were singing the lyrics that Jesus is our healer, and while we were singing, the Lord said, "Tell the people that I am healing people right now." I did, and immediately I felt warmth almost like being immersed in a warm bath. I knew I was being healed. Sure enough, after the service when I felt for the lump, it was gone.

In September of 1987, within a month after burying the second of the two beloved women, I discovered a new lump in my other breast. As too many women do, I put off going to the doctor. A few weeks later, while I ministered to people during the altar call, I urged anyone to come forward who needed healing. Several people came forward, among them a young woman who asked me to pray for her. She was a nurse at Huguley Hospital and wanted prayers because she had been diagnosed with breast cancer. She was going to have surgery on the following Tuesday. I prayed for her, and on Tuesday when she was being checked prior to surgery, doctors discovered that her tumor was totally gone. I never doubted for a moment that the nurse would be healed.

At that time I still hadn't visited the doctor about the lump in my breast. When I finally stopped procrastinating in October, I was diagnosed with breast cancer. I felt the same wave of nausea that many women feel when they hear the word. It sounded like a death knell.

I said the same prayer for myself that I had said for the young woman a few weeks before. There was no difference in my faith when I prayed for myself and when I prayed for the nurse. There was no difference in my faith in the doctor's office and my faith when I stood with the congregation five years earlier and received my healing.

The doctor told me I needed an operation right away. The scan indicated that the cancer was in an advanced stage, and she believed a radical mastectomy should be performed immediately. A biopsy confirmed the doctor's suspicions. During the post biopsy consultation, the surgeon illustrated how widespread the tumor was by drawing a picture. The lump was about the size of a knuckle.

The tumor flattened and then spread out all over my chest wall on one side. It extended down into my rib cage. It was in an advanced stage.

The doctor urged me to move forward immediately. She almost couldn't believe it when I said that I would wait until the next week. I insisted that I would only consent to the surgery after I had told the congregation at Steppingstone about my illness and sought church members' prayers in the Sunday service. To her chagrin, we scheduled the surgery for the first week in November. That was on Thursday.

I never doubted that the cancer would be gone when I reported back to the doctor. I believed that God would heal my body and take away the cancer, and on Sunday morning, I planned to preach on healing. No matter what happens to us, no matter what the circumstances, God's Word is true. God does not lie. We must stand upon His Word. That Sunday morning, I told the people of the church, and everyone started praying. The love of God reached out to me. The Holy Spirit came in, and we had an awesome service. God performed healing miracles in people's lives.

While we were praising and worshipping, I felt like I was floating above the floor. I couldn't tell if my feet were on the ground. Nobody said anything about seeing me hovering above the floor, but it didn't make a difference. I felt light as a feather, and when I preached, I continued thinking that I was floating. The glory of God descended over me, and I knew I was healed.

I still planned to report for the surgery. There were some people in the church who rebuked me for going back to the doctor if I believed I was healed. I had preached on healing many times. People had been healed in church services throughout my ministry, but I had never told anyone not to follow up their healing with a visit to the doctor. In fact, sometimes we need that confirmation. Nevertheless, some of the church members felt that if my faith had been strong enough, the surgery would not have been required. There were some people who walked right up and scolded me, saying that I should not have surgery and that I should stand solely on faith.

John disagreed with them. He insisted that I needed to have the surgery. If the doctors found that I didn't need it, they wouldn't go forward with it. Some of my critics insisted, "Well even if you are not healed, you should not have the surgery." I suppose they felt that it was God's will for me to suffer with the illness if I wasn't healed, but it is not God's will for us to be sick.

After we had scheduled the surgery, I had asked the doctor to schedule another biopsy on the same morning as the operation. I warned the surgeon that I would be healed in Sunday's prayer service, and I wanted another biopsy as confirmation. I firmly believed the tumor, if it were still there at all, would no longer be malignant.

I went in on Monday morning, and they did another biopsy. It was still cancer, and they proceeded with the mastectomy. As I was prepped for surgery, I continued to pray. I struggled with the contradiction between my experience on Sunday and the results of the second biopsy. I knew I had been healed, yet the doctors insisted I needed the surgery. As far as they could tell, there had been no change. As I succumbed to the anesthetics and drifted into sleep, I continued to claim my healing.

Afterward, the surgeon told me, "God heard your prayers." When they got in, the tumor had shrunk. It was not as large or as widespread as they initially thought. The feeders that the doctor had described as roots going down into my rib cage had turned loose. The tumor had shrunk so much that there was a big flap around the cavity where it had been. They hadn't done the radical mastectomy in which the chest wall muscles under the breast are removed in addition to all the lymph nodes under the arm. They performed a modified radical mastectomy. They did not scrape the bones and take out everything under my arm as they would have with the radical mastectomy. They took out some lymph nodes, but not all of them, and there was cancer in the lymph nodes, too.

It was a miracle that the tumor turned out to be smaller than it had been at first and that the complete radical mastectomy was not required, but the diminished size of the tumor was only half the miracle. Because the tumor had shrunk, radiation was no longer required. The surgeon had consulted with the oncologist before the surgery, and the two of them had agreed that I would need six months of chemotherapy and twelve weeks of radiation. After the surgery, the doctors consulted again, and the oncologist changed his analysis. The cancer was not in my bones, so the radiation therapy wouldn't help.

That was an answer to prayer. God had obviously moved in my behalf. It remains a mystery to me why I didn't receive complete healing. The cancer wasn't completely removed, but it was apparent that my condition had changed dramatically since the first biopsy.

Some people might try to rationalize why the tumor had not completely disappeared. Some would argue that if I had waited and prayed more the tumor would have completely disappeared. I don't. I just praise God unceasingly for the healing I received. The majority of the congregation displayed an outpouring of love that was very healing to me. I received so many flowers while I was in the hospital that my room looked like a florist's shop. When I came home, an abundance of food was brought in, and I received hundreds of wonderful get-well cards. I will never forget the encouragement and loyalty of the Steppingstone congregation.

There are a lot of things we don't understand. I'm not going to worry about them. I received complete healing, didn't I? Between the miraculous healing of the tumor by God's power alone, the science that enabled the surgery and treatment, and the skill of the doctors, I was healed. Maybe the lesson is that God uses man and the wonderful knowledge of science that He has given us to complete His will in our lives, just as He relies on Christians to complete the work that Jesus started with His death on the cross. We, the believers, are the ones whom God has used to complete the work of Christ by delivering the message of salvation to others. I don't know the whys.

I came to a conclusion that when you don't understand, just trust. All the way through the Bible, we are told to trust in the Lord. When you trust somebody, you don't need to understand. When you don't have all the knowledge about something and you believe anyway—that's trust. Children trust their parents. Like a parent, God knows things that we may not be ready to understand. He knows our limits and doesn't burden us with the details. I just trusted the Lord, and I learned a lot about trust from that experience.

Chapter 59

Spiritual Chemo

CHEMOTHERAPY WAS HARD. The surgery was the first week of November. During the first week of December, I started what was supposed to be six months of chemo. It was a very strong treatment. They hooked me up to three intravenous bags in each session that took about three hours. When I sat for my first treatment, the nurse who was hanging the IV bags on the hooks of the support tree said, "This one will get your hair. It is strong and kills the fast growing cells. Within three days of this treatment, you will wake up one morning and your hair will be on your pillow." Then she hung another one and said, "And this one will get your hair, too." Either of the medications by itself would have caused my hair to fall out. But the nurse wasn't done with her prognostication, "With both of these, you are going to lose your hair very quickly." Then she hung the third bag and didn't say anything at all about it.

There I was, pastor of a church. I had only missed two Sundays after the surgery. I had just gotten back in the pulpit, and now I was starting chemotherapy. By that time, many church members knew that the doctor had said my cancer was in an advanced stage, and many of them thought that meant I was going to die. Some of them were friends of the two women who had died of breast cancer the previous summer.

I feel like this experience endowed me with more compassion for people who have health issues and don't get healed. It does not mean you do not have faith. I knew I had faith, and I knew I believed. I was not fearful at all. The doctor and nurses thought I had a lot of faith because I was joyful. When they came in to start the treatment or disconnect, I was always cheerful.

I remembered a sermon preached by Jerry Savelle titled, "The devil can't get your goods if he can't get your joy." The joy of the Lord was my strength throughout the ordeal.

Because I was a pastor, some of the nurses talked to me about their problems. I talked with them about the Lord. There is always an opportunity to witness if you are open to it. One of the head nurses found out that I had counseled kids and their families about drugs. She told me about her sixteen-year-old son's drug abuse. She was very upset and asked my advice. I talked to her, gave her pamphlets, and counseled her about her son. After I started chemo, Sandy Browning brought me a booklet, *How to Survive a Night in the Lions' Den*. The nurse came in just as I finished reading it.

"Can I read that?" she asked.

I gave her the book. I thought it would bless her with her son.

I ministered all the time while I was in the hospital. God used me, even in my illness, to minister to the medical staff at the clinic, too. I have always understood that my ministry is sitting right in front of me. Not everyone is pastor of a church, but everyone has a ministry. At home, at work, at the kids' soccer game, taking out the trash, or lying in a hospital bed, each of us is presented with opportunities every day to say something about Jesus Christ to someone else, sometimes to people we have never met, sometimes to people we have spoken to a thousand times. Before I left the hospital, the nurse reported back to me how much the little book had helped and encouraged her.

Chapter 60

Hair Apparent

MY DOCTOR WAS telling me that my cancer was still in an advanced stage. It was a negative prophecy, and I recognized it for exactly that. Here I was, pastor of a church. The church was full of people every Sunday, and we had a great congregation, but the preponderance of things had me wondering if the time had come for me to step aside. I said, "Lord, I need to know if I am going to get over this and go on with my ministry. Could you give me a sign?"

The Bible says a woman's hair is her glory (I Corinthians 11:15). So I asked God to spare my hair as confirmation that His glory still rested upon me and as a sign the ministry would continue beyond this trial. I asked for a very specific sign so that I would have no doubt about it. Since just one of the intravenous therapies was expected to make my hair fall out and I had gotten two of them, keeping my hair would take a miracle. I admit it; if I were a man, I might not have asked for that sign. That was important to me, and besides, all the worldly prophets were predicting that my hair would fall out. What better sign could there be that my ministry was destined to continue than that the Holy Spirit overcame the prophecies of man?

I didn't tell anybody, except my close friends and prayer partners, what I had asked of the Lord until everyone saw that I had kept my hair. Then I told everyone about my request to the Lord. My hair never came out. That was a real testimony to everybody who knew me. The oncologist, my surgeon, and the clinic nurses were astounded.

They asked, "What is your secret to keeping your hair?"

I said, "Prayer. A group of women at church is praying for me right now. They are praying for my healing, and they are praying that I will not experience any bad side effects."

They said, "How wonderful. Everybody needs that!"

At one point the surgeon said, "Well, since you have hair, take good care of it. Don't put any dye on it and don't get a permanent because your hair is probably not going to be as healthy as normal."

I followed the doctor's advice and didn't get a permanent. My hair got pretty straight. It was fashionable to pull hair back and clip it, and I wore it in a ponytail a lot, but it was wonderful having that confirmation. It was a blessing to our congregation, too. Everyone acknowledged the miracle of my hair.

I had the chemotherapy concoction each month. Cory drove me to the clinic at about lunchtime on the day of my appointment. The treatment took all afternoon, and John picked me up after he got off work.

During the fourth month, the vein started collapsing when the nurse inserted the needle. Instead of going into my vein, the medicine was going into the flesh of my hand. It was very painful. I had been told that it would rot my skin. So they took out the IV and tried again. It took seven sticks to infuse all three bags. Later the nurse told me, "When you come back we may need to put in a port for the last two months of treatment."

When I started the course of treatment, the doctors decided they would not install a port so that it wouldn't be necessary to stick a new vein for each treatment. As John drove me home that afternoon, I dreaded the next month's episode. "Lord, I do not want to have to go through that." Having a port put in is an outpatient procedure, but it is similar to surgery, and afterward you have to keep the site clean so that it doesn't get infected. I wasn't looking forward to it. But the Lord spoke to me, "You don't need any more chemo. It has done all the good it is going to do, and if you take any more, it will only weaken you. It will actually work against you."

I was so excited. I knew the word was from the Lord. Even though I got sick the next few days—I was always sick within a day or two after a treatment and for several days afterward—I was excited because I knew the treatment had ended. I praised God despite the nausea and weakness. The treatment usually knocked my blood count way down. Even so, I went to church, and I never missed. I even preached on Sundays. At the time, Cory was on staff, but he didn't preach much. He was a Sunday school teacher and hadn't entered the pulpit ministry yet. So I preached every Sunday and taught on Wednesday nights. I preached three times a week, even during those times when, about ten days after each treatment, my blood count bottomed out and I became incredibly weak.

One Sunday morning I was so weak I could hardly walk. As I came into church, Pat Shetter was sitting in the pew near the front. I had to pass her to walk up on the steps to get up on the platform. I stopped and said, "Pat, pray that I have the strength to get up those steps," because I thought I might have to crawl.

She said she would. I am sure she was praying as I started up because I managed to get past the steps. I got a microphone, and as always, I stood off to the side while the worship leader began the music. Steve Bowersox was our worship leader at that time. He was really good. He worked with Integrity Music after he left the Steppingstone. Later he was worship leader at a big church in Jacksonville, Florida, and he founded the Bowersox Institute of Music, a non-profit organization dedicated to the development of worship musicians. He authored the *Worship Musician's Theory Course, Vocal Aerobics* and *The Worship Leaders Survival Kit,* and today is recognized as a leader in the area of advanced technology for churches.

As soon as Steve started the first song, the Spirit of the Lord hit me like a bolt of electricity. It went through my body, and I started dancing. I danced during the entire praise part of our service, and I was full of energy. When we got through with praise and worship, I preached and continued to be full of energy. By the time I got home, I felt weak again, but the Lord had brought me through the illness and exhaustion. He had held me up while I preached.

The next day I called the oncology clinic and cancelled my next appointment for chemotherapy. I told the scheduling clerk that I no longer needed it. Almost immediately, I started getting calls and letters from the clinic urging me to complete the chemotherapy treatments and warning me that my cancer was in an advanced stage.

The next time I went to the doctor for my tri-monthly check up and routine blood work, she told me, as she pressed around my neck to see if there were any new bumps, "Now you want to be sure you keep your appointments regularly because from the time we diagnosed you, you probably only had about two years to live." She added that she had two patients whose cancer was not as advanced as mine. One had died that week, and the other would probably die before the week ended. Each of them had had surgery about a year and a half before, and their cases weren't even as advanced as mine.

I asked, "Well, if I am going to die, why do I need to continue the check-ups at all?"

"We can monitor your condition, adjust your treatment immediately, and make you more comfortable," the doctor explained.

As she was speaking those words, it was as though a dark cloud dropped over me. It was trying to envelope me. The doctor left the room, and I began repeating, "By His stripes I am healed." I claimed healing, but at the same time I was fighting off the spirit of doubt and doom that the doctor had dropped as casually as tossing a napkin into the waste basket. I was trying to keep it off of me. It was a spiritual struggle, and I knew darkness was trying to overtake me through the power of the doctor's words.

My surgeon was a wonderful Christian woman. She was a member of a prominent Baptist church. She had prayed for me before she did the surgery, but in making the pronouncement that my death had been, and possibly still was, eminent, she was looking at the medical facts and basing her statement on her personal experience and education in the field of medicine. That was all she had to go by. She was telling me the cold, brutal truth and was simply trying to be honest, but her words were like a death sentence. I knew they empowered the devil to try to make what she was saying come to pass.

Up until then almost everything that had been said around me was positive. The people at church believed I was healed. My hair was evidence of Jesus' victory over my cancer. But when the doctor delivered her powerful prognosis, Mohammed Ali couldn't have punched me any harder. So I kept repeating, "By His stripes I am healed." Only the Holy Spirit could lift me back up. It was impossible to ignore what the doctor had said. A word, whether negative or positive, is a powerful force.

I rode home with depression in close pursuit. I felt a demon of cancer in the room with me all evening. It lurked in every corner and was waiting to pounce the moment I let my guard down. If I gave in to the doctor's words for one second, they would swarm over my health completely, and I would die. I had no doubt about that. I couldn't see anything with my natural eyes, but in the spirit, I could see that cloud.

The feeling hovered over me throughout the evening while I continued to pray and claim healing. I reviewed the Biblical accounts of healing, and I went to sleep speaking scriptures: "He was wounded for our transgressions.

He was bruised for our iniquities and the chastisement of our peace is upon Him, and by His stripes I am healed."

I woke the next morning and had forgotten about it. The doctor's words didn't cross my mind. I barely thought about what had happened the day before. I did my work around the house, got dressed, and went to the church. After I got into the office, Cory came in and said, "I want to tell you what happened. God woke me up during the night, and I had to pray for you."

I hadn't told anybody what the doctor had said because I didn't want to give any power to those words. I was not going to speak them out loud to anybody, not even to John.

Cory described a vision he had while praying the evening before. He said that he had seen a dark cloud hovering over me. He began rebuking the cloud as it drew nearer. He saw into it, and rather than a mist, it seemed to be made up of a cluster of insects like flies.

In some parts of the Bible, the devil is called Beelzebub. That means "Lord of the Flies," and the flies represented the demons that were pursuing me. Cory rebuked them, and they went away. Then he saw a praying mantis. It was trying to get its spiked forelegs around me. Cory rebuked that, too. After he had pressed on with the spiritual warfare, he looked up praying mantis in the encyclopedia to see what the vision may have meant. The word mantis derives from the Greek word for prophet or fortuneteller.

As Cory described the cloud, I realized that was the first time I had thought about the doctor's prognosis all day. I had gone to bed with a cloud looming over me. I had awakened perfectly at peace. The doctor's words were forgotten, but when Cory told me about the dark cloud, I remembered the doctor and how I had felt the night before. Immediately I knew what Cory's vision meant. The mantis represented the doctor's words. The doctor was prophesying my death. Those words were overcome by Cory's prayer.

Cory's vision exactly described what I had been feeling: a heavy dark cloud settling over me. The praying mantis bites the head off its prey, and that's what the doctor's words would have done to me if I hadn't escaped through prayer and constantly repeating the promises of the Bible. I know the cancer would have devoured me.

I knew that Cory had waged warfare on my behalf. Of course, I had, too, in speaking the words, "I am healed." While my constant prayer and recitation of the scripture took on the direct attack and kept the cloud from overwhelming me, Cory's intercessory prayer flanked the devil's attack. Through Cory's intercession, we had complete victory over the illness.

I said, "Cory, that is exactly what happened to me yesterday." I described the sensation that a cloud was trying to envelop me. I told him how I had rebuked the doctor's words. "It was like her words were a negative prophecy," I told him.

I have never doubted the power of intercessory prayer. The prayer group had prayed for President Reagan even when we had no idea how he would be attacked, and Cory prayed for me without knowing anything about the attack I was experiencing.

It is important that we pray for one another. Every Christian is fighting some battle. Though we know we will have the ultimate victory through Christ Jesus, we struggle daily with those things that would destroy our health, our faith, our finances, and our witness. We must pray constantly for one another. Prayer, the word of God, and faith are our most powerful weapons.

Chapter 61

Taking Your Lumps

E VEN THOUGH I had fought through to victory, my struggles with cancer weren't over. About a year later (1989), a knot came up in my side. It seemed about the size of a lemon when I first realized it was there. Then it just kept growing over several weeks until it was more like an orange. You could have seen it protruding out my side. It was so large it was getting difficult to wear my clothes. When I sat down or stood up, the burst of pain in my waist was excruciating. I nearly cried out.

John repeatedly told me I needed to get the problem treated, saying, "You have got to get to the doctor," but I was worried what might happen if I had to tell the congregation the cancer was back. I thought, after all we have been through, after all that the people in the church have been through with me, after the surgery and the miraculous recovery, what would happen now? The doctor had told me that if the cancer came back it would have metastasized, and it probably would be in a lot of places. I kept the lump and the pain a secret and continued to perform my duties as pastor. I still hadn't told anyone except John about it until one Friday when Richelle visited me at home. "I have got to either be healed or I am going to have to go back to the doctor, and then you know they are going to do surgery," I told my daughter.

I asked her to pray for me and to continue praying for me.

The next day, John was working and I was home alone. I spent the day talking with the Lord and crying out to Him while I was studying. Sitting on the sofa, I said, "Lord, how can I connect my faith with you? I know I have faith, but I can't seem to connect it to get this miracle." I started crying, "Lord, I know that you love me more than I can understand. I know that you love me more than my earthly father does, and I know that he loves me so much that if he could, he would make this go away. I need you, my heavenly Father, to make this go away."

I also said that I felt like I had not fulfilled the mission that He had given me. "I feel like I need to be here for this church and for my grandchildren." Of course, a lot of my grandchildren had not even been born yet. As I prayed and continued to plead my case to the Lord, I suddenly felt as though He had taken me into His lap to comfort me. I was like a little girl sitting in my father's lap with my head on his shoulder. I felt comforted, and peace came over me. Complete peace. I wasn't thinking anything. I wasn't thinking about my healing. I wasn't thinking about my ministry. I simply felt the love of God.

The burden was gone. After that, I went about the rest of my day as usual, except I was no longer worried about the lump or the pain. I was secure in the belief that I had turned all the issues concerning my health, my ministry, and even my grandchildren over to the Lord. Whatever happened would be in line with His calling upon my life.

The next morning, just like every morning for the past several weeks, the first thing I did was reach down and touch the lump. Just to sit up in bed could be painful, and I was in the habit of holding it as I moved around, getting out of bed. Many times, I had covered it with my hand, applying pressure to reduce the pain as I raised myself up.

When I put my hand over the lump, it was gone! My hand pressed in. I knew then that I was not going to have cancer again. God had totally conquered cancer in my body. I thought back to my prayer when I asked God, "How do I connect my faith with your power?" I realized the Holy Spirit had directed my thoughts to the Father's love. That was His answer—to humble myself as a little child and put my whole trust in the perfect love of the Father. That was the connection!

Let there be no doubt. Faith is first. Jesus said, "whatever things you ask when you pray, believe that you receive them" (Mark 11:24, NKJV). Galatians 5:6 says, "faith works through love" (NKJV), and I Corinthians 13:13 assures us, "and now abide faith, hope, love, these three; but the greatest of these is love" (NKJV). The Holy Spirit revealed to me that God's love connects us to His power. He brought me what I needed—the manifest presence and comfort of His love.

Chapter 62

The Russian Connection

N 1988 AND 1989, the Soviet Union relaxed restrictions that denied its citizens the right to move abroad. Many Russians took advantage of the new policy and left the country knowing that they may never be able to return home. Evangelical Christians, who had been subjected to years of ostracism and persecution by the government, were among those who left.

Immigrants to the United States were required to have a citizen sponsor before the government could issue a visa, and several refugee organizations throughout the state of Texas provided assistance to immigrants under the auspices of state and federal agencies. In 1980, the Refugee Service of North Texas provided assistance and helped relocate expatriates in the Dallas area. The agency helped find US sponsors for Russian refugees and provided translation services for refugees who had been relocated to Texas.

The *Fort Worth Star-Telegram* ran an article about a local church that sponsored a Russian family. The article described the conditions that Russian immigrants were leaving behind and the difficulties they faced in the United States. It described how the new arrivals to our country were amazed by the freedoms that Americans took for granted.

Sandy Browning spotted the article and immediately thought the Steppingstone could host a family, too. At least our church should be able to do something to help. She cut out the article and brought it with her to the next meeting of church elders, where she summarized it and proposed that the Steppingstone sponsor a family.

We had been praying for the Soviet Union in our prayer meetings for years. We especially prayed for the Christians in the Ukraine. While everyone in our church and our prayer group felt a burden for Ukrainian Christians, Sandy had a special burden for them. Every time we had a prayer meeting, she would say, "We have to pray for the persecuted church in the Soviet Union."

Soviet Premier Leonid Brezhnev's regime had begun a campaign against

Pentecostal Christians in 1961. The tribulations of Pyotr Vaschenko's family are chronicled in a book written during the four years that he and his family hid from Soviet authorities in the basement of the US embassy in Moscow. In 1978, the family, which became known as the Siberian Seven, traveled 2000 miles by train from Siberia to Moscow. Pyotr, his wife, and their three daughters, along with Maria Chmykhalov and her son, sprinted past Soviet guards outside the American embassy. Once they were inside the embassy, the Soviet authorities could not take them out.

They remained in self-imposed exile and isolation inside the embassy for four years. They couldn't leave the premises and take a walk. They couldn't go out for a meal or visit friends and acquaintances. If they left the embassy, they would be arrested. The embassy was their freedom and their prison.

In 1982, Pyotr's wife, Augustina, stopped eating. Three days later their eldest daughter, Lidiya, joined the hunger strike hoping that they could draw world attention and pressure the Soviet government to let them leave. We prayed for them every week in our prayer meetings. The two women were almost dead before a missionary organization, Christ for the Nations, offered to sponsor them, and the family made its way to the United States.

After Sandy presented the article, which described recent migrations of Russian families to the United States, our board agreed unanimously that we should sponsor a family. I called the agency. The refugee service's representative told me that there was an immediate need for a sponsor, and before we knew it, we had committed. It was a large family, more than we had expected: two grandparents and their three adult children. The older couple had a daughter who was not married and lived with them. They had two sons who were married with children. We had expected one household— one small family, one home, one set of parents and children—not three generations. We felt we had no choice but to sponsor the entire group. We had made the commitment, and the thought of breaking the family up was unconscionable.

The Steppingstone assumed the family's financial burden. We had to provide board, medical services, transportation, everything for the first three months they were here. We had to take them to get their green cards and then help them find work. We rented some property for them and paid the rent for the first six months. As they got jobs, they started paying a portion of their way. But it was our responsibility to take care of them until they had assimilated into our culture, and they could pay for their food, utilities, rent, and transportation.

Not one person in the family spoke English. Several people in the church volunteered to help teach them. One of our members had taught English as a second language, and she held classes at the church a couple of nights a week. The refugee organization provided translators who attended church services with the family. Although a translator wasn't with the family twenty-four hours a day, the team of translators and the family spent a lot of time together, and the family confided things with them that they didn't with us. The translators usually didn't tell us what the family members were telling them. They only translated when someone in the family spoke directly to one of the church members, and they translated church messages to the family.

All our conversations with the family members were courteous and respectful, but our efforts may not have been appreciated as much as many of us believed. We thought the family was grateful for our effort and for our sponsorship. We didn't know what they were saying to the translators or what the translators overheard as the family talked to each other.

The immigrant families were devout Baptists. Even by Bible belt standards, they were cinched pretty tight. They did not wear make-up. When the women were in public, they were expected to cover their heads. They always had scarves or handkerchiefs draped over their heads or had their heads wrapped when they went anywhere. We didn't know it, but the families were unhappy with the Steppingstone because the church allowed its female members to wear makeup and didn't force them to cover their heads. Possibly, the most insurmountable problem for them, something they even found insulting, was that the church had a woman pastor. They did not believe in women saying anything in church. The idea of a woman pastor was so inconceivable to them that it had never occurred to them to ask before they were placed with a sponsor. There were no women pastors in their homeland.

Women were not respected. We could see that cultural difference, but we didn't know the depth of disdain they had for our ministry. We were taking care of them, feeding them, paying their bills, and all the while they were dissatisfied, uncomfortable, and insulted.

The church was struggling to support the families. Financially and logistically, we were maxed out, but the provision was always there, and someone always came forward to help them with their needs. We were taking good care of them, such good care that the refugee services contacted me in December 1989, when an urgent need developed. A family was stranded in Italy.

"We have a family who had a sponsor that withdrew," the caller explained to me. "After the Ukrainian family left Russia, their church sponsor backed out, and now they are stranded in Rome."

They could not go back. Before they were permitted to leave Ukraine, they were required to renounce their citizenship. Abandoned in Rome, they were a family without a country. That must have been terrifying for them, but as soon as I understood what the refugee service was calling about, I was ready to answer. I was sympathetic to the plight of refugees, but there was no way our church could take on any additional responsibility. I was ready to answer almost from the moment the volunteer started speaking.

I knew the nature of the church body. The members of the Steppingstone were generous, but there was a limit to what could be expected of them. The volunteer continued explaining the family's situation. They would only be permitted to stay in Rome for a few days before they would be deported. I was trying to be polite, and I let the woman finish her sentence before I started to explain that the Steppingstone was so burdened with the three families it was already sponsoring that it was impossible to do more.

I wasn't even going to consider it, but those weren't the words that came out of my mouth. I said, "Yes. OK, we will take them," and I thought, what is wrong with me? I'm saying the wrong words. But it was too late. I had already agreed to take another family. Normally, I would not think of unilaterally assuming that the church would go along with me. I would never consider taking in another family without presenting it to the board, but I had already said, "Yes, we will."

"They will arrive on February 14," the volunteer informed me, and as simply as that, I had committed the church to sponsor another family. They still had to clear a lot of red tape, but the agency was firm about the date. The representative thanked me, and as I listened without really hearing, the dial tone buzzed from the receiver in my hand. I sat at my desk stunned, still wondering what had happened. I wasn't sure how to break the news to the church elders.

Despite the hardships we were enduring with the family that we already sponsored, the response from everyone was different than I had expected. I told everybody what happened, and they were happy about it.

On February 14, 1990, several church members caravanned to the airport. The Russian family that we already supported tagged along. It was very exciting, especially for them because they were going to have another family to talk to. The families talked together excitedly from the moment they met at the airport. The women hugged each other. The men hugged each other. It was like a family reunion. The Russian men talked excitedly to the patriarch of the new family, Sergei Bodyu, while everyone waited for their baggage.

All of us in the American entourage from the Steppingstone smiled happily while the two families apparently caught up on news from Russia. They seemed so happy. We didn't want to interrupt.

Within a few weeks after the arrival of the Bodyu family, their predecessors decided they had suffered enough of the liberal leanings of the spirit-filled Steppingstone church with its woman pastor. With their newfound freedom and mobility, the family started attending other churches. They liked a Russian church they had found in Fort Worth. I didn't think anything about that. I understood, or thought I did anyway. I wouldn't want to go to church where I did not understand the people and everything had to be translated. Even though they were learning some English, they were not fluent. Most of them still barely understood it.

A few months later the family decided to move to California, all three families. They had discovered a Russian community of other refugees from the same region they had migrated from. They even knew some of the families. They longed to be part of a Russian community, so they packed the cars that members of the Steppingstone had helped them purchase with all the belongings that they had accumulated, at least in part from the generous gifts from the church, and like the Clampetts, they set out for "Californee."

They had been in Burleson less than a year. We saw them off. Many members of the church were a little disappointed to see them leave, but at the same time, the church was thankful that it had been able to help a family adapt to life in America. It was something like a child leaving home. We felt joy and loss at the same time.

A year after the Russian family departed, we learned that the younger generations had not been as hostile toward the church as their parents.

They had grown to like us, and they had a different attitude toward me as a woman pastor. In 2014, one of the sons passed through Burleson en route to San Antonio. He stopped by to say "hello" and to let me know how much the family appreciated the Steppingstone's sponsorship. Their families have prospered in the United States. One of the children became a doctor. Another was graduating from military school in San Antonio, which was the reason for their trip.

When the family departed for California, the church's sponsorship ended, and the meager resources required to support two immigrant families no longer had to be shared. The church was able to provide for the smaller Bodyu family much more easily.

The Bodyus were different. They were charismatic Christians who believed as most members of the Steppingstone did. They didn't have a problem with a woman pastor, speaking in tongues, or any of the signs of the spirit.

Chapter 63

The Linguistics of Miracles

THERE WAS ONE problem, though. Sergei was dying. Doctors in Russia had told him so. He had a very bad heart condition. Although the small church sponsoring him would only learn of his illness after the family had arrived in America, Sergei had moved his family to this country because he knew he was dying. He knew that his teenage son and two young daughters would be taken care of in America. He was convinced they would be able to make better lives for themselves here than they could have in Ukraine. He knew they would be free to worship in the United States. They would be free of religious persecution whether socially or governmentally sponsored. He hoped he would be able to find work and support his family. While things had never been easy in the Ukraine, and he certainly didn't expect them to be easy in America, he knew that his chance of providing for his family was better. People still come to America because it offers more opportunity than any other country in the world.

The three adults found work quickly. Sergei found a job in a machine shop in Joshua. Xena, Sergei's wife, performed custodial duties at the Steppingstone academy, and Dima, their eighteen-year-old son who had left behind a fiancé in Russia, went to work at Bransom's grocery.

Dima's heart was still in Ukraine. His job in the grocery helped support the family while he managed to put a few dollars aside for himself each week. He was determined to return to Ukraine and marry Helen, the girl he left behind.

We had to go through the same process with the Bodyus that we had started with the earlier family. We got them a place to live. They were learning English. Dima and his sisters picked up English very quickly. The two girls started school immediately and were immersed in American culture. The elder was in junior high school. Her sister was just starting school. Someone gave the family a car, and we were getting their green cards. Otis picked up Sergei every morning and drove him to work. In the evenings,

Otis drove to Joshua and brought Sergei back home. Sergei's heart condition was so bad that sometimes Otis had to take him to the emergency clinic. They told him he had a degenerative heart condition and that there wasn't anything that would help him except a heart transplant.

The Bodyus had no health insurance, and there was no chance that Sergei would get on the list for a heart transplant. They needed the entire cost, $100,000 or more, just to get a stake in the game. There was no hope for him. He struggled to work every day and managed to put in a day's work only to be exhausted and sick when he got back home each evening. Once the church members found out about Sergei's heart condition, we began praying for him in our meetings.

Unrelated to the Bodyus, at least as far as I was concerned it was unrelated, in my personal prayer time, God instructed me to call a miracle Sunday. I was to plan for a Sunday of miracles. I announced it from the pulpit during a service in 1990. "Next Sunday is Miracle Sunday. Come expecting your miracle."

The following week, instead of delivering a sermon after the praise and worship was over, I announced again that it was Miracle Sunday: "Everybody who is praying for a miracle, come forward," I told the congregation. "It is time for us to get our miracles. Everybody that has come here believing God for a miracle, whether you need healing or whatever your miracle is, come down to the front." Waves of people flooded the aisles, landed at the base of the altar, and flowed across the room in front of me.

Although I knew where his family was sitting that Sunday, I wasn't thinking about Sergei. Miracle Sunday wasn't just for him, and the altar call wasn't focusing narrowly on him. Lots of people needed miracles in their lives. Almost everyone needs some kind of miracle. Sergei certainly needed one.

The Bodyus were sitting at the back of the building on my left, on one of the last rows. The people who picked them up and brought them to church sat with them each Sunday. I couldn't see Sergei, but I knew he was struggling. His face the color of ash, he couldn't sit up straight. He leaned over and put his elbows on his lap to hold up his body. Sometimes he would even put his arms over the back of an empty chair in front of him and lean over on it.

I started at my right and prayed for people who were lined up in front of the altar all the way across the building from one wall to the other, and I intended to start at one end and work through the entire line, praying for each person who had come forward. Cory and the elders of the church were praying for some people who had come forward, too. They were on the opposite side of the church where Sergei would go if he came forward for a healing prayer.

I had prayed for maybe ten people, and God spoke to me, "Call Sergei down. I am going to give him a new heart."

I didn't know if Sergei had already started down for prayer or if he was still sitting in the congregation. I stepped back up on the stage to see if he was at the opposite wall. He wasn't. I looked over the auditorium and saw that he was still seated.

I began to say what the Holy Spirit gave me. "Sergei, God wants to give you a new heart." When I began speaking, I knew it wasn't just me inventing and saying those things. The Holy Spirit had given me the word. I spoke God's healing word for him. I knew he couldn't understand a word of English yet. I was simply repeating what the Lord was saying to me. I was sure the translators would get the message to him, and I knew the people that brought him would get him to come down.

I didn't know that the translators hadn't made it to the service, and there was no one to help Sergei understand what I was saying. A translator may never have had a chance anyway. At the same moment I spoke his name, Sergei was on his feet and on his way to the altar. He strode quickly, briskly to the front of the church. I met him there. He chattered rapidly and excitedly, speaking to me in Russian. I could only understand one word that he kept repeating, "Russki, Russki."

"Receive your miracle," I said and laid hands on him.

I told him that he was getting a new heart. I closed my eyes as I spoke over him, praying in the spirit, and when I opened them again, his face was as pink as a baby's, even flushed. I had never seen him with color in his face. Even though I had seen healing miracles many times, I hadn't expected such a dramatic answer to my prayer. I didn't know it would have that quick of an effect, and I exclaimed, "Oh, you look better already."

He kept trying to tell me something, but I couldn't understand. He went back and sat down, talking all the while to his family and friends. For the rest of the service he was animated and vivacious. He praised God and was able to move, sit without leaning over, and stand. There may have been other miracles that Sunday, but that is the one I remember.

How could I forget it? As I walked into my living room after getting home from church, the phone was ringing. It was one of the people who had given the Bodyus a ride to church that morning. Ever since the service had ended, Sergei had been trying to talk to them. He had found his Russian-English dictionary and was trying desperately to explain something. He looked up sentences, word by word, trying to tell them what he was excited about, but he still wasn't getting his message across.

They phoned one of the translators, and Sergei repeated his message to her. Finally, he was able to give his testimony and tell everyone about the other miracle that had taken place that morning. When I had given that word, "God's giving Sergei a new heart," he heard it in Russian. I was speaking in English, and he heard it in Russian.

He understood every word I said. That was why he was talking to me and kept repeating the word Russki. He thought I had learned Russian. He told me over and over that he could hear me speaking to him in Russian. When he heard me speaking in in his native language he believed for his healing. He knew that God was speaking directly to him. God was giving him a new heart. The doctors had been telling him that he only had a few weeks or at most two or three months to live without a transplant or other treatment, but when Sergei went to work that week, he had the strength and endurance to get through his shift. He didn't die in a few weeks, or months, as the doctors had predicted. He confessed later that during the first couple of weeks after his healing, he sometimes had pain and felt the old symptoms of his illness, but he stood on the word and rebuked the devil. Many times, right after you have a healing, or any miracle for that matter, the devil will try to steal it from you, and if you give in and believe the devil's symptoms, then you lose your healing.

I know that from watching people, and a lot of people with healing ministries teach about the things you must do to keep your healing. Kenneth Hagin, among others, taught about the fight to keep your healing. Faith is not a momentary whim that comes over you on Sundays after an inspired sermon. It is not just being moved by the belief of others. Faith is hard work, and Sergei had a battle for a couple of weeks. Not constantly, but sometimes he felt his healing might be slipping away, and he actively re-professed it. He felt better from then on.

It's been over twenty years. For many years, Sergei worked at the Burleson Wal-Mart as a stocker. It was tough, physical work, from ten o'clock at night until six o'clock in the morning. At times, Sergei stood before the church and testified about his healing.

He knew he was healed, but he couldn't go to the doctor and confirm it. It wasn't as if he had been living here his whole life and had a lifetime of medical records on file in a doctor's office. Since the family had arrived in Texas, the only medical records he had were on file in the emergency room. Now that he was healed, he didn't go to the clinic anymore.

Members of the church didn't need to see doctors' records, anyway. The proof of God's healing power stood beside them in worship every Sunday. Sergei, who had been ashen faced, now had color in his cheeks. Sergei, who had been stooped in pain and barely able to raise his head, now stood erect and lifted his hands in praise. Sergei, who had not been expected to live long, was in the midst of them a week later, a month later, a year later, a decade later, sharing in worship with them and praising God.

God heals people today, even in a world where science is finding more solutions to health problems all the time, in a world where technology is worshipped as though the secrets of life lie in the next smaller particle or the next miracle drug. God's power is larger and smaller than science.

The Bodyus have been a blessing. In God's knowledge and sovereignty, he chose to put them here, and having them in our church has been a wonderful experience. Because of them, we got to witness a great miracle. Everybody is reminded of God's power every Sunday when they see Sergei. They had seen him as a dying man, and after Miracle Sunday they saw him vigorous and strong.

Chapter 64

The Nepal Connection

UT THERE'S MORE to the story of the Bodyus. One of the translators was a girl named Debbie, a young, red-headed American woman. She was married to a man from Nepal who had been sent to America for his education. When he had left home, his parents had cautioned him not to be seduced by the decadent lifestyle of the Americans. "Don't date an American," his strict Hindu mother had told him. "We don't want you to marry an American."

Once he had started to school, he supported himself by selling vacuum cleaners door-to-door, and he Americanized his first name to Bob. One evening Bob's rounds led him to knock at the door of a Fort Worth minister. The minister invited the young man into his home, and somewhere between sweeping dust out of carpets and getting stains out too, the conversation turned to religion. Before long, they were into a comparative study of Christianity and Hinduism. Bob accepted Christ as the savior of his soul and the only vacuum cleaner powerful enough to sweep away a man's sins. He started attending the church where his host ministered, and somewhere along the way, he started dating the pastor's daughter. That was Debbie.

Debbie was devout. She had been studying Russian because she intended to become a missionary to the Soviet Union. Partly to increase her understanding of the Russian language and the people of Russia and partly to help foreigners who were trying to make a home in the United States, Debbie had volunteered as an interpreter for the North Texas Refugee center. God, with a little help from Bob, changed her plans.

Debbie and Bob married not long before the Bodyus arrived in America. She was one of the interpreters who rotated in and out of the Bodyu household during the first few months of 1990, and she attended church at the Steppingstone with them regularly. She wasn't there on the Sunday that Sergei received his healing, but she heard about it soon afterward, and it wasn't long before the young couple was commuting to the Steppingstone every Sunday.

Bob's faith grew throughout his stay in America. As frequently happens though, he became convicted with a burden for the people in his home country who remained Hindu or Buddhist or who worshipped in the mosques of Islam. Hindus comprise more than eighty percent of Nepal's population, estimated at twenty million in 2006 by the US State Department. Buddhists make up a little more than ten percent, and Muslims number less than five percent. Christians account for less than one percent of the population.

There's good reason for that. Nepal, like India, had legal restrictions against proselytizing. The Constitution of 1990 stated that "Everyone shall have the freedom to profess and practice his own religion as handed down to him having due regard to ancient practices; provided that no person shall be entitled to convert another person from one religion to another." Witnessing for Christ, whether on the streets or in private homes, could get you thrown into jail. It might even get you executed. It was a crime to convert native Nepalese to Christianity, and no one knew better than Bob, whose family was in a prestigious position in Nepal society, the potential costs of bringing Christ to the masses. Members of his family were leading people in their town, and the Nepalese people were very conscious of class. His father's position was similar to the position of mayor in a US city, and he was a local leader of the Hindu faith.

Nevertheless, Bob was convicted for his family and friends and for all his countrymen. Within a couple of years after his conversion to Christianity, Bob knew God was calling him to the ministry in his homeland. He and Debbie studied for the ministry at Christ for the Nations, and as soon as they were finished with their training, they began their missionary journey. The Steppingstone church found itself supporting a foreign mission. After they moved to Nepal, the Steppingstone was their principal means of support. We sent six hundred dollars a month, which is about all they needed. A dollar over there could be stretched a lot farther than here, although there's no telling how much our Lord had to do with it.

Not too surprisingly, it was six months before even one person who attended services in their church publicly professed Christianity, but they were diligent, and slowly others began attending the church. Eventually, they established churches in several villages. In Nepal, bodies of believers could not have the words "church" or "Christ" in the name of the organization, so the young missionaries had to come up with names that represented their ministry but didn't specifically label the places where they assembled as churches. The first church they organized in Nepal was called the Steppingstone. What homage to the church in Texas.

When Nancy Harmon, who founded Love Special outreach ministries in 1968, visited the Burleson Steppingstone in 1995, she told me that a friend of hers had recently been in Nepal and had visited a church called the Steppingstone. "That's our church," I exclaimed. I told Nancy about the two young missionaries and explained that they had led many to faith in Jesus Christ and established meeting places throughout the country. The Steppingstone was living up to its name around the world.

Bob and Debbie are still missionaries. They come to America every three to four years, and they make a point of visiting our church. Bob forwards newsletters and e-mails keeping me abreast of the latest news from Nepal, where attitudes toward foreign religions still make it a dangerous world for Christians. Some people who converted to Christianity were beaten to death, and for a little while, they were living under such fear that Bob sent Debbie and the children to Katmandu, one of the country's larger cities. The local resistance to Christianity and the mob mentality made it too dangerous for them in the smaller towns.

As you are reading this in the comfort of your home or on a plane or even on the bus to work, wherever you are at this moment, put this book down and pray for the Christian missionaries throughout the world. Many are in countries where the message of love and peace is considered anathema, and many are in danger of becoming martyrs for Jesus Christ. They're not dying to spread violence and hatred. They're not dying to receive material rewards in the hereafter. They're not dying and taking other lives with them. They, like our Savior, Jesus Christ, are dying so that others will have an eternal life, and the very least we can do for them is pray for their ministries.

Then pray for your country. In the United States, the Christian faith is under siege. Legislation, executive orders, and even Supreme Court decisions almost daily assault Christian beliefs. If you are a Catholic, Mormon, or evangelical Christian, you are already designated as a terrorist by people who are responsible for training US military personnel. If the statists continue to usurp more power and authority, you may soon find it is illegal to profess your Christianity. If current trends continue, regardless of whether liberals or conservatives control the White House and Congress, every case heard in criminal courts will be subject to review by a bureaucrat who is employed by the national government. Apparatchiks empowered to determine that a crime was motivated by "hate" will have the power to summarily supersede the findings of the courts. Bureaucrats will have more power than state courts to determine the appropriate punishment for those who commit acts of aggression. Bureaucrats will determine what doctors you can see and when you can see them. They will determine your course of treatment. By treaty and not by constitutional amendment, the police and the government will have the power to come into your home and inspect it for weapons. All these things have been proposed in recent years. They will happen, unless we few remaining, who honor the precepts upon which this country was founded, are willing to stand for our beliefs rather than surrendering our constitutional rights to a government run amuck.

As Christians, we cannot condone any violent act against another human being. All crimes are hate crimes. In granting unprecedented power to bureaucrats, the Congress will undermine the balance of powers that preserves American liberty. As bureaucrat-in-chief, the American president will assume supreme authority to determine your movements and your lifestyle. Already today, if you make a moral stand based on fundamental Christian beliefs, you are subject to derision, ridicule, and financial ruin. The next step is ostracism and then imprisonment.

Yesterday you had a choice to become a Christian and to live a life based on Christian values. Tomorrow you may not. Yes, it seems laughable, but possibly within your lifetime, when you or someone you love is rotting in a political asylum because they attempted to defend themselves when someone took away their Bible, only the jailers will be laughing.

Chapter 65

The Russian Reconnection

DIMA BODYU HAD left Helen behind. He had intended to marry her, but he was still a teenager when his parents uprooted him. Almost immediately, after his family found a place to stay in America, he was lobbying to get Helen to the United States, too.

An attorney, who was a member of the Steppingstone church, began working with him. There was a lot of red tape, but by December, Helen stepped off a plane at DFW and drove home with the Bodyus. Almost as soon as she got here, we had a wedding. It was Christmas, and all the decorations were red. All the women wore red dresses. It was a beautiful wedding, and it was the perfect time because the marriage also marked the beginning of a new outreach ministry sponsored by the Steppingstone.

Dima had already made a commitment to return to Ukraine and preach the gospel. He attended classes at Christ for the Nations (CFN), a Dallas based training academy that has prepared young people for the missions fields since the early 1970s. To support himself he worked as a security guard at the school. Shortly after Helen's arrival, she entered the CFN training program, too. After they had both graduated from the missions program, Dima and Helen returned to Melitopol in Ukraine.

Under Glasnost, a policy of openness instituted in the Union of Soviet Socialist Republics (USSR) by Premier Mikail Gorbachev, and with the eventual dissolution of the Soviet Union in 1991, many of the travel restrictions for returning expatriates had been removed. The young couple was able to return to their native country to preach the gospel.

Their plans had been modest, but God had bigger things in mind for them. Dima became the assistant pastor of a 500-member church. The church had met in a house until freedom came and they were able to rent a building. Shortly after Dima's arrival, though, the pastor decided to leave the church and pursue more formal training in the Bible. He departed for Bible college in Sweden stopping on his way out the door to name the twenty-three-year-old Dima as head pastor during his absence. Dima, barely more than a teenager and just out of Bible school, was the senior pastor of a church. We used to laugh together when he described the difficulty he had when people came to him with their marriage problems. He would tell them, "I'm just a *keed*," (as he said it). But whether he still considered himself a kid or not, God had given him a man-sized task. Christians in Ukraine had been deprived of the Bible for so long that they had very little understanding of the Word. Their Christian beliefs were mixed with their culture to the extent that it was hard to distinguish one from the other. They didn't know much scripture, and their theology was a little…different. Dima, fresh from his training at Christ for the Nations, had received a thorough education in the Word. He had listened attentively and soaked in the preaching and teaching at our church, too. We teased him about being a *"keed,"* but the Ukraine kid was ready because God had chosen him for the job.

He didn't have the luxury of developing his ministerial skills under the guidance of a senior pastor. Right from the start, he was in charge of a church and responsible for delivering the sermon each Sunday. He wasn't without a mentor though; he had several of them: Matthew, Mark, Luke, John, Peter, and Paul. While the senior pastor was away, Dima developed under the tutelage of the apostles, and the Bible was his textbook.

After the pastor returned from his sabbatical, Dima willingly returned to his subordinate role, but there was a hunger for Christ, and Dima began speaking in meetings throughout Ukraine. Before he knew it, he had started a church in a neighboring town. Then he organized another. He and Helen were planting churches all over Ukraine. Since the mid-1990s, they have planted more than fifty churches.

Once again, God was performing the miracle of spreading the message of Jesus Christ throughout the world from the little church in Burleson, Texas. The miracle didn't stop there. Each of the two missionary families, supported in large part by the contributions of the members of the Steppingstone, didn't stop at establishing one community church. Our missionaries in Ukraine, like our team in Nepal, became itinerant preachers, carrying on the work of Paul, Peter, and the other apostles and establishing Christian organizations throughout their respective regions. They established churches and then returned to them to preach from time to time, offering leadership and guidance. Dima organized a Bible college in Melitopol where they taught the pastors and elders of the churches.

Chapter 66

Building Ukraine

I N 1995, THE government owned all property, but after the demise of the Soviet Union, the new Ukrainian government needed money so badly that it rented and in some cases sold buildings to anyone who was willing to pay. Dima's church got an opportunity to rent a large meeting hall. It resembled a theater with a stage. It was perfect for speaking to a large congregation. Later that year the government decided to sell the building.

Dima returned to the United States and reported that his church had an opportunity to purchase the building. The state was demanding $10,000 as a down payment. Dima didn't have that kind of money. Combined, all the churches he had established couldn't come up with that much money. The country was still suffering the throes of a severe recession, and many of the church members were as poor as church mice.

Nancy Harmon was visiting the Steppingstone for our anniversary service, and she heard the news. She asked me if she could take up an offering specifically for the Russian church. If Dima couldn't raise the $10,000, the church would have been out on the street. Six hundred faithful worshippers in Melitopol would have no place to meet.

Our church members came through. They gave the ten thousand dollars for Dima to use as a down payment on the building, and he promptly forwarded the money to the government. Almost two years later, the final purchase terms had not been finalized, though. Dima reported to the Steppingstone in 1997 that the government had decided it would not allow the sale of buildings for use as churches. In an effort to strictly enforce new policies that separated church and state, the government was disallowing the sale of any property to religious organizations.

However, the government was so broke that it couldn't refund the $10,000 down payment. So, Dima negotiated the final terms of a sale. At first, the government imposed an excessive demand of $200,000 full payment for the building by September 1, but Dima continued bargaining with various officials and agencies and eventually he negotiated a final price equivalent to $60,000. That was still a lot of money, more than the members of the Ukraine church ever could have raised. Even though church members had sold their furniture, their jewelry, and their cars in an effort to save their church, they were only able to raise about $10,000 more. They needed another $50,000.

On Dima's next trip to the United States, he shared the church's situation. "If we don't have the additional fifty thousand, we will be out on the street," he told me bluntly.

My vision of overflowing all the churches in Burleson and of building a church that could hold more than one thousand people on Sunday mornings flickered in my mind. Dima had a similar dream and mission in Ukraine. God would send a revival to Burleson, and the church needed to be ready to handle the masses of new Christians who would be seeking spiritual guidance. He was doing the same thing in Ukraine, and they needed to prepare for the coming revival, too. How could the church in Burleson provide funds for a church in Ukraine?

Much was at stake. When I presented it to the people of the Steppingstone, I said, "We've got a building that we can meet in. Whether we ever get another one or not, we have a building; they don't." The Steppingstone had raised about $75,000 for its new building, and to some of the members of the church it sounded as if I was asking them to reallocate our building fund for the Ukraine church. Some of the Steppingstone's church leaders even said, "Well, we can just give that out of our building fund."

That wasn't my intent, and I said, "No, people gave that to our building fund." It was a matter of trust and commitment. We had collected our building fund for a specific purpose. To have given over the money from our building fund would have been a violation of a trust. You could argue that once someone gives money to the church, it is the church's right to dispose of it as it sees fit, but the people who had given to the building fund for our church had given specifically for our building plans. In most cases, the money donated to the building fund was in addition to their tithes. So those funds were earmarked for a specific purpose. I would not violate that trust, much as I refused to violate my father's trust when we decided to become a church. Nevertheless, I believed that saving the church in Russia was essential. I told our congregation that the Steppingstone was to raise the entire $50,000 from new offerings dedicated to the ministry in Ukraine.

The Lord spoke to me as if the fate of our nation depended on the success of the church in Ukraine. I know that may sound dramatic or even pompous, but missions and churches throughout the world have relied on the charity, resources, and spirit of American churches for many years. If American churches do not remain dedicated to God's command to spread the word of Jesus Christ throughout the world, God may well decide that his blessings should go to countries that support outreach. I felt strongly that the survival of America and the church in America depended on our support of the message of Christ throughout the world.

It was important that we raised the money for Ukraine. In a way, our church's giving was a profession of our faith. Somebody came up to me after we took up the offering, and repeated, "Well, we could give our building fund money."

I said, "No, the Lord said we were to *raise* it. I think it has probably come in." Sure enough, when we counted it, we had $50,000. It was a miracle. We had raised the entire amount.

Dima transported the money back to Ukraine. Before he left, we went to the bank to get the cash. He couldn't take a check. We notified the bank in advance so that they could have enough cash on hand. We deposited the checks and cash that we had received in the offering, and I wrote a check to cash on the church's account. I stood beside Dima while the teller counted out fifty thousand dollars in one hundred dollar bills, five hundred brand new ones, banded, crisp, and totally flat, like a stack of typing paper, a ream of 500 sheets about two inches thick. Dima bought a money belt. It was camouflaged. It didn't look like a money belt at all. Stuffed into it, the cash was invisible. A few years later, after the Steppingstone had struggled through building its new auditorium, Dima and the senior pastor of the church in Ukraine visited the United States. "I'll never forget that this church paid for our building," the pastor said. By that time, I had almost forgotten about it, but it was rewarding to know that the funding provided by the Steppingstone church had meant the difference between survival and dissolution for the church in Melitopol.

Each person who contributed to that special collection gave sacrificially. That kind of giving is part of worship, and raising the $50,000 in obedience to God's will was an intercessory act. A church in America saves a church in Ukraine, and because of that, churches in America are blessed. The

Steppingstone saved the church in Melitopol, and the church in Melitopol eventually became the hub of fifty other churches in Ukraine. Dima has planted a lot more churches since then, and it all started with the sacrificial giving of the people in the Steppingstone church.

I believe that sacrificial giving to rescue other ministries, like the donations by Steppingstone members to save a church in a foreign country, is one of the things that maintains America's prominence and status as a blessed nation. Because of the faithful, sacrificial giving of the Steppingstone and other churches like it, the Holy Spirit continues to intercede on our behalf and protect us from dangers that the rest of the world is vulnerable to. When America fails to lead other nations in giving and in spreading the message of Jesus Christ, we may no longer be blessed in the same ways that we have been in the past. I have never taken up an offering that was as important. I know in my heart that our giving led directly to the Holy Spirit's intercession for our nation in some way. I hope someday God will reveal to us why and how intercession works. Maybe some prophet will tell us.

We were blessed to sponsor the Bodyu family and be a part of Dima's work in Ukraine. Today, his ministry stretches far beyond that. He has established churches in Alaska and Israel. Many Russian Jews migrated to Israel in the last century, so there is a close link between Russian and Jewish communities. Dima's ministry started with our sponsorship of the Bodyu family. One church member who felt a burden for the people of Ukraine ignited a fuse that exploded in a series of miracles. God, no doubt, could have called on others and used other resources to support Dima's ministry, but we are blessed that He chose to use the Steppingstone/Lighthouse church.

Chapter 67

School Daze

ALWAYS FELT THAT the Steppingstone had a special obligation to youth and children. As the church grew and the Steppingstone ministry became more diversified, we looked for ways to extend that outreach to the young people in our community. At the beginning of the 1991 school year, the church opened the Steppingstone Academy. I hoped the school would offer the community an alternative to public schools where any mention of God, especially a Christian God, had been anathematized. Public schools expelled God, and the only way to get Him back in class seemed to be for churches and other religious organizations to sponsor Christian academies.

Schools have their own fiscal and administrative challenges, including staffing. Members of the church provided much of the administration, and Martha Myers, our principal, was a member of the Steppingstone. Three or four people of the church were teachers over the course of the next few years. Most teachers, however, were from outside the church. Mark Collins, who was inducted into Baylor University's athletic Hall of Fame in 1989, taught at Steppingstone Christian Academy for a few years. He made the 1980 Olympic relay team, but President Carter cancelled the United States' participation in protest of the Soviet Union's invasion of Afghanistan, the only boycott of the Olympics by the United States in the history of the games.

We started with four grades, counting kindergarten, and the school was a huge hit. Many people wanted their children to be educated in Christian schools, where they knew that the values taught were consistent with theirs. After the first year, we wanted to add another tier of grades, the upper division of elementary school. We wanted all our students to be able to continue their education in our school, and of course, if we hadn't added at least one grade, we wouldn't be able to provide that continuity. However, we didn't have the space for additional classes. With enrollment increasing for the grades that we already offered, we desperately needed more space.

We contacted many of our neighbors trying to purchase property. The families owning the two houses south of the church, between our buildings and the creek, had been living in their houses for years and weren't going anywhere. Others, across Dobson, weren't interested in selling either. We even tried to buy a portion of the playground of Nola Dunn School, across the street on the north side of the church. We contacted the Boys Club about purchasing some of its property to the east.

Across a small street at the northeast side of the church, a row of duplexes occupies the next block, and the one nearest our building was available for rent. The "street" was little more than a driveway to get to our parking lot and the Boys Club's athletic fields. If we could rent one or more of the duplexes, then we would at least have a short-term solution to the space problem. I contacted the owner.

After I explained that the school was associated with our church, he refused to rent the duplex to us. He said he didn't believe in God. God had never done anything for him, he stated. Even though he wanted to rent the property, he had no intention of renting it to us.

There was a history there. The man had attempted to obstruct our building efforts before. Several years earlier, during our first construction of a sanctuary, the church had bought T.J. Bransom's father's house. He had owned a narrow strip of land between Miller Street and the Boy's Club's ball field. It was at the back of the original lot where we had built the Steppingstone Youth Center. With the acquisition, the church owned the block between Dobson Street and Rigney Way, the small lane that was barely more than a driveway. We bought two narrow lots outright, and T.J. gave us a copy of the deed and filed it.

We figured we were ready to build, but when Richard Lowe, our builder, who was also on the city council, applied for the permit, he was told that the city had taken a big part of the lot. The city owned a fifteen foot easement on each side of Rigney Way, according to their records. That meant that we would not be able to expand as we had planned. We would have to revise all our plans. We had already designed the expansion to build as close as possible to the lot line. Up until we tried to get the building permit, no one had said anything about easement or ownership issues.

The city had little to gain from the keeping the easement. Even though the narrow street provides access to the Boys Club's property, most traffic, then as now, was for the church. Richard recommended that we ask the city to close the street. We didn't want to completely close it, but we wanted to be able to build as close to the edge of the lot as the law allowed. If we were able to close fifteen feet we would have a little more room for our new sanctuary. After Richard had explained our circumstances to city administrators, the city offered to surrender the easement. That would give us another fifteen feet to develop as we needed. It still wasn't enough to accommodate our original building plan, but it was something.

The city contacted the owner of the duplexes to let him know what it was planning to do. When the city gave up its right of way, it would give the church fifteen feet on our side of the street and it would give the owner of the duplexes a matching fifteen feet on the other side of the street. But the owner wanted no part of it. He was willing to sacrifice the additional fifteen feet if it would interfere with any development for the church, and apparently he believed that by refusing the offer, he would block the church's construction. After conferring with him, the city secretary contacted me and told me that the city had decided that, since the owner of the duplexes had declined the city's offer, Burleson would make the entire thirty foot easement available to the church. Before concluding our call, she warned me that the owner of the duplexes evidently had something against God.

The change didn't affect the paved portion of the street, but with the modification, we were able to continue according to our original expansion plan. Ultimately, in an effort to prevent the church from building, the owner of the duplexes had facilitated the expansion. God does work in mysterious ways.

It wasn't surprising when the duplex owner refused to rent it to us a few years later. He had already shown an extreme prejudice against God. He was courteous and respectful to me personally, but he was angry and bitter. When I told him my name, he knew immediately who I was. He asked if we were going to use the duplex for the church. I told him no and explained it was for the school. He wouldn't even consider the idea of renting to the church, even for the school.

I couldn't help feeling sorry for him, despite his almost confrontational refusal. He was never disrespectful or discourteous, but he spoke harshly about God. He had no use for either God or the church. Ordinarily, I would have reacted out of Christian conscience and offered scriptures and consolation for someone who was so hurt and openly hostile toward God, but I didn't. I only let him know I was praying for him. There was little more I could do.

I'm always a little surprised by people who insist they don't believe in God but seem to be holding a grudge against Him. I asked why he didn't believe, and the truth spewed out like lava. His pent up rage against God found an outlet. His wife had been ill and had died. God had not intervened. I could hear the pain in his voice, and I wished there was something I could do to change his mind—not just in reference to the school, but in his relationship to the Lord.

With no way to acquire additional lot space, we continued our plans to add grades and to start the school year making the best use of the space available in the church. We planned to get portable buildings to handle the additional classes.

A few weeks before school started, I got a call from the duplex owner's real estate representative. The owner still would not rent the property to our school, but he would consider selling the duplex. The catch was that if the church wanted the property, it would have to buy all three of the duplexes in the next block. It was an all or nothing proposition.

I was elated. Not only would we have adequate space for the added grades, but we would be able to expand the school and the church's outreach as we needed for the foreseeable future. The only thing bothering me was that something must have happened to change the owner's heart and mind. A few weeks later, at the closing, I asked the real estate broker about it. He didn't know what had happened either. He was amazed. He had handled many of the owner's real estate transactions, and he was surprised when the owner called and told him to sell. It was an unusual move. "This is the only property he's selling," he said.

At the time of the purchase, we had committed to adding more grades, and by the time we closed the sale and had possession of the first duplex, it was nearly time for school to start. The men of our church converted the living spaces into classrooms. They worked night and day in the stifling August heat.

Almost five years later, the real estate representative called and asked if the church would like the former owner to buy back any of the duplexes.

I asked why.

"The owner knew how bad you wanted that first duplex, and he thought maybe he had been a little hard on you by making you buy all of them. So he offered to buy a couple of them back." By then, of course, we had converted all of them.

"Oh, no, we love having them," I said.

All of God's miracles aren't spectacular. God's not ostentatious. He doesn't need to be. He's God. Some of his miracles are small, like changing the heart of the owner of a property. His miracles are all around us, happening every minute.

I thought about calling the owner to see if there was anything I could do for him. He may have had a change of heart, but I didn't have the information to get hold of him because he only contacted us through the real estate broker. The number I had looked up the first time I called wasn't good anymore. I don't know if he had moved or changed his phone number, but I wasn't able to contact him.

Chapter 68

Educational Building

THE DUPLEXES AND Sunday school classrooms were soon filled with students through the eighth grade. Eventually, in order to continue the education of children who had attended the Steppingstone Academy and were ready to matriculate into high school, we had to add more space.

We drew up plans for a new educational building and awarded the construction contract for $300,000, but we had raised only $140,000 for the new construction. In one lump, we received a donation of $100,000 from a man whom many of us knew. Everyone associated with the church had always thought he was very poor. That increased our building funds to $240,000, but we still needed $60,000 more at the end of 1992. We had to begin construction by January if we were going to have the building available for K through 12 classes for the 1993-1994 school year, but we couldn't begin work until we had all the funds.

On the last Sunday of 1992, a member of our church handed me a check for $60,000. I was thrilled. My first thought was to call Dad, but I considered waiting until the next Sunday when I would announce to the entire church that we had all the funds necessary to begin construction. On the other hand, he and Mother had supported the ministry since its inception. I knew he would be as happy as I was that we finally had enough money to start the next phase of our campus, and I couldn't wait. As soon as I got home that afternoon, I called him. He was as excited and happy as I knew he would be.

I am as grateful to God for allowing me an opportunity to speak to Dad that Sunday as I am for the miracle of finally reaching our building fund goal. It was the last time I spoke to him. He died the following Friday of heart failure.

My parents had given to the Steppingstone throughout its history, and I knew that Dad tithed at church, too. I didn't fully realize the extent of his giving until after he had died. Condolences poured in from all across the globe. Many of the letters stated how Dad had helped sustain a ministry. It was a blessing to discover how respected, appreciated, and revered he had been even outside our small community.

About that last $60,000, the man who donated it and helped us meet our goal was the step-father of Troy Brewer, a dynamic young Christian who had recently started a food bank ministry and was in the process of starting a church. Who could have known that twenty years later the Lord would lead me to turn the building and all other church property over to Troy who would replace me as pastor.

In March 1993, we broke ground. Mark Emmert and his building crew went to work immediately and finished the building in time for the start of school on September 1, 1993. With the additional space, we were able to offer all four high school grades.

We dedicated the education building to my parents, Frances and Clyde Lewis. My parents had played such an important role in launching the ministry that it was only appropriate that their contribution should be recognized in some way. God would have found a way to fund it, I'm sure, but He used my parents, and that has always been a blessing to me.

We used the two-story building for all Sunday school and educational activities, as well as classrooms for the Steppingstone Christian Academy. Enrollment had grown to 125 students in grades K through eleven, and with the additional 11,000 square feet of educational space, the school at last had room to grow for the foreseeable future.

The dedication service recognized everyone who had donated their time and labor to finish the Lewis Building in only three months. My husband John, Cory (who was then assistant pastor of the Steppingstone), Richelle, several church elders and board members including Mickey Morris, Joe Ed Spencer, James Clamon, and Sandra Browning were also on hand.

For several years, the church and school grew together. We had a number of notable commencement speakers, including Arlene Wohlgemuth, state representative; Judge John Neil; Marcus and Joni Lamb, the owners of Daystar Television; and Justice Tom Gray of the 10th Circuit Court of Appeals.

The church managed to keep the school open for twelve years while costs of subsidizing it grew to $75,000 annually. I believe that it was the will of God for us to have it. We may not know until we get to heaven how much was accomplished in those twelve years, how many lives were put on the right course, but I know that God blessed lives through the school.

Justice Gray spoke at our last graduation in 2003.

The Education Building completed in 1993 was dedicated to Frances and Clyde Lewis.

Chapter 69

Daystar

MARCUS AND JONI Lamb's address at one of our graduation exercises wasn't the only time they spoke at our church. They had moved to the DFW area in 1990 after they sold the UHF television station they had built in Montgomery, Alabama. They spent the next three years trying to acquire a television station in north Texas in obedience to the Lord's call. A visiting evangelist in 1990 told me about them, and soon we had scheduled Marcus to bring the message during one of our services. Joni accompanied him and led the praise and worship.

Their services often included a prophetic word, and in one of them, Marcus singled out my eldest grandson. Jeremiah was only fourteen-years-old, but Marcus laid out his future exactly as it eventually transpired. When he graduated from high school, Jeremiah was awarded a full scholarship to Oral Roberts University. He began his ministry as youth pastor at the New Life Church in Colorado Springs, and today he serves in that church as an associate pastor.

After Marcus and Joni purchased channel 29, a low powered television station in Las Colinas, I traveled to the station a few times to answer phones during their fund raisers, although the little station's signal was weak and didn't broadcast very far. Often, during the frequent phone lulls, I wondered how the station would ever succeed. I had no doubt about the dedication and talent of Marcus and Joni. They were fabulous, but the phones didn't seem to be ringing.

Jeremiah and I were guests on their programs a few times, too. Jeremiah was still in high school, but he described Marcus's prophecy and how it was already being fulfilled in his life.

One afternoon while I was manning the phones, I was wondering once again how the station would survive when God spoke to me about it. "I'm raising up this station and this ministry. It will go around the world." He told me that He could trust Marcus and Joni with that ministry. He had called them to it, and He would build it. I was sitting there thinking *can this be the Lord speaking to me?* when I looked up and Marcus was standing in front of me. I just blurted out the word. "This ministry is going to go everywhere," I announced, "because He said He could trust you with this ministry."

During the next few years, I hosted a television program at the station, and I presented my studies on the faith of the founding fathers including John Adams, who stated their convictions that our nation is founded on God's laws as He gave them to us in the Ten Commandments. Revisionists might try to tell you differently, but the evidence is overwhelming that the founders of our nation believed in a God who endows all men with the rights of life, liberty, and the pursuit of happiness, and that these concepts are meaningless in absence of a deity.

On one occasion when I was walking into the building, Marcus and his brother were standing in the foyer. Marcus introduced me and the three of us talked briefly before I reminded Marcus of the word I had given. He certainly remembered it, he said. It had given him courage to branch out and buy stations in other markets.

By the end December of 2003, Daystar had moved into its new International Ministry Center, which includes two state-of-the-art production studios. Today, the network operates over seventy television stations in major markets across the United States. The ministry has gone worldwide, just as God had told me it would. In 2006, Daystar became the first Christian broadcaster to be licensed to operate in Israel. It reaches into over 200 countries and is still growing.

Chapter 70

Steppingstone to a Lighthouse

THE STEPPINGSTONE CHURCH lived up to its name. Throughout its life, the church on Dobson was a steppingstone for other ministries. We rechristened it as the Lighthouse church when we added the new sanctuary, but that didn't change our mission. The Steppingstone was a Christian youth ministry in Burleson, the assembly of a body of Christians for worship, and a Christian alternative to public schools. It was the steppingstone for establishment of Christian ministries in India, Nepal, Ukraine, Israel, Alaska, Mexico, Peru, and even Mansfield, Texas.

I often think about the wonderful ways God used the Steppingstone ministry. I focus on the success that God gave us all through the trials that we confronted during the early years of the new millennium. God always brought the church through. He always brought me through. He never failed, and He will not fail. I believe the city of Burleson has a destiny in reaching the world for the Lord, and I believe that our church will be important in fulfilling Burleson's destiny. I described the Steppingstone's journey and my expectations for Burleson to Dottie Wilson of the *Burleson Star*, and in an article titled, "A Part of a City's Destiny," in its September 13, 1984 edition, the newspaper reported:

> Gloria Gillaspie believes there is a destiny upon the city of Burleson, and she wants to be part of it. The petite, attractive woman is in a position not only to be a part of that destiny but to be a driving force in its implementation.
>
> She is Burleson's only female pastor, the soft-spoken founder of the Steppingstone church and Youth Outreach. Soft spoken, yes, for Gloria counsels and witnesses in gentle tones. But her knowledge of the Bible becomes evident after only a few moments of time spent talking with her, and her understanding of people and their needs is equally abundant.
>
> A Burleson resident for many years, she witnessed problems

within her own neighborhood among the youth and began to have a vision for a youth center. Out of that the Steppingstone was born. Her parents donated the property on [Dobson and] Miller street in Burleson, and the small house on the corner began to be a popular Saturday night gathering place for youth.

The movies and Christian music concerts may have been what attracted the youth to the Steppingstone, but they also responded to Bible study and drug counseling. And they continued to come. Their numbers grew, and their families began attending the Bible studies, too. In January of 1982, the church was established, adding a Sunday worship service to the week's schedule. The congregation has grown from a core group of about 50 members to a present number of 250 members.

"The Steppingstone has always been a faith venture. We receive no financial support from other churches," she explained. "We built the new facility in 1979 without any financing, but a month after completion all bills were paid," she said with a smile.

Gloria was ordained by a Full Gospel Fellowship when the Steppingstone became incorporated. But the decision to become the pastor of the church did not come without a great deal of searching her heart to be sure it was the right decision.

"One of the hardest things for me in making the decision was the opinion of the community and whether they would accept me," she said.

She has found for the most part that the community was very accepting and responsive to her as pastor of Steppingstone. She recently started attending meetings of the Burleson Ministerial Alliance at the urging of several local pastors. "I was really reluctant about that at first," she admitted. "But they have been wonderful and very helpful," she said. "There are those few people who want to believe that the Bible says women should be silent in the church," she commented. "Everyone is entitled to their own interpretation of the Bible, but I have always read I Corinthians 14 to mean that Paul was correcting people for making women be silent in the church. I'm not offended, though, when people ask me my understanding of the scripture.

Our goal at the Steppingstone Church is to see a real move of God's spirit to bring a great revival to our city, one which will affect all the churches. It will involve a change in the community, a returning to strong family principles," she said. "I believe it will happen, and I want to be part of that."

Though her own family had some adjustments to make when she entered the pastorate of the church, they were a close-knit group and have worked through the problems caused by the increased demands on her time and energies. She and her husband, John, have four children: Shanda Parks, Richelle Smithee, Stuart Gillaspie and Otis Gillaspie.

"They grew up here, did their dating at the Stepping Stone," she said. Concerned that they might feel pressured into coming to the Stepping Stone she told them once that they should follow their own feelings if they should ever choose to find another church. She was pleased when they responded that they couldn't imagine wanting to attend church anywhere else.

Chapter 71

Rediscovering America's Heritage

RECORDED MY RESEARCH on the religion of the founding fathers and the doctrine of separation of church and state in a series of programs called *Rediscovering America's Heritage* that aired on the Daystar network when it was still in its infancy. I went to the network's Las Colinas facilities to record the series.

The First Amendment guarantees that the government shall not interfere in religion, but it doesn't say that churches, Bible rooted morality, and Christian people should stay out of politics. The doctrine of separation of church and state was birthed in a Supreme Court ruling in 1878. The court excerpted phrases from a letter written by Thomas Jefferson three quarters of a century earlier.

The Baptist community of Danbury, Connecticut had written President Jefferson seeking assurance that they would not be discriminated against because of their religion. In their letter, the Danbury Baptists stated that religion is "a matter between God and individuals—that no man ought to suffer in name, person, or effects on account of his religious opinions." Jefferson's concurring reply consisted of three paragraphs, the first a salutation and the last a close. The central paragraph, the body of the message, stated:

> Believing with you that religion is a matter which lies solely between Man & his God, that he owes account to none other for his faith or his worship, that the legitimate powers of government reach actions only, & not opinions, I contemplate with sovereign reverence that act of the whole American people which declared that their legislature should "make no law respecting an establishment of religion, or prohibiting the free exercise thereof," thus building a wall of separation between Church & State. Adhering to this expression of the supreme will of the nation in behalf of the rights of conscience, I shall see with sincere satisfaction the progress of those sentiments

which tend to restore to man all his natural rights, convinced he has no natural right in opposition to his social duties.

Jefferson confirmed that government should stay out of religion, not the other way around, unless religion was used as an excuse for shirking a person's "social duties." Clearly, his concept of separation was that (a) government shall not sponsor one religion or one sect over another and (b) that each of us should have a right to worship where we choose, when we choose, and how we choose as long as our religion does not conflict with our obligation to obey the law.

In 1878, the Supreme Court referred to Jefferson's letter for the first time when it dismissed a Mormon's argument that he had a religious obligation to exercise polygamy. The first use of the separation concept by the courts was to refute an argument that religion could be used as a defense for breaking the law.

Since 1878, however, the courts have increasingly used the clauses of Jefferson's letter to legitimize agnosticism and atheism as the only acceptable forms of public, religious expression, thereby granting those religions exactly what the first amendment forbids. They have subverted the intent of the original constitution and of Jefferson's interpretation of it. By banishing God from the public domain, atheists, humanists, and libertines have elevated their religion to the law of the land.

Thomas Jefferson's reasoned but casual paragraph has been used as the basis for alienating the church and the state for the last 130 years, and those who proselytize atheism, who would banish Christ from the classroom and strike every Christian symbol from the edifices of state, have leveraged their entire argument on a concept that never existed. It's all smoke and mirrors.

I hadn't had much experience in the television medium when I presented my study of the founding fathers and the ways that their messages were usurped to promote a nationalized apostasy. I presented my arguments simply, with minimal video editing as if I were standing at a lectern in front of a classroom.

I interviewed political figures on the program, too. The Hon. Joe Barton, who for many years represented a portion of Johnson County in the US Congress, was one of them. Joe has played a large role in the life of Steppingstone church, and if you ask him, I have little doubt that he will tell you that our ministry has played no small part in his life. As I told the Lighthouse congregation in the celebration of our thirtieth anniversary in April 2012, Joe Barton is a man of his word. At the same service, Congressman Barton reminisced about those interviews saying that I asked hard and sometimes penetrating questions that he hadn't expected. That was high praise from a man who has held the same office for almost as long as the Lighthouse ministry existed and who has been interviewed and scrutinized by professional journalists on national news programs like *Meet the Press* and *Face the Nation*.

America was established as a Christian nation. The founding fathers meant for us to respect the beliefs of others, but there is no evidence that they would have promoted humanism as the sole religion of a godless theocracy. There is no evidence that those founding fathers believed in anything but a single deity. There is nothing that suggests that they considered themselves gods or that they would have elevated government to the status of religion—quite the contrary.

Today the name of the Christian God has become anathema to American government and many of those who ostensibly represent the American people and the American way of life. Unless something changes, it can only be a matter of time and His patience before America becomes anathema to God.

Chapter 72

Revival

THE BROWNSVILLE REVIVAL in 1995 was a landmark event in the Pentecostal community. If you're a member of a spirit-filled church, you probably know all about it. It started in a Sunday church service at the Brownsville Assembly of God church in Pensacola, Florida, June 18, 1995.

As soon as I heard about it, I jumped in with both feet. I wanted to be where the Spirit was moving. My sister and I went to Brownsville for three days. We weren't disappointed. You can't be disappointed when the spirit of God is moving and people are getting saved, whether it's one by one or by the thousands. The spirit was at work there.

I had felt the spirit move just as strongly many times in services at Steppingstone. Brownsville was good, but we were having a strong move of the Spirit at home, too.

Sometimes, as I spoke on Sundays, I looked into the congregation and thought wind was blowing inside the building. Sometimes it was so powerful it was almost like rushing water. I had to look to see if a fan was blowing. Many times, I was slain in the Spirit just sitting on the pew.

On several occasions, as we entered into praise and worship a dense cloud, almost a mist, would fill the building. It was so thick I could not see the back of the auditorium. When Steve Solomon, a pastor who hosted a popular radio program called "Praise in the Night" was a visiting speaker at our church, he suddenly stopped in the middle of his sermon and exclaimed, "It's gold in here." Always before, the mist had been white. We were experiencing the manifest presence of the glory of God.

I didn't tell any members of the church about my response to Brownsville. Many of them planned to visit the Florida revival themselves, and I didn't want to influence or interfere with any work the Holy Spirit might do in their lives. I did not come back and tell them that I felt the Holy Spirit as strong in the Steppingstone.

Gary Mitchell and several others made the trip to Pensacola. After the others visited Brownsville, many of them reported the same feeling about it: "The spirit is as strong here as it is there." Their perceptions and observations confirmed mine. Brownsville was, no doubt, experiencing a revival, but the spirit was working the same way week in and week out at the Steppingstone church. Of course, our church could not have the same notoriety. Our congregation wasn't as big. While Burleson is on the periphery of the Dallas-Fort Worth metropolitan area (the metroplex), it is not at the heart of a city, so we didn't get the publicity of the Brownsville revival.

That may have been a good thing because the Brownsville movement had detractors both inside and outside the Pentecostal church. There are always people who condemn any spiritual activity, and there are always good Christians, pious people, who judge all spiritual movement by their own immediate experience with the Holy Spirit. That is, if they have never talked in tongues, they don't believe in tongues. If they have never healed the sick or been healed by faith or seen the healing of a family member who has suffered for a lifetime, then they don't believe in spiritual healing or they relegate it to the times when Jesus or the twelve disciples walked the earth. If they have never seen a prophecy spoken in a church service come true, then they don't believe in prophecy even though the Bible itself is a chronicle of prophetic word and its fulfillment. If they have never been smitten to the floor after having anointed hands laid on them, then they don't believe in the possibility of being slain in the spirit even if they have seen it a hundred times. If they have never received a financial blessing after giving to the church or others, then they think the prosperity message is hooey.

I didn't go to Florida with a preconditioned mindset, except that I never go anywhere without expecting God to work miracles. I have tried not to stuff God into a box with my worldly expectations and dictate to Him how it is appropriate for the spirit to move in another person or in the church. I acknowledge that manifestations of the spirit can be completely affected, but I don't feel it is my job to judge every individual case. Nor do I judge those people who don't exhibit the spiritual gifts.

A Holy Spirit movement was breaking out in many places. Churches were reporting it all across America especially in Rodney Howard Browne's revivals and the revivals led by many of the evangelicals who were popular in those years. It was a time of great growth in the church.

Chapter 73

Overcoming

GOD BLESSED THE Steppingstone church. The Holy Spirit moved in our services, and our congregation continued to grow. In 2000, The Steppingstone launched construction of a new assembly hall on the lot next to the church campus. It was an ambitious project that would double the capacity for our Sunday morning services.

Since the first days of my ministry, I have believed that God will bring a great revival to the United States. People will become hungry for the gospel, and there will be so many new Christians that the churches will not have room for them all. The new believers, as well as Christians who are suddenly revived, who awake, arise, and shine will need places to come together in worship and to share the riches of God's word. The church, both as the body of Christ and as a building, must be ready for the overflow.

Despite the secular world's tendencies to dismiss Christianity and spiritual visions, people all over the world sense that the end time is approaching. Non-Christian theories about the end of the world abound. Films and television sink a little further in the mire of apocalyptic heresies with every new blockbuster and each new prime-time lineup. People study Nostradamus and the Mayan calendar (until it ran out) rather than reading the Bible. Apocalypse sells, and the media seem determined to guide us into it relying on soothsayers and sorcerers, teenaged super sleuths and scalawags for salvation. Belief in anything will save us, it seems, except faith in God and Jesus Christ, His son. People sit for mind numbing hours and lay their souls at the digital, high-definition altars of ghost whisperers and mediums, superheroes and x-files, and one protagonist after another who outwits the devil to save all mankind.

The Christian church builds places where we can worship precisely because it believes that the rest of mankind will eventually see the light, and the church must be ready when it does. We have an awesome responsibility.

If we fail, souls will be lost to eternal damnation because we didn't do the one thing that our God commissioned us to do: Arise. Shine.

When the Steppingstone church started building its new sanctuary in 2000, I didn't have to pick up a hammer. I didn't have to connect spars to a crane, although maybe I should have. The building was practically completed by late 2001. The two biggest jobs remaining were laying the carpet and building the speaker's platform. Gary Hood, a member of the church who was a builder and contractor, had gone into the new sanctuary to get measurements. From the outset, Gary had planned to construct the speaker's platform. He had told us to make sure that the builders didn't include it in their construction estimates because he wanted to build it himself. Now that the building was almost finished, he felt that he could start planning. He and Cory were looking at the building together, and they noticed a large crack at the peak of the sanctuary's roof. Gary could tell right away that it was a lot more than just a small crack or a painting oversight. The sheetrock seemed to be splitting right at the apex.

The two of them got into an unfinished area on the second floor. The area will be finished out as a balcony someday when expansion is necessary, but then and now it's unfinished. They were able to see right up into the framework. Immediately, Gary realized what the problem was, although he didn't want to believe it. "There's no bracing for the trusses, and they're rolling," he told Cory.

I was sitting in my office when they came in with the news. I wasn't sure what it all meant, but it didn't sound good. With Cory and Gary in the office to explain the problem, we called the construction company. We had a very good relationship with them, and I assumed they would send someone over immediately to see what was happening and start fixing the problem. Instead, the contractor denigrated Gary. "Oh, he's a just a home builder, and he probably doesn't understand the construction," the project manager told me. "There's nothing wrong with that building." He didn't say anything about sending someone over, even though we had told him about the cracks in the ceiling, too. His tone was different than it ever had been when speaking to me before. That was the first time I had ever had a conversation with him when he seemed like he didn't want to talk to me. He said there was no need to have his engineer look at it. That was the first sign that there was a bigger problem than met the eye.

Within a few weeks, we realized we were going to have to get an expert to look at it ourselves. We contracted an engineer to inspect the construction and help determine what we needed to do about it. When the engineer came downstairs after his brief inspection, his analysis was much the same as Gary's. "You need to put a yellow ribbon around this building," he pronounced. "It's dangerous." As soon as the written report made it to my desk, we sent it off to the building contractor. Weeks passed with no response.

In the meantime, the church funded two additional, independent studies by different engineering firms. Each report could be summarized with the same simple statement: it was bad. Two of the three firms said that the problems couldn't be fixed and that the building could probably never be occupied. One of the engineers even suggested, "Maybe you should just tear it down and start over." As rowdy as worship in a Pentecostal church can get, there was no doubt in my mind he was right. The roof would cave in on the congregation the first time Cory blew the shofar, a Ram's horn trumpet similar to the one that the Israelites' priests used to announce holidays. Shofars were probably used during the daily march around Jericho for seven days until the walls came tumbling down. I could almost see our walls tumbling down, too.

None of the engineers suggested a solution. Only one thought the building could be salvaged. He didn't know how, but he thought it might be possible. He agreed with the others that the building could not be occupied as it was. They studied the blue prints and individually confirmed that, if the building had been constructed as designed, there would have been no problems. The blueprint clearly indicated that bracing for the trusses should have been installed. After three reports, the construction company could no longer deny the obvious. They sent their engineer to conduct a survey of the building, and he had to concur with the others. But despite all the studies and the conclusions of their in-house engineer, the construction company offered no recompense or solution. It was clear they had cut corners in the construction, but they hadn't made a single gesture toward offering any kind of remedy, whether monetary or ameliorative. They didn't offer to try to engineer a solution. They certainly didn't offer to follow the recommendations of the independent engineers and pull the building down and start over. In fact, they made it clear they intended to do absolutely nothing.

The most disastrous effect of the shoddy construction wasn't that we couldn't occupy the new building. It was that people started leaving the church. Can you believe it? People gave the excuse that they were leaving our church to worship elsewhere because the new building couldn't be completed. We still met in the old sanctuary. We had been meeting in it for more than ten years, and it wasn't as though the engineers had condemned our whole campus. They had only told us not to move into the new building. At the rate our congregation was shrinking, it wouldn't take long before we didn't need the new building anymore.

As far as paying for the repairs, the Steppingstone church had exhausted its financial resources long before the issues with the trusses had been discovered. Before construction had started, our building fund was about eight hundred thousand dollars, and we had used that entire amount as down payment. We had borrowed an additional million from a local bank, and it had all been spent on the building.

Even though I knew things would eventually work out as the Lord intended them, I couldn't see how it was going to happen. If I had not known that God works miracles in the body of the church in the same way that he works miracles in an individual's physical body, and if I had not witnessed, first hand, God's miraculous power, I may have been dejected. I thought about ways to get out of the mess we were in. During a trip to a conference in Chicago, I was preoccupied with the problems with the building. The church had taken out a million dollar life insurance policy for me several years earlier, and I offered that to the Lord if it was how He wanted to pay for the repairs or reconstruction. He could have taken me in my sleep, and I would have only had another reason to celebrate. He didn't take me up on it. I'm still here.

As we are all prone to do, I was thinking in the physical. Perhaps I wasn't giving God full credit for His authority over all things. He always has a better plan, and sometimes we just have to wait for Him to work it through others. Not everyone gets healing for their illnesses when they ask. Sometimes God waits. Sometimes He waits for us to be ready for Him to act. Sometimes He waits just so that we will recognize a miracle for what it is.

Praise God when things seem like they're going nowhere because at those times He's moving just like a submarine tidal wave that may not be seen on the surface of the ocean, but as it approaches land, its awesome force becomes obvious. We can neither understand nor account for His timing, but I believe there is a reason for many of God's delays. Maybe a delay will lead to someone's salvation. It's impossible to know. So praise God. Someday we may get access to a tiny part of God's reasoning, and we may understand some of the intricacies of His mind. When we do, we will no doubt be like the angels who unceasingly sing God's praises because they unceasingly discover new things about His awesome glory.

When I got back from the Chicago conference, I was told that Patsy Dumas, whom I have known most of my life and who was an officer at the First National Bank of Burleson, had called and wanted to meet with the board. When we met, she brought along the bank's president and other loan officers. She told us the bank had gone out to a sister bank and gotten an additional loan. They tagged the financing onto the existing loan somehow so that the church only had to make one monthly payment to First National, and they took care of the payment to the other lender. That was an answer to my prayers because we couldn't get any money to fix the building ourselves. God had continued working in miraculous ways when it seemed that every solution of man had failed.

Over the months since he and Cory had discovered the unsecured roof trusses, Gary Hood hadn't been able to stop thinking about it. He prayed and asked God how to fix it. And God showed him. Gary drew up plans and submitted them to one of the independent engineering firms that we had consulted with earlier. The firm signed off on his plan.

Instead of destroying the whole building or tearing out the roof entirely, Gary's plan just required the construction team to open the roof, install bracing, and then reseal the hole. Maybe it shouldn't have been so difficult to figure out. After all, doctors do it all the time when they perform surgery. And that's exactly what Gary's solution was, surgical reconstruction. They cut a huge hole in that roof. It may not have been microsurgery, but to me that was just like a surgeon's incision. They didn't tear out any of the infrastructure. They went in and fixed it.

One of the consulting companies had suggested that, during the reconstruction period, we should keep the air conditioner running and try to maintain an inside temperature of about eighty-five degrees Fahrenheit to preserve the building, so the air conditioning was always on. When the repair team first opened the roof, cold air gushed from inside. The frigid air had been trapped in the attic. At first it was a mystery, but as the repair team got inside the roof, they found that air conditioning vents had not been completely installed. They weren't pulled together and wrapped. They were disconnected, and cold air was streaming out into the attic. If we had not opened the roof to make the truss repairs, we never would have found the air conditioning problems. Our cooling bills would have been out the roof, so to speak, and we may never have understood why it was so difficult to keep the sanctuary cool on Sunday mornings. While they were fixing the roof we had to have the air conditioning system's venting properly re-installed, too. Then we discovered the walls weren't properly constructed either. They didn't have the bracing required to connect the walls to the roof.

I never got a chance to ask the representative of the original construction company how he felt about Gary's plan for the repair. When we had first reported the problem he had said that Gary was just a local builder and suggested that we didn't understand the intricacies of the construction of a large building like a church, but it was Gary, that same man whose opinions had been denigrated, that eventually saved our building. Gary, the local builder ostensibly lacking the requisite sophistication and education, was the only person who had even offered a solution. Professional engineers from four separate firms, if you count the company that had originally con-structed the building improperly, had only stood and scratched their heads while Gary bowed his in prayer and respect for the Lord. And look who the Lord sent an answer to. I'm not saying that the independently contracted engineers were not Christians. I don't know that, but I know that Gary was praying for an answer. It didn't come quickly, and Jesus did not crawl up on the roof and make the repairs himself. He didn't send angels to make the repairs, but I think we got the next best thing, an inspired plan for repairing the church. It was a miraculous answer to our prayers.

The church retained a lawyer to represent us as we continued negotia-tions, if you want to call them that, with the construction company that had botched the job so badly. The attorney's investigations showed that the company had a long history of failures. It had declared bankruptcy and changed its name repeatedly in order to avoid fulfilling its legal obligations. Before our church was built, a school in a nearby town south of Cleburne had sued them. A large church in the Dallas-Fort Worth metroplex, whose roof had actually caved in, had caused them to declare bankruptcy and change company names. After the fiasco with our church, they continued to operate in the Dallas-Fort Worth area under a series of new names.

Butch Korb attended our church. He served as one of our attorneys as we continued negotiations with the construction company. He probably provided as much as $100,000 worth of services though he never charged us a cent. The lawyer we had retained worked closely with Butch, passing along some of the routine work. Butch was a Godsend because the attorney we had retained charged fifty dollars an hour. The attorney passed as much as he could to Butch so it wouldn't cost us any more than was absolutely necessary, and Butch spent a lot of time on our case.

Because of the construction company's history, our attorney was really walking a fine line. We wanted to force them to compensate our damages once we went into arbitration, but we didn't want to exert so much pressure that they declared bankruptcy and walked away from their ethical obligations to compensate us for the costs of completing the building.

Up to this point, a casual observer with no knowledge of the company's history could have chalked up all the problems to egregious oversights and maybe even incompetence, but you know what they did next? Once we got a settlement in which they agreed to compensate us for the repairs we had already made, they tried to obfuscate and avoid the payout, even though the money was coming from their insurance companies and not directly out of the company coffers. The settlement wasn't that detrimental to them. They were only required to compensate us for our expenses to complete the repairs. While our attorney was confident that we would have obtained a stiff judgment, with heavy punitive damages for their malfeasance, we couldn't take the chance that they would declare bankruptcy and wiggle out of their financial obligations as they had in the past when they had been sued by other customers. We felt it was best to take the little that we could get. Despite the agreement, they seemed determined to deprive us even of the small monetary concessions they had made in arbitration.

The builder owned two insurance policies that could be related to our claims. Each policy was with a different insurance company and covered a portion of the builder's obligation to us. They filed an incorrect claim with each insurer. What one insurance company was supposed to be responsible for was filed on the other insurance plan and vice versa. It was a delaying tactic designed to stall payments so that the builder would eventually have to pay nothing. There was a time limit on their obligation to pay at all, and if they stalled long enough they would wiggle out of any payment. It may not have been coming directly out of the builder's pocket, but maybe they figured their insurance costs would sky rocket if they actually had a payout. Who knows? Because of the inappropriate claims, each of the insurance companies responded with a denial. Neither one was liable for the claims cited by the builder. Finally, time had run out. Our attorney reported to us that there were no remaining avenues of legal recourse.

During the attempts to settle the claims, administrators for the two insurance companies figured out what the construction company was doing. They realized the predicament that our church was in, and how the building contractor had put us there, and praise God, claims representatives from the two companies got together. They went ahead and paid what the contractor had agreed to pay us in the settlement. The insurance companies could have gotten out of it. There was no longer a legal requirement for them to pay us. Each of them could have denied the claim that the contractor had filed with them and let it drop, but they didn't.

God is great. His miracles are boundless. There can be little question that we overcame a deliberate frontal assault by forces of evil through prayer and faith. God performed a whole series of miracles during the darkest hours of our church's history. Just think about it. He led Gary and Cory to a discovery of the unbraced trusses before we had occupied the building, before the roof came crashing down on us in a Sunday service. He planted an idea for fixing the building construction in Gary's mind. He led our friends at First National Bank of Burleson to find a way to help us with financing our repairs despite the best plans of the devil to thwart all our attempts to build a church. He led us to discover other construction errors through our repair of the roof. Finally, he led two insurance companies to compromise on a way to compensate us when the builders were doing everything they could to avoid any kind of payment. He turned every disaster into victory.

We had started construction on the new sanctuary in 2000. At that time, we had two services every Sunday morning with a total attendance of a little over 500 people. The new sanctuary was designed to accommodate up to 700 people before the balcony area was opened. It easily would have been enough to combine the two services and still have room enough for modest growth.

Cory and Gary discovered the faults in the construction when the new building was nearing completion in December 2001. At that time, church attendance was still high. We were not able to occupy the building until 2004, and by that time, combined attendance in Sunday services had dwindled to two-thirds the size of attendance in 2000. Those kinds of figures weren't calculated into the church's losses. There were no punitive damages even though the members of the congregation who had moved to other churches between 2001 and 2004 had taken their tithes and their building fund offerings with them.

We were almost three years behind schedule, and the financial damages to the church as a result of the poor workmanship and malfeasance were incalculable. Nevertheless, the church was still intact. Our ministry survived.

Four years late but still on time, the Lighthouse Church started meetings in the new sanctuary on October 4, 2004.

As we neared the end of that period, Brandi Jobe, a gospel singer, modified one of the songs that she frequently sang in our Sunday services. The song was about Jesus' resurrection of Lazarus. It ends with the phrase "four days late but still on time." In the last line of her song Brandi changed the lyric to "four years late but still on time." When everything is lost and there is no way out of a dilemma, God can still overcome. It's never too late to trust Him.

The Bible is a book about bad things happening to good people. It describes the troubles people have had and how God brought them through. Our Christianity doesn't guarantee that we will not have problems. Instead it says, "Many are the afflictions of the righteous, but the Lord delivers him out of them all" (Psalm 34:19). He walks with us through the valley of the shadow of death. He never tells us that we won't have to walk through that valley, but He assures us that we don't have to walk through it alone.

Yet many people today seem to believe that if you have problems and storms in your life, God isn't with you. Our congregation dwindled during the years when our building stood almost finished but unoccupied. Many people believed that our struggles were a sign that God was somehow displeased with the church, but how can you believe that when He performed such miracles to bring us through it. God didn't create our problems. Men did, dishonest and disreputable or incompetent men, who cloaked theft in business attire. God solved our problems. He brought us through despite the devil's best efforts to use such men to bring us to ruin. Praise God. We win. We always win when we wait on and trust in the Lord.

Chapter 74

Dancing with Jesus

Is that Jesus praying, Nanny,
For the lady on the floor?
Once He touches someone, Nanny,
They only want Him to touch them more.

Do you see the angels, Nanny,
Gathering round above
Singing praises while she lies
Wrapped in Jesus' love.

They're so beautiful. They glow, Nanny,
When Jesus passes through.
Why are you staring at me so, Nanny?
Don't you see angels, too?

Don't cry, Nanny, not for me.
You shouldn't be that way.
He took my little hand, and see
Now I dance with Him all day.

I'm dancing with the Savior, Nanny,
And I can tell you a secret, too.
He told me not too long ago
He's holding a dance for you.

Maisie loved to dance. She was the oldest of my great-grandchildren, the daughter of Shanda's son, Jerome. At four-years-old, she sang songs about Jesus, and she talked about Him all the time. She sang praise songs constantly. I believe that, in her innocence, she understood more about Christ's message than many adults ever will. Jesus loves children. They are closer to Him than adults. Maisie certainly was.

We didn't think her dedication and constant praise of the Lord was unusual because she went to church all the time. Her parents, Jerome and Karen, worked with the youth pastor at Steppingstone. They were always at youth meetings, and Maisie had heard all the Christian music. She loved it. During praise services on Sunday mornings, I could sometimes pick out her voice despite the roar of the instruments to my right, the choir behind me, and the sea of souls who had come for worship. When she wasn't at church, Maisie played Christian tapes and sang along. There was little doubt that she would someday be a praise leader.

She loved the songs "I'm Trading My Sorrows," and "I Can Only Imagine." She was a delight to the church and to me. I'm sure she was a delight to the Lord, too.

Maisie's life was a dance with Jesus. Born with a heart murmur, she was perhaps in step with a slightly different rhythm than most children. Perhaps she knew how close she was to being in Jesus' arms at any time. Her heart beat to the step-drag-step-drag rhythm of a waltz rather than the quickstep tatta-tat that most children's hearts are timed to. She often talked about heaven with her parents and with me, her "nanny." Her teachers from vacation Bible school and her Sunday school teachers saw something wonderfully different about Maisie.

She never left a service without saying bye to me, usually with a hug bigger than she was. As soon as she got out of children's church or the nursery, she ran to the auditorium and found me. No matter where I was when she got into the building, she would holler, "Nanny," as she ran to me. She dashed to me with her arms raised, knowing as surely as she knew that Jesus loved her, that nanny would pick her up. After she had her hug at the end of a service, she was ready to go home with her parents. I grew to expect that hug. I would have missed it if I hadn't gotten it.

In July 2001, Alberta Quigley, an evangelist especially liked by the young people and the children, visited Steppingstone. She took the time in her services to minister to people one by one, delivering a personal word for each of them. The website of John Gan Ministries describes Quigley's ministry.

> This woman's ministry stirs up the gifts in everyone. Her love to see everyone come into the fullness of God's calling has changed my life. God's anointing on her stirs the crowd to participate and minister...We all have perfect gifts from above, and you just may find out what that is as God stirs you during one of her ministry sessions.

The altar services often lasted as long as the message and sometimes even longer when Alberta spoke. The church met every night from Sunday through Wednesday during the week she was at the Lighthouse. One night Maisie boldly stepped up to the front during the altar call while the Reverend Quigley was ministering and laying on hands. So the evangelist said, "And what do you want from the Lord?"

Without missing a beat, Maisie replied, "I want to go be with Jesus."

Wednesday was the last night of the series, and it was the longest altar call of the entire week. Despite the late hour, no one left. Normally, even though it was summer, people started leaving as soon as the message was over, and people continued to drift out throughout the altar call. After all, they had jobs, and children needed their sleep even if they didn't have to worry about homework or school the next morning, but that night it was nearing 11:00 p.m., and no one had left. We were all still standing, singing, and praising God.

Alberta was praying for people, and some lay sprawled on the floor, slain in the spirit. I sat in the front row of the congregation. I was watching a woman who lay on the floor as Alberta moved on to another who had come forward. The lady lay motionless at the base of the podium with a peaceful smile, enraptured, touched by the spirit. Maisie left her seat next to her mother and sneaked up beside me. We watched together.

"Is that Jesus that's praying for her?" Maisie whispered, tugging at my sleeve. I couldn't see anyone standing near the woman. She was lying on the floor alone. Excited, Maisie answered her own question, "It is. That's Jesus." There was no one that I could see.

"That's wonderful," I said anyway. Almost before the words were out, Maisie gazed up at the ceiling.

"Nanny, see the angels?"

"Where? You see angels?"

"Yes, they're everywhere." Maisie pointed up drawing an arc across the ceiling with her finger following the flight. Her finger moved about the room, up and down but always as though it was following the motion of an invisible butterfly.

"See it, Nanny. Don't you see the angels?"

I couldn't lie to her. "Oh," was all I managed to utter, while trying to think of the right response. I was still searching for an answer when Karen sat beside us.

"She said she's seeing angels," I explained.

"Yes, she's been seeing angels all through the service; the whole evening, she's been looking at angels." For the rest of the service Maisie watched the angels float about the room singing heavenly praises to Jesus Christ. She gave me her customary hug before walking away holding her mother's hand.

It was summer in Texas. Hot. It was so hot that anyone not in an air-conditioned room was preoccupied with the heat. Maisie, too. Her parents lived in the country outside Burleson, and a week after seeing Jesus in the meeting, she played in a wading pool. Karen was in the kitchen just a few feet away listening to Maisie and Brooke, Maisie's three-year-old sister, giggle and splash. Karen had just noticed that they had gotten quiet and the splashing had stopped when Brooke called, "Maisie, get up. Mama, Maisie won't get up."

I sat in the pastor's study musing over the week's message. Cory burst into the room. "We just got a phone call. Maisie has drowned."

Without leaving any messages or notifying anyone, Cory, Richelle, and I scrambled from the church. We didn't tell anybody. If somebody had come in, they wouldn't have known what happened to us. We didn't think about it. We just jumped in the car.

Karen had dialed 911 before calling us. The emergency assistant had instructed her in CPR, but she hadn't been able to get Maisie's mouth open. Her daughter's jaw wouldn't budge. It was only minutes until the paramedics arrived, and Karen called Cory while they worked.

Cory, Richelle, and I sped to the country. Richelle called Karen from the car. "Turn around," Richelle said. "She's alive. They're flying her to the hospital." Cory turned around and headed back toward Fort Worth. We supposed the paramedics had resuscitated her after all.

"Go straight to the emergency room," Karen told us over the phone. "We'll meet you there."

The waiting room was different than I had expected. Rather than pointing out the chairs in the lobby after we told her we were there for the little girl who had been brought in from Burleson, the receptionist said, "Come with me." She ushered the family into a room where we waited privately. That really told us Maisie's condition was grave. Praying, we filed into the room and waited.

The paramedics had gotten Maisie stabilized before they put her on the helicopter, but en-route they lost her again. They continued to work with her all the way to the hospital, and they must have continued to try to revive her even after she was delivered because every now and then someone reported, "It's not good. It doesn't look good."

We kept praying. Even when it seemed hopeless, we prayed that God would raise her. I thought at times that my prayer would be answered. Then I saw Jesus walk into the room where they still tried to revive my darling. I saw the huge room, without the privacy curtains that would normally hang around the bed of an emergency room patient. Jesus was smiling, and he had his arms stretched out as though to catch a child that was running into them. A few minutes later, the doctors told the family they had stopped trying to revive her.

Someone in the group suggested that we should pray for God to resurrect her, but I disagreed. I knew that God had shown me He was taking her. I knew what He was telling me, because we had already asked for Him to send her back to us, and that prayer had remained unanswered.

At the church, people were praying, too. They had started arriving as word had circulated among church members. People who hadn't heard began arriving for the midweek service by five in the evening. As they arrived, they began praying.

I know that there was enough prayer and enough faith that if it had been God's will, He would have raised her. You know, God's ways are not our ways, and we have to trust Him. Besides, our prayers were answered even before we started praying. Maisie had already been resurrected into the bosom of the Lord.

We went into the room where Maisie lay. It looked exactly as I had seen it in my vision. It was a large open area with the table in the middle. Maisie was still on the table where they had tried to revive her. I knew then that my vision had been from God. It was really hard for me, but it was easier having seen the Lord himself waiting for her.

The recent memories of her, especially those of the previous week when she had seen the angels and when she had announced her heart's desire to be with Jesus, consoled me and the rest of the family. She always wanted to go be with Jesus. She danced to the Christian music and said she was dancing with Jesus. It's as if she was already there, in heaven with Him, at times. I think she saw beyond this realm. Obviously, she did because she saw angels, and sometimes when she said she was dancing with Jesus, I think she might actually have been. We couldn't see Jesus, but who's to say she couldn't?

It's not like heaven or Jesus is that far off. He and heaven are only a heart-beat away. There's no huge gulf that we have to cross to be with Him. Maisie could see across it. When she died, it wasn't as though it was frightening or terrible. She was already there, in heaven. She had been all along. Suddenly, instead of standing on the earth and looking into heaven, she was standing in heaven and looking back.

She looked like a doll lying there. She was so pretty.

A doctor said later that it appeared she had a seizure, probably caused by her bad heart and the hot weather. She had probably fallen head first into the pool and drowned. Because she had a seizure, her jaw was clamped shut.

I don't have any answers about why children die, but there is no question that Maisie's time here was blessed; her testimony was as influential as anyone who has lived, what we think of as, a full life. A lot of people got saved as a result of her life.

Jesus said that one soul is worth more than the whole world to Him. He said that if you gain the whole world and lose your soul, you have nothing. Maisie had everything. She was one of his messengers. Many of Karen and Jerome's family members were saved because of Maisie's life and her death. The Lord needed to send a child like her so that He could perform His work in the lives of her family. Many of those who knew how she loved Jesus were saved.

She talked to people about Jesus incessantly. She had cute little ways of starting the conversation. "Do you know Jesus?" "Are you saved?" She was always talking to people about salvation. It was on her mind all the time. What a powerful witness for the Lord. Jesus was always foremost in her thoughts, and that's the role He should play in our lives. If we know Jesus, we should be dancing with Him and celebrating incessantly.

Could Jesus have resurrected Maisie? Of course. "The things which are impossible with men are possible with God" (Luke 18:27). But after seeing Jesus enter the room, I didn't feel that it was right to pray for her physical resurrection. "Suffer little children to come unto me and forbid them not: for of such is the kingdom of God" (Luke 18:16). No one was ever more pre-pared to enter into the kingdom of God than Maisie, and Jesus explained that to us in the next verse of Luke: "Verily I say unto you, Whosoever shall not receive the kingdom of God as a little child shall in no wise enter therein" (Luke 18:17). Maisie was so full of the Holy Spirit that she was overflowing, and it came bubbling forth in every word and action. She knew the unalterable truth that somehow manages to remain a secret from most of the world, even though Christians like her are shouting it from the rooftops: the secret of salvation. Our time, our existence, is a unique and wonderful blessing given of God. We are all chosen to become His children. He chose us when He breathed life into us. The only question is "will you choose Him?" Maisie did.

We have all watched young children play. They are so wrapped up in the moment and in the thrill of what they're doing that nothing else matters. They have no cares or concerns or burdens. They play with absolute abandon. Perhaps that's what Jesus was talking about. Certainly, Jesus was referring to children's innocence, too. The most common interpretation of these verses is that we must ask to be forgiven of our sins and enter into God's kingdom as innocents. But that's not all of it. Our relationship with Jesus isn't a walk; it's a wonderful dance. Accepting Jesus is becoming like a child at play, laying aside all the cares and concerns of our worldly responsibilities and feeling nothing more than the excitement of being with Him. That's what it will be like in heaven. When we have that kind of relationship with Him, we bring heaven into our lives. Maisie was so full of excitement about Jesus she could burst. That's dancing with Jesus. And when we're dancing with Jesus, sharing God's Word isn't a chore, a charge, a challenge, or a choice, it's as natural as a giggle.

At those times when I miss my great-granddaughter the most, I close my eyes and see her still laughing and dancing with Jesus.

Maisie

Chapter 75

More than Conquerors

NOT EVERYONE FELT the same way about Maisie's death. A few families with small children left the church. Some even said that they were leaving because they feared something similar could happen to their children. They believed that if a death like that can happen in the pastor's family, then maybe they weren't protected. What a sad and horrible misunderstanding of scripture.

The Bible does not guarantee that we won't go through hardships. Any message that teaches Christians that they are not susceptible to the same tribulations on this earth as non-believers is an aberration of the message of salvation. Such messages are delivered by and tailored for people who think only in worldly terms.

Jesus said, "In the world you will have tribulation; but be of good cheer. I have overcome the world" (John 16:33, NKJV), and "I will never leave you nor forsake you" (Hebrews 13:5, NKJV), which says to me that whatever trials we go through, He is with us and will bring us through in victory by His grace and power. I love what the word says in Romans:

> What then shall we then say to those things? If God is for us, who can be against us?... Who shall separate us from the love of Christ? Shall tribulation, or distress, or persecution, or famine... Yet, in all these things we are more than conquerors through Him who loved us. For I am persuaded that neither death nor life... shall be able to separate us from the love of God which is in Christ Jesus our Lord.
> —ROMANS 8:31–39, NKJV

Our faith does not guarantee protection from problems or heartache. The stories of Christian martyrs in the century after Christ's death prove that Christians have been threatened and persecuted because of their faith since Jesus walked the shores of Galilee. With the exception of John, each of the disciples who walked with Christ was executed for his beliefs. They suffered hardships throughout their lives for what they believed.

God comforted me in the weeks after Maisie's passing with the story of Stephen. If you know Stephen's story that may seem odd. Stephen was one of the deacons in the first church. He was not one of the twelve disciples, but his faith was as strong as anyone's in history. He had the kind of faith that Maisie had, joyful and absolute. The first of the new disciples mentioned by name in Acts 6, Stephen was so full of the Holy Ghost that he couldn't stop preaching the word.

He preached about Jesus' life boldly, with reckless abandon of thought for himself. He performed great wonders and miracles among the people. He was captured and brought before the council, and those who were persecuting him saw his face as if it had been the face of an angel. Standing before them, Stephen recounted the history of the Jewish people and how Jesus was fulfillment of the scriptures that foretold of the messiah. Then he calmly looked into the heavens and proclaimed, "Behold, I see the heavens opened, and the Son of man standing on the right hand of God" (Acts 7:56). For that, they stoned him. Exactly as Jesus himself pleaded for the souls of his tormentors, when Stephen lay dying, he said, "Lord, lay not this sin to their charge" (Acts 7:60). What wonderful faith and forgiveness. That's the way it is when you're dancing with Jesus.

According to historians, Stephen was young. He may have been anywhere from seventeen to twenty-one. In many ways, he was still a child. The Bible says there was great lamentation over him. The apostles loved him as though he was a child, and yet his is one of the most impressive acts of sacrifice recorded in the Bible.

The consoling peace that I found in Stephen's story wasn't shared by some in the church. At that time, we entered into a period of trials that affected our church and our congregation. It wasn't long after Maisie's death that we discovered the problems with the new building.

In the years following Stephen's death, Christians were scattered from Jerusalem because of persecution, yet the word of God grew and multiplied. They went everywhere sharing. Many of these early Christians had seen Jesus crucified. Some had seen Him after His resurrection. They knew of Peter and John and how they had been delivered out of prison by angels. God had performed tremendous miracles to save them.

The church could have said of Stephen, "Why did God let him die? Why didn't God send an angel to stand between him and the stones? Why didn't God work a miracle?" The whole ministry of Christ could have ended right at that point if the early church had been rooted in the world and not in the word.

The church today is a lot like the disciples when Jesus still walked with them. He told them he was going to die, but they didn't accept it. They could not comprehend it. When Jesus told his disciples, "you will be delivered up" (ESV), He wasn't speaking just about those twelve. He was speaking about those that followed them, too. He was telling them and us that many will be put to death. Jesus said, "In this world you will have tribulation, but be of good cheer. I have overcome the world" (John 16:33, NKJV).

In one of his letters Peter wrote, "Think it not strange concerning the fiery trial that will try you..." (I Peter 4:12). Peter is telling us that we can expect hardship and strife. Christians are not immune to the ills that all people suffer, "the whips and scorns of time, the oppressor's wrong, the proud man's contumely, the law's delay, the insolence of office or the spurns that patient merit of the unworthy takes" (Hamlet 3.1.1763-1767). As the children of Adam, we can expect hardship.

But Jesus is the overcomer. He overcame death. He can overcome whatever we go through. That message hasn't sunk in yet for many of us. Even though He told them He was going to die, Jesus' disciples couldn't believe it. Then, when He died on the cross, they thought all was lost. He had already told them that He would die and in three days He would rise, but the concept was unfathomable to them until it had actually happened.

We live in anno Domini. Even our calendar recognizes that we are living in His time. We should be able to see things from a different perspective than the followers of Christ who walked alongside him. We're on the power side. We're on the side of time after the Holy Spirit has been poured out. We have the power of the Holy Spirit, yet we're so much like the disciples in the days before they were baptized in the Holy Spirit. We're self-centered. We don't want to go through anything uncomfortable. It's like we don't think we should have to.

Maisie died, and the Lord had to comfort me in my sorrow. Her death doesn't mean I'm not blessed. It doesn't mean I'm not going to have blessings in the future. It certainly doesn't mean that Maisie regrets one moment that she lost here with me. She's dancing with Jesus.

After Maisie died and the church building was found to be flawed, I saw the reactions, the discouragement, and the lack of faith. I began to see how flawed the church is, not the building, the body. As with much of the Bible and religious experience, the challenges facing the Lighthouse in the physical realm reflected problems in the spiritual realm. Maybe as a church body of believers, we weren't ready to occupy the new meeting hall yet. It's not as though there are no biblical precedents. After all, the Israelites were not permitted to occupy the Promised Land until they were ready.

There were no flaws with the building's design or planning. The flaws were with the execution, the construction. God has a perfect plan for our lives, too. Where the problems come in are with the execution, our decisions to ignore or violate the plan for the sake of expedience or other selfish reasons. At first, it looked as though the building would have to come back down and we would have to re-build it from the ground up, but that just wasn't feasible, just as it's not feasible for us to start our physical life over again after we fail to do God's will. We accept our flaws, with God's grace fix them, and go on serving the Lord.

As we went through the agonizing years of the construction, I walked every day by faith. Eventually God made a way for the building to get fixed. It's actually stronger and better than it would have been if it had been built right to start with because it's had so much reinforcement. In designing the improvements, the architects and engineers not only compensated for what was wrong, but the changes improved on the design.

In the same way that we have overcome the flaws in the building that has become the Open Door Church, God's going to work in our lives until we overcome the flaws in us. Where our faith is weak, He's going to make us strong. The Lord has shown me things about myself through every experience we've had in building this church and this ministry. He showed me areas of pride and weakness, and He showed me areas of faith and strength. Every one of us has strengths and weaknesses, and we should praise God for any experience that shows us how we can walk closer with Him.

We began meeting in the new sanctuary on August 8, 2004. On October 4, Pastor Harold Nichols of Grace Temple, a longtime personal friend, delivered the dedication message and a prayer for the church, which was renamed

The Lighthouse Church of Burleson. State and national representatives who had become my personal friends over the previous thirty years spoke, too. Joe Barton, still US Congressman, spoke as a special guest of honor. State Representative Arlene Wohlgemuth delivered the exhortation. I later told people, including reporters from local papers, that the Lighthouse Church was probably the strongest building in town. It had been built twice, and God had a say in the final design of the reinforced building. It was a glorious celebration of victory, and every service in it is a reminder of God's grace and power.

STATE REPRESENTATIVE ARLENE WOHLGEMUTH AND US CONGRESSMAN JOE BARTON
PRESIDED OVER THE DEDICATION OF THE NEW SANCTUARY IN 2004.

GLORIA AND JOHN CELEBRATE THEIR 50th WEDDING ANNIVERSARY WITH THEIR
CHILDREN (L-R) OTIS, STUART, RICHELLE, AND SHANDA.

Chapter 76

Israel

J ULY 27, 2008, was the night of my return from the third annual conference of Christians United for Israel (CUFI) in Washington D.C. Our
Christ was a Jew. So how can anyone condemn the Jews as the race who
crucified Christ? Anyone with a little background in the Bible knows that
both Romans and Jews participated in Christ's death. The Jews may have
condemned Him, but it was the Romans who carried out the sentence. All
mankind, Jews and Gentiles, participated in the crucifixion.

We all crucified Christ: "For all have sinned and come short of the glory
of God" (Romans 3:23). Jesus died for the sins of all people: "For God so
loved the world that he gave his only begotten son, that whosoever believeth
in him should not perish, but have everlasting life" (John 3:16). The birth,
life, death, and resurrection of Jesus may have been a fulfillment of Jewish
prophecy, but Christ gave His life for us all: "But now in Christ Jesus
you who once were far off have been brought near by the blood of Christ"
(Ephesians 2:13, NKJV). We Christians join the Jews as God's chosen people
through the blood shed for us on the cross when we receive Jesus as our
savior.

That doesn't diminish God's covenant with the people and nation of
Israel. God made a covenant with the descendants of Abraham that cannot
be broken, but through Christ's death, he created a way for anyone to buy
into the contract, and it doesn't cost us a dime. Jesus paid the price, His
blood, and redeemed us from the curse of the law. He became cursed for us,
"(for it is written, 'Cursed is everyone who hangs on a tree') that the blessing
of Abraham might come upon the Gentiles in Christ Jesus, that we might
receive the promise of the Spirit through faith" (Galatians 3:13–14, NKJV).
Christians share in the covenants that God made with Abraham and Jacob,
but while we share in the covenant, we still recognize that the nation of
Israel is separate, and many Biblical prophecies that mention Israel pertain
to the nation of Israel and not the body of Christ, the church.

The Bible foretold the dispersion of the Jews across the globe, and the prophecies of the Old and New Testaments described how Jews from all over the world would migrate back to the land that God had given them. The migration started at the end of World War II and continues today. The return of the Jews to Israel is intricately intertwined with the end of the age of man.

Israel is, without doubt, the most hated nation on earth. You would think they must have committed some of the most heinous acts in history since the state of Israel was recognized a little over a half century ago. The truth is they are hated simply because they exist and because the fulfillment of biblical prophecies related to them prove that God exists and that the Bible is true. Jews are not universally hated because they have enslaved others or committed genocide in the name of racial integrity. Their very existence is an affront to many of the countries of the Middle East. Despite the fact that inter-Arab wars pre-date the delivery of the Jews to the Promised Land, some of the Arab nations seek to destroy the nation and the people of Israel. They won't be content until every last Jew on the face of the earth is dead. These are the same people who say they doubt that the Holocaust of World War II ever happened. They are the same people who, once they get their hands on nuclear weapons, will not hesitate to destroy the nation of Israel and its ally, America. They are the same people who would turn their hatred, and their weapons, on God's other children, Christians.

During CUFI's Night to Honor Israel, the Washington, D.C. Convention Center was packed with attendees waving American and Israeli flags. Israel's Ambassador to the United Nations, Dan Gillerman, Pastor John Hagee, and Senator Joseph Lieberman were the speakers. Senator Lieberman opened his speech by saying, "I am your brother Joseph." He went on to say, "You have come to Washington as Americans of faith with a purpose. You are Christians, united for Israel. And may God bless you for, and in, your work."

The day is coming, and it may not be far in the future, when all people will be forced to choose between the God of Abraham, Isaac, and Jacob and some other god. As Christians, we worship the same God as the Jews, and along with Israel, we may suffer extreme prejudice in the end times. We may be forced to choose between God and medical care, God and our jobs, or even between God and our lives. The Jews, because of their unique covenant with God, will have no choice. Many of them know this. The young man who sat next to me on my American Airlines flight from Washington to

Dallas-Fort Worth after the CUFI conference was aware of the isolation of Israel and of the close ties between Christians and Jews. He became interested when I described the conference to him.

At one of the most precarious times in Israel's history, we traveled to Washington to remind our nation and the world that Israel does not and will not have to stand alone, I explained to him. Christians will stand with them. I explained that Christ was the Messiah that the Jews had waited centuries for.

He smiled and said, "My wife will be happy to hear about our conversation." She was a Christian, and she had witnessed to him many times, he explained. The man did not give his life to the Lord during our flight, but I have to believe that God put me in the seat next to him for a reason. I will never know if he later became a Christian, but we agreed that the bond that unites Israel with Christians is essential to the survival of that nation. Our support of Israel must never falter no matter what stance the government of our nation takes.

Chapter 77

Cabbage Patch – Heart Surgery

THE COWBOYS, MY favorite team, hadn't been in the championship game on February 7, 2010. They had ended a thirteen-year playoff drought and beaten the Eagles in the wild card round during the first week of the series only to be knocked out of post-season play by the Minnesota Vikings in the divisional competition. But that had been three weeks earlier, and I didn't have a favorite between the two teams, Saints and Colts, that played for the NFL championship. Unlike lots of fans in Indianapolis on Monday morning, I had no reason to be sick. The weather couldn't be blamed either. It had been in the mid-forties with clear skies throughout the weekend and into the morning. I got up and started getting ready to go to the church, my typical Monday morning routine.

Researchers have stated that the risk of a heart attack is 33 percent higher on Monday than on any other day, and on that Monday following the big game, I personally contributed to all the statistics about Mondays and the day after the Super Bowl. I still hadn't had breakfast when I felt a pain in my chest. I tried to ignore it, but it only got worse. I took two aspirin and decided to sit for a few minutes. The pain subsided some, but didn't completely go away, and I decided to read my Bible until I felt well enough to go to the church.

I never felt very well, but decided to go anyway. At midday, I stopped by a store to pick up some refreshments for the board meeting, scheduled for later that evening. While I was shopping, the chest pains came back. I only had a few items, but as I stood at checkout, my chest got tighter and tighter. I considered asking if someone could carry my purchase to the car, but decided against it. It wasn't as though I couldn't make it to the car, but the pain was still growing. I got into the car, set down my purse and reached for my phone to call John. I was suddenly having a lot of difficulty using my arm. I dug for the aspirin that I carry in my purse and put a couple into my mouth before I pressed the speed dial buttons. I told John where I was and asked him to pick me up and take me to the hospital.

He had me to the ER within minutes. They checked me in and immediately started running tests. The symptoms hadn't lied. I was having a heart attack. The tests showed I had four clogged arteries. Two of them were almost completely obstructed and two of them were very bad. They scheduled the surgery for the next day.

Once they had my chest open, doctors decided to complete the by-passes for the two life-threatening arteries that were completely clogged, but they stopped there. I guess you could say they called the game on account of cabbage. My heart was so diseased that they decided to do only the absolutely critical work.

Cardiomyopathy is the technical term for an enlarged, diseased, and deteriorating heart, and my condition was so severe that the only viable alternative was a transplant. They didn't think my heart would hold up to more, so they just did enough to keep me alive.

During the surgery and in recovery, I was aware that the Lord was with me, and I remember feeling His overwhelming presence. It filled the room. It was so glorious I felt as though I may have been in heaven already. I asked if it was my time to go to heaven.

"No," he said. "Your work isn't finished. You will live to see the fulfillment of the vision I gave you." He went further and gave me some specific instructions about the Lighthouse ministry. Cory and Richelle were trying to launch a church. They had begun preparations and were looking for a place. I guess it was natural for me to think that the heart attack was a way for God to tell me it was time for me to surrender my role as senior pastor and turn over the ministry to others. Instead, he told me that it wasn't yet time for me to leave the full-time ministry. I was lying there, ostensibly under anesthesia, and God was telling me I would fulfill the vision he had given me and that Cory and Richelle were supposed to start a new church. My work in preparing the bride of Christ for his return was not finished.

Despite what God was telling me, the nurses were telling Shanda and Richelle that it was a miracle I was alive. They compared the surgery to opening up cabbages. CABG is an acronym for coronary artery bypass graft. Doctors and nurses just call it "cabbage." I was a miracle cabbage, they said, and they confessed that they hadn't thought I was going to survive the surgery.

Although they had patched me up well enough to send me home, I needed a new heart. The doctors told John all about the cardiomyopathy. He had discussed it with Shanda. If the doctors told me about the cardiomyopathy during post op or while I was in the hospital following my surgery, I didn't remember it. I knew they hadn't healed me. I was very sick. I felt overwhelmed—the simplest challenges began to seem like insurmountable obstacles. I often felt that I wasn't going to live much longer. At one point, I confided that feeling to John.

He rebuked the statement immediately. "I don't want to hear you say that again."

Recovery was slow. After three months, I started driving again, but I couldn't escape the sense that I didn't have much longer to live. It helped that my brother predicted some of my emotional reactions. He had bypass surgery a few years before I did, and he warned me that my emotions would be on edge, that I may be depressed, and that I may even cry for no obvious reason.

"If you know it's coming, then you can understand a little better what's happening when you suddenly break into tears," he told me. He was right, and I'm glad he said something. I was still surprised when it happened.

I cried at the drop of a hat. Richelle was still working at the Lighthouse, and on any given day, I might step into her office to consult about some problem with the utilities or to let her know how to manage payment of a bill. It could have been just about anything. Before the surgery, I would have given these minor issues little thought. Let's face it, the ministry is not a good life choice for someone who needs economic security, but after the surgery, even the slightest problem could set me off. I'd go in and I'd say, "Richelle, I don't know if we're going to have enough money," and it was like Moses striking the rock. I burst out with a gusher. Almost immediately, I'd recant, "Richelle, I'm really not worried. I don't know why I'm crying." I knew that the funds would most likely come in with the Wednesday night collection, and on Thursday we would have enough for the bill, but that didn't keep the emotions in check. I couldn't help it. It was like my heart got broken a thousand times a day. When you're a pastor, a lot of things get said to you or about you that could hurt your feelings. That's a given. You learn to take it in stride, but after the surgery, I couldn't deal with them.

The Bible associates the heart with emotions a lot, and the heart truly is where our emotions reside. Each insignificant incident hurt my heart. It was nothing like the pain of a heart attack, but it hurt.

Cory and Richelle Smithee. Cory was Steppingstone's Associate Pastor for twenty-three years. Richelle, Gloria's daughter, served as Worship Leader and Secretary for eleven years. The Lighthouse church helped them establish a church in Mansfield, Texas.

Chapter 78

Road to Healing

Cory and Richelle were concerned. They knew how I struggled. They could see that I had no energy, that my emotions were unpredictable, and that I was not improving. They continued preparing to launch a church, but they were conflicted because they didn't want to abandon me or the Lighthouse. They offered to stay. If the Lord hadn't already instructed me to allow them to leave and start a new ministry, I would have said, "Yes, oh, yes, please." The Lord had made it clear to me that it was important for them to continue their plans, so it was important that I follow through despite my personal feelings or even their loyalty or sense of obligation to me or to the Lighthouse church.

My brother, Grady, was concerned, too. After his heart attack and bypass surgery, the doctors had quickly reduced the frequency of his follow up visits. He got better. But as the year went on, I was weaker and more easily fatigued. The doctor required more frequent follow up visits for me than he had for Grady, who had only been required to see the doctor once every six months.

I struggled just to get up out of a chair. On Sundays, whether I preached or not, God gave me the energy to get through the service. God has always given me energy to preach. He has always given me the energy to do His will, but after church was over, whether I preached or not, I barely had enough energy left to get out of the church. People asked, "How are you doing it?" I answered, "Well, I'm trying to keep up," and that was the absolute truth, but I couldn't wait to get home and collapse on the couch.

It was a monumental effort to keep up with my duties. Otis and guest speakers started leading the services more often, but there was still a lot of work to do during the week. Some people seem to think that a pastor works one day a week. That's somewhat like believing that professional athletes only work when they are on the field or that lawyers only work when they are arguing a case. A lot of work gets done between Sundays. At least for me,

Sunday had always been the easy part, and now I was becoming too sick even for that. The day-to-day work of a church pastor was becoming overwhelming.

Although Otis spoke often, he couldn't preach every Sunday. He ran a business in Joshua, a few miles south of Burleson, and his business and other ministries carried him all over the state. One of his regular customers lived west of Mineral Wells. For years, the customer had taken pride in telling Otis that he was an agnostic. Every time Otis visited, the man greeted him with a playful reminder of his agnosticism. They often took a few minutes to sit and talk. On a call to design a new water system in 2010, Otis headed him off at the pass, "Are you still agnostic, Roy?" The preemptory question should have elicited a "yeah" or "maybe," at least a "whatever."

That day, however, Roy wanted to have a serious discussion. He asked Otis to come in and visit for a while. "I want to show you something," he said. He led Otis into the house and pointed to several paintings decorating his wall. There was one beautiful, western painting in particular that Roy drew him to. He pointed out the details, the veins in the horse's neck, the mane, and the eyes. It was amazing art. "The artist is a friend of mine," Roy explained. "He painted these for me. He's a good Christian man, just like you are. He even believes in faith healing, like you do."

Otis waited for a punch line that never came.

"I have an interesting story to tell you," Roy said. "Why don't you have a seat?"

Intrigued by the direction of the conversation, Otis sat and listed to Roy's tale. Roy and the artist weren't just friends. They were the best of friends. Sometime since Otis' last visit, Roy and his artist friend had taken their wives on holiday and rented a cabin together. "I have this bad knee," Roy said. "I really needed a knee replacement. It hurt me to take a step. It even hurt when I sat—hurt all the time." Chuck, Roy's artistic friend, had noticed the limp and the grimaces. He was well acquainted with them, and his compassion for his friend finally got the best of him.

"Roy," said Chuck. "I want you to sit down in that chair right there. God's going to heal your knee."

Roy balked like a worn out, old horse that's just been spurred in the flanks. "You know I don't believe in any of that stuff."

"I don't care if you believe in it or not. I've got enough faith for both of us. Now sit down." Getting down on one knee before the Lord, Chuck prayed for Roy.

Roy looked at Otis as he finished his tale, "And I could walk. There was no pain or anything at all. I walked to the window and pretended to look out while tears swelled in my eyes." It was clear to Otis that Roy was struggling mentally and emotionally with what he said next, "I'm still agnostic, but this has got me puzzled." They talked a while. Roy didn't give his heart to the Lord that day, or maybe that's the wrong way to say it. He didn't give his mind to the Lord that day. He was still trying to work through it intellectually and was tripping over his brain on the road to salvation.

About a year and a half later, Otis made a trip to Graford to see another customer in the area. He took along a friend, Chris Morris. "We went out to Graford and saw the customer," as Otis has described the trip. "We were on our way back, and as we were going through Mineral Wells, I told Chris to pick a place to eat."

Chris looked up the road and saw a barbecue restaurant ahead. He said, "Let's eat there."

They pulled over and went inside. As Otis entered the small eatery, he noticed several prints of western paintings lining the walls. Many of them looked very similar to the pictures hanging in Roy's home. Otis couldn't recall the artist's name, but he was pretty sure these were samples of his work.

As Otis stood at the register to pay for the meal, Chris, who had never met a stranger, noted aloud how cute the shop owner, Nancy, was; then, he turned away and started exploring other people with all the enthusiasm of a spelunker who has just discovered a new crevice. Nancy took Otis's credit card, but the reader didn't work. After tinkering with it for a moment, Nancy told Otis that she would have to go into the back office and reboot the computer. She told him it may take a few minutes and encouraged him to look at the artwork adorning the establishment while she tried to get the system working. "That man right over there painted them." She pointed as she disappeared into the office.

Otis looked over at an aging cowboy. He tried to remember the name of the artist whom Roy had described. Chris stood next to cowpoke's table. They were talking like old friends embellishing shared and all but forgotten reminiscences. Otis looked at one of the paintings. Once he saw the artist's name, he remembered instantly, recognizing the signature. It was the same as the one on the paintings in Roy's home: Chuck Dehann.

He went over and joined in the conversation and asked the cowboy if he knew Roy.

"He's one of my best friends," Chuck retorted. Within minutes, the three men were old friends.

"So we got to talking and one thing led to another," Otis would remember the conversation later. "And I asked Chuck if he'd be willing to come to our church and speak for us."

Within a few weeks, Chuck Dehann spoke at the Lighthouse Church in Burleson for the first time. Before Otis introduced him, most members of the church had never heard of Chuck Dehann. When he spoke, it was more like listening to a cowboy uncle as he stowed his tack after a long ride than listening to a sermon. At the end, if you had been listening, you just expected to be healed. Half the congregation must have been at the altar at the end of that service.

As people were prayed for, they left.

John had decided to leave, too. I had sat with him through the service as I usually do when we have a visiting speaker, but during the altar call, I moved up to the front of the church to pray and lend support if I was needed. I wasn't able to do much. I didn't feel well enough to stand, but I was able to sit in the front row and pray. John sent Shanda up to let me know that he was leaving, and to remind me to be prayed for, too.

I stood and made my way into the prayer line. As Chuck prayed for me, the Holy Spirit came upon me. It is an indescribable feeling. In one sense, it's like having warm oil poured over you, but then it permeates into every cell. It is almost as though you are conscious of every individual cell in your body all at once. It was the most unusual thing that had ever happened to me. As I stood there, I felt the energy of the Holy Spirit charging every cell. I was filled with energy. I hadn't felt that invigorated since at least two years before the heart attack.

The service ended, and I went home. Since my surgery, Otis had started taking our visiting ministers to lunch after church because I never felt like doing it myself. Before the heart attack, I had enjoyed taking them out. The intimate details of people's personal relationships with the Lord aren't always brought out in sermons, and it is a great blessing to hear each one's personal testimony. It's like an old hymn, "Tell me the story of Jesus. Write on my heart every word." Each personal story is similar to every other. At the same time, each is unique and special. You can't hear the story too many times. I missed those luncheons. I was sure that Chuck's life story would be a blessing, and I was sorry I had to miss it. As I walked in the door at home, I said, "I wish I had gone to lunch with them," and I realized I could have.

Chuck preached again that night. I didn't go forward for healing. I didn't need to. I've been…normal…ever since. In earlier years, I had been compared to the energizer bunny. Everybody said, "She never runs down." But I had. Now I'm the energizer bunny again. Maybe I've lost a step or two because of age, but I have energy, strength, and vitality.

My next quarterly visit to the cardiologist was scheduled during the second week after I was healed. I was on an alternating schedule. Every other visit I saw the physician's assistant instead of the doctor, and this time I was scheduled to see the assistant. When she asked, "How are you doing?" I couldn't wait to tell her. I was still bubbling with energy and praise. I could still feel the Holy Spirit.

"I am doing great. God healed me," I said. I told her that we had a visiting minister who had the gift of healing. "He prayed for me, and I am healed," I announced.

She was excited about it, too. "Great, I'm so glad to hear that," she burst out, just like I had burst out. The most recent sonogram of my heart had been completed during my previous quarterly visit. She told me that my heart had continued to deteriorate after the surgery and that the prognosis wasn't good, but she could see the change in my energy and was excited for me. I was scheduled for another sonogram, and we were both eager for my next visit with the cardiologist in three months. That was when I would hear the results.

"I heard you were feeling really well, and the sonogram showed your heart *is* strong." The doctor's analysis in my next appointment was emphatic after he reviewed the sonogram's results. He seemed surprised that the results were that good.

The emphasis was on the word "is." That was the verification I had of a miraculous healing. Of course, I still have a sonogram every six months, and the report continues to be very good.

I have been healed miraculously. It still amazes me, all the details God worked out to arrange the circumstances that led to my healing.

Chapter 79

Thirty Years as a Church

NEAR THE END of 2011, we began planning to celebrate the church's thirtieth anniversary. Otis and Shanda organized the festivities. They didn't let me know everything they were doing. They wanted it to be a big surprise, and it was. When the day arrived, I was amazed by all the people who attended.

For many it was a homecoming. People came who had attended our first Steppingstone church service and were Charter members. The relationship with some went back even further. They had been teenagers who attended Bible study at the Steppingstone Youth Center before we organized the church. Some had contributed to the center in one way or another. Many more had been members of the Steppingstone or Lighthouse church over the years but had moved away or found other church homes. Some had started ministries of their own. It was wonderful to see all of the people who had worked and served and worshipped God with us, some for up to twenty-five years. Many had attended for shorter periods and yet had an impact in the building of Steppingstone and Lighthouse ministries. Without some of them, my ministry may not have developed quite the same.

In addition to all the past members and friends, my family came. My brothers and sisters were all there. My sister Bettie Morris and Lowell, her husband, came from Rowlett. My sister Mary and her husband Roy Mercer came from Glen Rose. My brother Grady Lewis and his wife Janice attended from Burleson. Ercel and his wife Elizabeth and their children came up from Ciudad Victoria, Mexico, where he pastors a church. I didn't know they were going to be there. It was a wonderful treat when I saw them all file in and sit on a pew together.

It was one surprise after another. A lot of celebrities attended. Otis introduced Congressman Joe Barton. He had been a friend of the ministry, and I had served on his advisory committee for more than twenty years. He briefly addressed the crowd and delivered a proclamation to our church. Many other state and local officials delivered proclamations, too. Texas Governor Rick Perry sent a proclamation. Representative Rob Orr and soon-to-be congressman Roger Williams, and his wife and daughters, were there. Mayor Ken Shetter proclaimed the day as Gloria Gillaspie day. Proclamations by the school board and the Chamber of Commerce were presented, recognizing our church and congratulating us on our thirty years of church ministry in Burleson. It was wonderful to see the people we had known through the years.

After the service, we adjourned to the youth hall, which had been beautifully decorated, and where a huge meal waited for us. Everyone moved about stopping to gab and reminisce. After dinner, an open mike was available for anyone to come up to the platform and speak and share their comments and memories about the church. There were many wonderful testimonies of what God had done through the ministry of the Steppingstone and Lighthouse. We all enjoyed hearing them. It was a wonderful day to remember. There was so much to put in my scrapbook—all the proclamations and well wishes and cards and letters of congratulations.

I had told Otis and Shanda not to make the anniversary celebration about me, and while many people spoke about the ministry that had become the Lighthouse church, a lot of them expressed their appreciation for me personally, and I dabbed away more than a few tears. Hugs were in such abundant supply that I still feel the warmth from them years later as I describe them here.

Chapter 80

Open Door Church

THROUGHOUT THE YEARS, visiting evangelists and speakers prophesied that our church building would someday be filled to capacity. Members of our church who are blessed with a gift of prophecy have predicted an outpouring of the Holy Spirit that will swell through the church. June Green, George Burger, church elders, and Otis spoke about visions and dreams they had about our church building. They reported seeing the church full of people worshipping the Lord. Some evangelists who came to speak in the years since we built our new auditorium prophesied that the building would be full and that we would add a balcony that would overflow. Most of them were unaware that the high wall at the back of the church hides an unfinished balcony that is only waiting for the need to arise.

My visions also played a prominent role in our decisions to start several building projects, including the construction of our new assembly hall. In my vision, I saw people standing outside waiting to get in.

The little building, where young people first gathered in praise and worship and to tell others about Jesus Christ, was demolished in one of our construction projects many years ago. Our church has grown from that seed. I am pleased that we have built a campus that has spread beyond the limits of that original lot. Additional property has been purchased over the years, and the Lighthouse campus, including the duplexes that house various adjunct ministries and the parking lot, spreads over four acres. More than 20,000 square feet of space were added with the new sanctuary. With a few meeting rooms and the pastor's office, the total size of the new building exceeded 21,000 square feet, yielding a total of 41,000 square feet of meeting rooms, halls, offices, and the sanctuary.

The buildings, however, are not the church. The people who have recognized Jesus Christ as their savior are the church, and there have been so many. I am very thankful that my work and vision has been shared by so many others. I am thankful for each person who was led to Jesus through the Steppingstone and the Lighthouse, whether I was the one who led them to our Lord or it was another young person or another member of our church. If not for our ministry, many people in and around Burleson, Texas, may never have been introduced to our savior.

Many young people who were saved at the Steppingstone went on to start ministries. They waded into the torrent of souls being swept toward the abyss. They reached out to others. Christianity is the first Ponzi scheme, except no one loses. Everyone who becomes a Christian is rewarded with a place in heaven.

One of the young men we witnessed to in the early years of our ministry was Troy Brewer. The Steppingstone was one of the ministries that reached out to Troy and many young people like him, although he has said that the greatest attraction of the Steppingstone at that time in his life was the girls who handed out tracts at popular teen hangouts in the 1980s.

On a trip to Little Rock, Arkansas, in 1986, Troy accepted Jesus Christ as the Lord of his life, and immediately he was imbued with a messianic spirit. He had to tell everyone he met about Jesus. Many of his family members were saved, too, and several began attending church at the Steppingstone.

There are a lot of parallels between the way that Troy's ministry evolved and the way that the Steppingstone became a church. In 1995, Troy started a food outreach ministry and soon realized that God was leading him into full-time ministry as a pastor. Like me, he never set out to be a pastor. He just wanted to help people. He was already witnessing and ministering to the spiritual growth of people who came to the food bank. Soon he was leading them in worship and praise. Before long, he had started the Open Door church in Joshua, Texas. Many of Troy's family members who had become part of the Steppingstone family left our church to join him in building his new ministry.

By 2013, membership in the Open Door church had swelled to over 1,000. The Open Door Food Bank distributes more than a million pounds of food to hungry people in our area of Texas every year, and through another ministry, SPARK World Wide, Troy and his wife, Leanna, have established orphanages that shelter, feed, and clothe more than 1,600 children in India, Uganda, Peru, and Mexico. Troy's burden for children is like a mirror image of the Steppingstone in its earliest years, and the ministries he leads complement those of the Lighthouse.

The Open Door church had been meeting in a building that was formerly the Baptist church of Joshua, Texas. Joshua is just a few miles down the road from Burleson. In fact, the city limits of the two towns are permanently locked together. Troy was like a nineteenth century itinerant preacher, only he traded in his horse for membership in a frequent fliers club and a web site. He made the circuit speaking at satellite churches every few months and returned home to Joshua as often as he was able. In early 2013, Open Door church had been making plans to launch a satellite in Burleson, too.

Given all this, it may be no surprise to you that God spoke to me again. I understood in an instant of revelation that God's mission for the Lighthouse church included Troy's ministry. After the thirty year anniversary and following the heart attack and open heart surgery, even though I had been healed, I realized I was getting to retirement age. I had led the Steppingstone Youth Center for six years, and before that, I was youth pastor for fourteen years. My personal, full-time ministry was about to inch past the half-century mark. I began to think that I needed to pass the baton.

Since the heart attack, I had been in constant prayer for guidance. I prayed and asked the Lord what He wanted me to do. In June 2013, I was waiting patiently on the Lord. I had often speculated that God might select this person or that as my successor. God is grooming a lot of dedicated people in and around Burleson as pastors. I'm glad it wasn't my decision. I couldn't have made a choice. I kept waiting to hear something from the Lord. The indecision was swept away in an instant on the morning of June 9. I was on the platform praising the Lord and worshipping during the Sunday service, and the Lord spoke to me very distinctly and said, "You are to merge this church with Open Door church, and Troy Brewer will be the senior pastor of the merged ministry."

I had known of Troy and had observed the growth of the Open Door ministries for many years. God's blessing was on each ministry that Troy and Leanna started. I had admired his ministry, the feeding program, and the orphanages that they supported.

God had spoken to me distinctly, authoritatively, and with urgency. He wasn't just telling me to offer the Lighthouse properties to Open Door Ministries; He was directing me to take immediate action. "Do it now." So, the next day I began trying to reach Troy, who is very busy. He's usually moving so fast that when you see him, he's already gone. I called a few phone numbers and wasn't able to reach him Monday. I was planning to attend a meeting on Tuesday, June 11. I knew that Troy often attended the Christian Heritage Foundation's meetings, and the best way to catch him seemed to be by standing where you knew he was going to be. So I asked the Lord, "If this is really you talking to me, and I have really heard from you,"—I knew without a shadow of a doubt it was the Lord, but I prayed just the same—"Lord, let Troy be at the meeting and make it possible for me to speak to him and set up an appointment."

The next day when I walked into the meeting, the first person I saw was Troy Brewer. I went to straight to him and asked if I could have a meeting with him.

He said, "Yes, when?"

I suggested that we should meet soon and asked if he could come to the Lighthouse the next morning (Wednesday, June 12) for a meeting in my office. I let Otis know about the meeting and asked if he could be present, too. Otis was the associate pastor, and it seemed appropriate for him to be informed of God's direction for the church even though I had not yet discussed the merger with the church board. Otis and I were waiting when Troy arrived. When Troy sat down, I cut to the chase: "How would you like to take over this church and merge your church with ours with you as the senior pastor?"

When I said it, he put his head in his hands as though he may have been overwhelmed and caught off-guard by the proposal, but when he looked up again there was no surprise in his eyes. He said, "The Lord has already told me this is what you were going to say to me in this meeting." What great confirmation. I couldn't have asked for anything more.

Just after we had scheduled the meeting, he had been wondering why I would want to meet, and he asked the Lord about it. He still hadn't left the conference when he had a vision of me handing over the keys of our church to him. Before our Wednesday meeting, he had spoken to some of his church leaders and told them that I wanted to meet. They came to the same conclusion. They were shown what I was going to say to Troy. They had already prayed and felt like it was the Lord's will. Troy's team was in agreement with the merger even before I had ever made the suggestion to him. The only remaining, preliminary hurdle was the presentation of the idea to the Lighthouse Board of Directors. I met with them at the end of the following week and described my meeting with Troy. It took them by surprise, but each of them acknowledged it was the Lord's work.

Cindy Mahon, an elder and board member, asked, "Have you told June about this?" June Green is a prophetess in our church. She is also my cousin. We've known each other all of our lives. She's been a big part of the Steppingstone and Lighthouse ministries from the beginning of the church, and even from beforehand. She was an intercessor for me, and a great blessing to our church ministry. I hadn't spoken to June about the change.

"Why do you ask?" I responded to Cindy.

Over the years, God showed June many things that determined the direction of our church, and she had recently told Cindy that the Lord had revealed there was about to be a change in leadership. June knew that something was going to happen soon, even if she didn't yet know the specifics. Moreover, she knew that whatever it was, it would begin in June, and by September it would all be settled.

June knew that retirement had been on my mind. She had been praying about it. The first week in September began Rosh Hashanah, which is the Jewish Holiday of the beginning of a new year. It was a perfect time for the beginning of a new ministry born from the marriage of the Open Door and Lighthouse churches. The merger was finalized by the end of September, just as God had told June. Her revelation was another confirmation that the merger was God's will.

It is an amazing testament to His faithfulness. He spoke to me first, but He gave the same message to Troy that He gave to me, and then He heaped on one confirmation after another. The leadership of the Open Door Church endorsed the merger, acknowledging God's will. When I spoke to my board, not a single member objected. Everyone could see that this was God's plan. Then He confirmed it with June's prophecy.

The merger went smoothly, and six months later, the combined church was steadily growing. The membership increased by hundreds in the first three months of 2014. In January and February, 197 people accepted Jesus as their savior and were born again into the kingdom of God and added to the church.

The spirit of God is speaking to people and witnessing to many in our congregation. We feel it in every service. We are on the verge of a great move that is going to break out and spread far beyond our church borders and the borders of this city. We have anointed, powerful services. It is amazing what God is doing. We give all the glory to Him.

The Lord appeared to me during my heart surgery and told me that I would see the fulfillment of the vision that the church would be filled to capacity. We have two services on Sunday mornings with total attendance up to 1,400 people. If we had only one service, the church would overflow each Sunday. People would be standing in the hall. It is such a wonderful blessing to me.

The year 2014 was the year of promise. Fourteen stands for promises kept. God kept his promises—to me and all the other people that He's spoken to and given visions to of the ministry called Steppingstone, then Lighthouse, and now Open Door. In the book of Revelation, Jesus spoke to the church of Philadelphia. He said, "I have opened a door to you that no one can shut" (Revelation 3:8, TLB). The door has been opened, and no man can shut it. I am so pleased with the pastor that God appointed to assume my role in this church. I am excited about the things that the Open Door ministries are about to do.

Leanna oversees the SPARK (supporting, parenting, and raising kids) ministry that supports 1,600 orphans over five continents. The food bank feeds thousands every month. The church's ministry to the homeless in Fort Worth cooks food and serves meals. It's a wonderful ministry and a blessing of the Lord, and I'm overwhelmed by how blessed I am that the Lord has brought me to this point. Now I see the fulfillment of things that He showed me back in the seventies and eighties. God is faithful.

Troy's daily radio broadcast recently went into syndication, and he now reaches hundreds, perhaps thousands, of believers every day.

As he wrapped his fingers around the keys, Troy knew that I was doing a lot more than giving him our church building. I was handing off the responsibility of administrating the ministry of the Lighthouse church and the care for the souls that make up its congregation.

I officially retired as pastor of the Lighthouse church in September 2013, after thirty-two years as pastor, thirty-eight years since founding the Steppingstone Youth Ministry. I had seen the ministry grow from a small, four-room house reaching out to scores of young people to a magnificent campus capable of reaching out to fifteen hundred people in each service, every week. January 2014 marked the fiftieth year of my ministry since I took the role of youth pastor.

GLORIA INTRODUCED TROY BREWER AS THE NEW SENIOR PASTOR WHEN LIGHTHOUSE CHURCH MERGED WITH OPENDOOR.

It really began even before that when I stepped into the aisle completely unsure of what my next step would be. Since that first step, seventy years ago, I haven't always known what the next step in faith would be. There have been a lot of surprises along the way. They never end, and I am confident they never will. I know I will spend eternity discovering new things that make me exclaim, "Praise God." What a glorious adventure life is.

What a blessing it is to be in full-time service of the Lord, not that we are not all full-time minsters. We are. There can be no greater joy than knowing you are in His will. For many of the years that the ministry has existed, I did not accept a salary, but my reward has never been measurable in dollars and cents anyway.

Some people have asked why, if I was ready to retire, I didn't hand off the pastor's job to Ercel, my brother, or to Otis, or to my grandson Jeremiah Parks who is associate pastor of a 14,000 member church in Colorado Springs, or to my daughter Richelle and her husband Cory. There were a lot of people who felt as though my personal investment, both spiritual and financial, in the building of this ministry meant that I somehow owned the church and the ministry. It's true that my parents supplied the initial funds to start the Steppingstone ministry, and they sustained our church at times when other resources all but dried up like a creek bed in August, but I don't think my father would have believed that he was buying a church. Nor does John believe that the property or the church belongs to us, despite the sacrifices he has sometimes made to keep it going. My father believed in my ministry, and he contributed to it as he contributed to the Gospel Tabernacle in the years when he was a member there. Father knew he was contributing to God's ministry, not mine.

Many people seemed to expect me to designate a new pastor, but while this has been my ministry in the sense that I have performed as the chief executive, it is God's church and God's ministry in every other sense. God has performed each of the miracles throughout this ministry. It has all been for His glory. I was encouraged by this fact often through the years when faced, at times, with what seemed to be impossible situations. I heard the Lord say, "Don't worry. This is my church." He proved it again when He chose Troy Brewer to lead the church as my successor.

Of course, the end of the Lighthouse church doesn't signal the end of my ministry. In some sense, it expands it. Laying aside the administrative burdens of being a pastor frees me to spend more time in prayer, Bible study, and personal witnessing. Now I can accept speaking engagements that I may have declined in the past. These are the areas of my ministry and my personal walk with God that I have wanted to develop more fully over the last several years, but the responsibilities of leading a church have precluded those efforts. So, while I am, in one sense, retiring, in another sense, I am increasing the time that I can devote to another aspect of the ministry. I am a prayer warrior, and I look forward to spending more time in prayer. I love to study the Bible. I have loved it since I first became a Christian sixty-five years ago.

TROY AND LEANNA BREWER LEAD OPENDOOR MINISTRIES TODAY. OPENDOOR AND SPARK ARE WORLDWIDE MINISTRIES.

I have been designated Pastor Emeritus of the Open Door church, and it just may be that this is God's way of rewarding my years as a pastor. God blessed me with a ministry, and I am glad to have served Him in the way that He chose for me. I have accomplished things, or God has accomplished things using me, that I would never have thought possible when I set out to build a youth center. Everything I have done has brought me closer to Him. Every step I've taken has been learning to walk in faith, and I revere and cherish each moment.

As I think about the vignettes that have made it into this book, I think about some of the things that I've left out, many no less miraculous than the stories that made the cut. Some of them are excluded because they simply didn't occur to me at the right moment. I hope that you've read some story that touched you in a special way. If so, I'd like to know. My prayer is that you found something that encouraged you in your walk with the Lord, and that you will find the impetus or the faith that you need to Arise! Shine! Be blessed.

Chapter 81

Getting to the Point

So what's the point? Why write a series of stories about my life? The point is that God's miracles are unceasing. He wants to work miracles in and through us. I am and you are one of His miracles. Every day of my life is one of His miracles. Each day of your life is a miracle, too. Awake every morning knowing that Jesus is your savior and proclaim it out loud.

The point is that He has infinitely more miracles to perform, and He wants to use you to perform them. The greatest miracle of all is when someone discovers Jesus Christ is God's own son and that He gave his earthly life so that we may be born again as His children. But, His use of you is up to you. Arise in the glorious light of His presence in your life every morning and shine by serving Him. Tell one other person about Jesus. It doesn't matter whether you tell them about Him in an e-mail, face-to-face, or on Facebook. Shining for Jesus is telling someone else about Him. It doesn't matter if you preach a sermon to them or just say "God bless you." If God has a message for them that He wants you to deliver, somehow He will make it known. Just be open to it, and Arise, Shine!

Contact the Author

You may contact Pastor Gloria Gillaspie at:

PO Box 1403, Burleson, TX 76097

or

gloriagillaspie@yahoo.com